The Good Financial Management Guide

National Mentoring Network

NCVO Publications

The Good Financial Management Guide

Haroon Bashir

National Council for Voluntary Organisations
London

Published by NCVO Publications
(incorporating Bedford Square Press)
imprint of the
National Council for Voluntary Organisations
Regent's Wharf, 8 All Saints Street
London N1 9RL.

© NCVO 1999

All rights reserved. No part of this publication
may be reproduced, stored in a retrieval system or
transmitted, in any form or by any means,
electronic, mechanical, photocopying or otherwise,
without the prior permission of the publisher.

First published 1999

A catalogue record for this book is available
from the British Library.

ISBN 0 7199 1539 2

NCVO – voice of the voluntary sector

NCVO is the representative body for the voluntary sector in England and acts as its principal collective voice.

Established in 1919, NCVO now has over 1000 members – from large 'household name' charities to small self-help groups involved in all areas of voluntary and social action.

NCVO also has close links with government departments, local authorities, Members of Parliament, the European Union and the business sector, and ensures the views of the voluntary sector are communicated to key decision makers and opinion formers.

NCVO provides access to information, advice and consultancy through specialist staff, networks, events and publications. Legal, financial management and fundraising advice is provided as well as many consultancy brokerage schemes. There is a free Voluntary Sector HelpDesk which is available on 0800-2798 798 (calls are toll free).

Apart from this publication, NCVO publishes a monthly magazine, NCVO News, and other materials on law, governance, european funding, human resources and planning for voluntary sector managers. For further information, call the HelpDesk on the above number.

If you are interested in becoming a member of NCVO, please call the membership team on 0171-713 6161, or write to The Membership Team, NCVO, Regent's Wharf, 8 All Saints Street London N1 9RL.

Acknowledgements

Like any project of this kind several people have kindly given their time and support to make this publication a reality. The Community Investment team at NatWest are to be thanked for undertaking the initial research into financial management advice needs, for their financial support which helps to ensure that this Guide can be published at a lower price than would otherwise be possible and for their valuable input.

The many individuals in NCVO for encouragement and support, namely, Susan Cordingley, Director of Operations, for persuading me to start this project, David Cameron, Publications Manager, Samantha Barber for proof reading, Fiona Keating for design input, Bill Feinstein, Head of Services, and Catherine Wood, Head of Finance for their on-going support as 'readers' of the many drafts that were produced.

This project has also benefitted from the considerable expertise of an external advisory group who have provided a range of technical input to help steer the content and format of this Guide, namely:

David Taylor, NCVO Honorary Treasurer; Patrick Allen, Head of Regeneration Directorate, DETR Jo Ash, Director, Southampton Voluntary Services; Timothy Bigden, Timothy Bigden & Associates Pippa Clark, Community Enterprise/ Development, NatWest Pesh Framjee, Head of Charities Unit at Binder Hamlyn Chartered Accountants Laurence Gandy, Director, North West Kent Council for Voluntary Service Juila Gibbens, Community Enterprise/ Development, NatWest Bill Hulton, Chairman, Local Investment Fund Andrew Robinson, Manager, Community Enterprise/ Development, NatWest Shirley Scott, Director, Charity Finance Directors Group; June Street, Executive Manager, Dacorum Council for Voluntary Service

Haroon Bashir

Contents

Sponsor's Foreword **ix**

Introduction **1**

1. Structuring the Organisation for Financial Strength **4**
2. Financing the Mission **30**
3. Budgeting **56**
4. Resource Management **110**
5. Special Financial Tools **151**
6. Charity Accounts and Financial Management **177**
7. Tax and Voluntary Organisations **185**

Glossary **210**

Sponsor's Foreword

NatWest has been involved with the NCVO's Financial Advice programme since it started in 1995. We believe that effective financial management of voluntary groups is key to meeting the increased demands being placed upon them today.

We see our involvement in the programme as part of our own education, learning about the issues and problems faced by the sector and, with the aid of our resources, passing this information on. The programme supports the work that we undertake within our own organisation. It's very much about communication and education, from developing new and innovative products which meet our customer needs to taking every opportunity to talk about the sector with our staff – a process we know will help them understand and be better able to serve you.

The innovative way in which the final stage of this year's programme is being delivered demonstrates both NCVO's and NatWest's belief in the content of the guide and in the importance of participation in the learning process. The guide was written to be used and we know you will find it invaluable.

Pippa Clark
Community Enterprise/Development
NatWest

SUPPORTED BY
NatWest

Introduction

This guide is concerned with the financial management of voluntary organisations, at both the strategic level and the operational level. It aims to meet the needs of a wide range of voluntary organisations, regardless of their constitution, their size, their areas of activity and whether they are local or national.

WHY IS A GUIDE TO FINANCIAL MANAGEMENT NECESSARY?

Widespread changes are taking place in the voluntary sector that will affect every organisation within it. Here are some of them:

- The report of the Commission on the Future of the Voluntary Sector initiated a far-reaching debate on voluntary action in the UK.[1]
- During the 1990s the gross income of general charities increased by £4.7 billion in nominal terms; but research shows that it is only the very largest organisations that are showing any appreciable growth.
- There are signs of very modest growth in smaller organisations, which can be explained by the arrival of National Lottery funding. It is the middle-sized organisations – those with an annual income between £100,000 and £10 million – that are being squeezed. These organisations are not investing in fundraising, are heavily reliant on generating earned income and do not have significant investment assets.
- The legal framework within which voluntary action takes place has also continued to evolve, as a result of national legislation – such as the Charities Acts 1992 and 1993 – and of European legislation that affects voluntary organisations as employers: for example, the National Minimum Wage and the Working Time Directive.
- A major milestone in charity accounting practices was the introduction by the Charity Commission of the Charity Accounting Statement of Recommended

---

[1] *Meeting the Challenge of Change: Voluntary action in the 21st century*. NCVO Publications 1996.

Practice (SORP) in October 1995. At the time of writing the Commission was reviewing the SORP, recognising that some of its details need to be clarified.
- Equally important has been the commitment of the present government to review charity taxation. The voluntary sector is by no means exempt from tax: although exemptions exist for direct taxation (income tax), indirect taxation in the shape of irrecoverable VAT costs the sector up to £400 million a year.

Everyone involved in voluntary action should be aware of the impact these factors can have on their organisations:

- The trustees, who are charged with the stewardship and governance of the organisation.
- The management team, who must work with the trustees to formulate policy and deliver services.
- The staff and volunteers, who need to be motivated by a clear mission and clear values to carry out their day-to-day functions.
- The finance officer (professionally qualified or otherwise), whose role is being transformed from 'police officer and score-keeper' to 'business partner' working across organisational boundaries to deliver a strategic and value-adding finance service.

This guide will enable the reader to understand how these changes are affecting voluntary organisations and in particular, their impact on financial management at a strategic and operational level.

An issue that has received much attention recently is the role of trustees in financial management and the division of responsibility between the trustee board and management. Chapter One, 'Structuring the organisation for financial strength', looks at governance across all three sectors and addresses the question of responsibility, specifically the responsibility of trustees in relation to financial management. How this question is answered can mean the difference between financial success or failure for a voluntary organisation.

Chapter Two, 'Financing the mission', looks at strategic intent: how to strike the balance between the mission of the organisation and the resources it has available. It proposes a framework for long-term strategic planning that will help managers and trustees to decide which charitable programmes to adopt.

Only when the strategic objectives have been decided can the wider question of management information and budgeting be addressed. This is the point at which any inadequacies in financial planning, control and monitoring become evident. Chapter Three, 'Budgeting', translates the mission into financial terms and comes up with a financial blueprint for achieving mission-orientated goals. This chapter also looks at how to prepare (and revise) budgets and how to enable staff to participate in the process.

The aim of budgeting is to allocate an organisation's current resources so that it achieves its programme goals, and effective asset management will maximise the value of those resources. Chapter Four, 'Resource management', looks at strategic options such as forming alliances and outsourcing; at cash flow planning and investments; and tackles the tricky issues of restricted funding and charity reserves.

The fifth chapter, 'Special financial tools', shows how the financially astute voluntary organisation will use techniques such as ratio analysis – which will enable it to assess performance and identify trends so as to ensure liquidity – and cost accounting, which allows management to make informed decisions based on a proper analysis of costs.

This is followed by two chapters which clarify some of the bigger issues in charity accounting. 'Charity Accounts and Financial Management' outlines the issues brought up by the Statement of Recommended Practice (SORP) and 'Tax and Voluntary Organisations' outlines the position surrounding taxation and VAT in particular.

Each chapter of the guide begins with a summary of the contents and concludes with:

- References to further reading.
- Resource tools.
- Case studies showing how theory has been translated into practice.

1.
Structuring the organisation for financial strength

1. The governance debate	3. The trustee board
2. Models of governance	4. The financial management role of trustee boards

1. THE GOVERNANCE DEBATE

Throughout the world, institutions of every kind – government, public bodies, voluntary organisations and commercial companies – are under increasing pressure to be more transparent about what they do and more responsive to the people they serve. This has led to demands for higher standards of accountability, behaviour and performance. Commercial practices that were condoned in the past – such as insider trading – are no longer acceptable and accounting rules are becoming tighter. Similar tightening up is taking place in government and public life in general.

This section briefly describes the main developments in governance in the private, public and voluntary sectors. It will be of particular interest to the trustees of voluntary organisations, given the increasing professionalisation of the voluntary sector and the renewed emphasis being placed on the legal obligations of trustees. In any voluntary organisation, a precondition for financial strength is the clear definition of the roles and responsibilities of trustees, paid staff and volunteers. Without this clarity of roles, responsibility for income generation and expenditure will be dissipated and with it, any hope of control.

DEVELOPMENTS IN THE PRIVATE SECTOR
'In some respects, being a non-executive chairman seems a dog's life. The money is good, but not that good. The job is part-time, but only if things are running smoothly. And if they are not, you lack the detailed knowledge to sort things out.' Sir Denys Henderson, *Financial Times*, 22 July 1998. Over the last ten years there has been a shift of attention away from how organisations are managed to how

they are governed. This was partly the result of a series of prominent corporate failures in the late 1980s. The collapse of companies such as Blue Arrow, Coloroll, Polly Peck, BCCI and Barlow Clowes – to mention only a few – caused company directors, institutional investors, auditors and financial advisers, supported by government, to engage in collective soul-searching on how to prevent such failures happening again. And by the mid-1990s, the perceived high levels of executive pay, particularly in the privatised utilities, added a new dimension to the governance debate.

The result was a series of Committees and Codes – the most prominent being the 1992 Cadbury Committee on the Financial Aspects of Corporate Governance – that have had a major impact on British corporate life. The main aim of these codes has been to find ways of making executive directors more accountable for their actions to a group of stakeholders, in this case the shareholders. Before the 1992 Cadbury report, the structure of corporate boards had prevented this, as such boards which were dominated by executive directors who diluted the ability of the independent non-executives to exercise their accountability function. The quote from Sir Denys Henderson above sums up the current state of affairs.

Against this backdrop of prominent corporate failures, the Cadbury Committee set out to address the low levels of confidence in company financial reporting and auditing, which have often been blamed for enabling the abuses of executive directors to go undiscovered. The Cadbury report, however, goes beyond financial audit procedures to examine board structures and models of corporate governance. The committee developed a Code of Best Practice in Corporate Governance which is based on principles of openness, integrity and accountability. In addition, the position of non-executive directors has been strengthened by the establishment of audit committees that report directly to them.

These developments in private sector governance have had, and will continue to have, a major influence to how the public and voluntary sectors develop their own governance structures.

Developments in the public sector

The public sector has often had a bad press too, particularly over its supposedly inappropriate use of public money. The 1979-97 Conservative administration began a process of reform and restructuring that has had a major effect on the way governance has been addressed.

The central theme of these reforms was the need to improve efficiency through greater competition, as pressure to reduce public expenditure and local taxation became politically fashionable. This policy was implemented by introducing private sector management practices – for example, performance indicators to assess the quality of services, and multiple audits to ensure best value for money – and by removing elected members and replacing them by appointees with business experience.

The reforms culminated in widespread structural change during the 1980s and 1990s, when many public services were removed from the direct control of local authorities and instead run by quangos, operating under contracts with central government. Independent trusts were established to deliver services in the NHS; Training and Education Councils and Local Enterprise Councils (TECs and LECs) were set up; and further education and the then polytechnics were removed from local authority's financial control.

This growth in quangos, coupled with the increase in central government control, has raised concerns about the membership of such bodies and their accountability. There is talk of a 'governance gap', of the danger of creating a closed professional elite that would ultimately control these quangos. In response to such concerns, the Nolan Committee published its Second Report in 1996, *Standards in Public Life: Local Public Spending Bodies* (Nolan II).

Nolan II focused on the conduct of local public spending bodies and reaffirmed the seven principles of public life set out in Nolan's first report: selflessness, integrity, objectivity, accountability, openness, honesty and leadership. In addition, Nolan II emphasised the duty of public bodies to have proper arrangements for ensuring local accountability of centrally funded bodies.

The third Nolan Committee report, *A Report on Standards of Conduct in Local Government* (Nolan III), published in July 1997, set out to consider an overall ethical framework for local government, and how this framework might be adapted to different circumstances. After extensive consultation, the committee decided that Nolan III should focus on these issues:

- Conflicts of interest and codes of conduct.
- Officer/member relationships and decision-making process.
- Ombudsmen, audit and surcharge.
- Planning.
- Contracting, local authority companies and joint ventures.

The first two issues are of particular interest to this guide. Nolan III recommends that a code of conduct be developed that deals specifically with local authority councillors who also act as charity trustees. As a result of those recommendations, NCVO and the Local Government Association have published their own guide.[1]

The introduction to the code states: 'There are increasing calls for good governance in the public, voluntary and private sectors. This requires greater clarity about the relationships between local authorities and voluntary organisations. A written agreement setting out the roles, relationships and responsibilities of local authority members and officers who serve on the boards of voluntary organisations would be a significant step towards good governance. The several different legal forms which are adopted by voluntary organisations have implications for roles, responsibilities and potential liabilities of board members. It is highly

---

[1] *Are you sitting comfortably? A code of practice for local authority members and officers serving on the boards of voluntary organisations.* NCVO/LGA 1998.

appropriate for relationships to be examined afresh in areas where local government structures have been reorganised because of the likely changes in personnel on the local authority side.'

The code elaborates on the types of written agreements that should exist, including the relationship statement; job description and reciprocation; reporting arrangements; and liability and responsibility statement.

To sum up, the public sector has been deeply involved in the governance debate. The widespread structural changes – and the concerns over accountability arising from those changes – have resulted in codes of conduct seeking to establish good governance. At the same time, the push to make local authority services more economic and effective has introduced many private sector management practices.

DEVELOPMENTS IN THE VOLUNTARY SECTOR

Section 97 of the Charities Act 1993 defines trustees as 'the people responsible under the charity's governing document for controlling the management and administration of the charity, regardless of what they are called.' In fulfilling this responsibility, trustees may delegate the management of the day-to-day affairs to an executive committee (a committee of paid staff in this instance) whilst themselves concentrate on governance. This delegation of duties does not, however, absolve them of being held accountable in law for the activities of the voluntary organisation. Given the legal position, governance issues and practices are therefore particularly relevant to trustees. Beyond the question of probity, the professionalism of trustees is leading them to seek greater accountability and effectiveness.

The voluntary sector economy has until recently experienced a period of rapid growth, driven initially by the former Conservative administration's decision to contract out the provision of local services to the voluntary sector. Social housing has moved from being a local authority responsibility to housing associations, who have been encouraged to take a commercial approach to managing the housing stock and finances. Further growth of the sector has been fuelled by the care in the community programme.

Inefficiencies in the public and voluntary sectors are bound to cause greater public concern, as both sectors rely on the good faith of the general public. Recent NCVO research into public trust and confidence in charities revealed the following:

- Very limited understanding of what charities are doing.
- Concern about the voluntary sector's relations with the state (some respondents fear that gap-filling 'lets the state off the hook').
- Lottery publicity has opened up the debate about what is a deserving cause.
- Many see the voluntary sector as full of competing charities.
- Demand for greater transparency, for example about administration costs.
- Perceived lack of information on which to base giving decisions.

The above results, together with the revelation of failings in certain 'household name' charities, has shaken public confidence and forced the Charity Commission to act.

The Charity Commission responded by introducing the Charities Acts 1992 and 1993 and by increasing its own supervisory role. The general review also led the Charity Commission and NCVO to publish the report On Trust, which examined the function of charity trustees, the role of committees and the level of training and support they received.

The three-year Board Development Programme at NCVO offers participating organisations the opportunity to undergo a 'health check' specifically designed to help boards get to grips with their strengths and weaknesses. The overall aims of the Programme are to:

- Establish a framework for effective governance.
- Create tools for governance based on sound principles, in line with legal rules and regulations.
- Develop good practice guidelines to help foster better board relations.

In response to the changes in the social housing sector, the Housing Corporation has developed codes of conduct, to be implemented by all housing associations, which address the competence of management, accountability, independence and diversification.

For the voluntary sector, the debate about governance culminated with the *Report of the Commission into the Future of the Voluntary Sector*, better known as the Deakin Report, published in July 1996. This contained 64 recommendations for action by the voluntary sector, central and local government, business, trusts and foundations, intermediary organisations and funders of the sector; one of the most important of these recommendations was that a Code of Governance for voluntary organisations, similar to the codes produced by the Nolan Committee, should be devised and publicised.

A significant response to the Deakin Report has come from the Joseph Rowntree Foundation, which has proposed a code of practice on the governance of voluntary organisations. This code is intended for voluntary bodies that deliver services with the benefit of public funding, and that seek to be effective and accountable. Such organisations will, the code states, be clear and open about their work and conscious of their social responsibilities. The code covers:

- *Effectiveness*: showing clarity of purpose, being explicit about the needs to be met and ways in which resources are managed.
- *Accountability:* evaluating effectiveness and performance, dealing with complaints fairly and communicating to all stakeholders how responsibilities will be fulfilled.
- *Standards:* having clear operating standards.
- *User involvement:* making arrangements to involve users of services.

- *Governance:* having a systematic and open process for making appointments to the governing body, setting out the roles and responsibilities of members.
- *Volunteers:* having clear arrangements for involving, training, supporting and managing volunteers.
- *Equality and fairness:* ensuring that policies and practices do not discriminate unfairly.
- *Staff management:* recruiting staff openly, remunerating them fairly and being a good employer.

Important in taking forward the recommendations of the Deakin Report has been the establishment of numerous groups to address: charity taxation; the sector's relationship with government and business; future funding of the sector; quality assurance systems; a research strategy for the sector; charity law reform; and closer working between intermediary bodies on issues affecting the sector.

The working party on relations between government and the voluntary and community sectors launched the Compact between Government and the Voluntary Sector in November 1998. The stated aim of the Compact is to create 'a new approach to partnership between Government and the voluntary sector and community sector. It provides a framework to enable relations to be carried out differently and better than before . . . The Compact is a starting point for developing our partnership, based on shared values and mutual respect.'

As the link between proper governance and quality assurance becomes more widely accepted, the Rowntree code of practice is being further developed. However, the pursuit of quality and continuous improvement is not new to the voluntary sector: the commitment to deliver the best possible services to beneficiaries has been a major driving force for many years.

Most voluntary organisations are highly motivated to deliver high standards of service. But in the absence of the criteria used in the private sector – such as profit or return on investment – trustees, management and staff need other ways of measuring their performance. There are, however, various obstacles:

- Market or customer satisfaction is rarely a measure of quality.
- Voluntary organisations often have a monopoly on providing certain services, therefore continued high demand is not necessarily an indicator of quality.
- Many end users are 'silent': for example, elderly or mentally ill people may not be able to make an informed view of quality.

For the last ten years, voluntary organisations have been under pressure to show that they have achieved, and maintained, verifiable quality standards. This has increasingly been at the insistence of the purchaser of services, especially local authorities, or the donors who fund activities: for example, TECs require voluntary sector providers to commit themselves to gaining The Investors in People award. There has also been concern among the wider public about the probity and performance of the voluntary sector.

These concerns prompted the Deakin Commission to recommend that 'a clear understanding of standards is important for voluntary organisations of all sizes. Even in the smallest organisations, issues of reliability, availability and consistency can be important for all users and volunteers alike.'

As a result of the Commission's recommendation, the Quality Standards Task Group was set up at NCVO in July 1997. After wide consultation, the Group recommended that the voluntary sector should:

- *Establish quality principles.* These would describe an organisation's fundamental beliefs that form the basis for its whole management ethos.
- *Commit to the concept and practice of continuous improvement.* This would provide for the systematic and methodical enhancement of an organisation's capabilities and performance.
- *Introduce the Excellence Model as the appropriate quality framework.* This would facilitate the determination of the overall success of an organisation, based upon an accepted set of management principles as well as values.

The Excellence Model was originally developed by the European Foundation for Quality Management and is promoted in the UK by the British Quality Foundation. The proposed principles for the voluntary sector state that a quality voluntary organisation:

- Strives for continuous improvement in all it does.
- Uses recognised standards or models as a means to continuous improvement and not as an end.
- Agrees requirements with stakeholders and endeavours to meet or exceed these the first time and every time.
- Promotes equality of opportunity through its internal and external conduct.
- Is accountable to stakeholders.
- Adds value to its end users and beneficiaries.

How voluntary organisations can use the Excellence Model to help them plan better forms the basis of the next chapter.

2. Models of governance

Governance in the voluntary sector has become a hot issue since the Deakin Report. The comprehensiveness of the report reflects the diversity of the voluntary sector and the complexity of its relationships with the rest of society. The challenge to the sector has been clearly outlined, and the response so far has been positive; but much more needs to be done.

If there is a common thread to the governance debate, it is the desire for the activities of the executive group responsible for day-to-day management to be overseen by a non-executive group independent of day-to-day management but legally and financially responsible. This is the 'stewardship model' of governance, which many regard as a negative one. There are other forms of governance relevant to the voluntary sector, and these will now be examined.

Stewardship model

According to agency theory, the owners of an enterprise need to face the fact that managers – their agents – are likely to act in their own interests, rather than in those of the owners. In this model, therefore, the main function of the board is to control the managers. The implication is that the directors of companies should be independent of management, and that their primary role is stewardship: safeguarding the resources of the organisation and monitoring and, if necessary, controlling the behaviour of managers.

The regulations applying to charitable trusts embody similar ideas about the role of governance. Under trust law, the trustees are appointed to look after the money and resources donated by an individual or group and to see that their wishes are carried out. In the same way, the principal role of the trustees of a voluntary organisation is to see that staff and management carry out the objectives of the organisation.

Partnership model

In this model the board, and the major shareholders, are seen as the partners of management, and the board's prime function is therefore to add value to the organisation by improving its top decision-making. To achieve this requires five major changes from the stewardship model: board members should be selected for their expertise; boards should focus on new strategies and policies, not just on reviewing past performance; directors should be given better access to company information; board members should devote a substantial proportion of their time to governance; board members should be appropriately rewarded.

Political model

Thinking about the governance of organisations has also been influenced by the principles of democracy. For example, many voluntary and non-profit organisations are set up as membership associations, and their constitutions state that the governing body should be elected by, and represent, the membership.

In this 'political' model, the role of the board is to represent the interests of one or more stakeholder groups in the organisation, expressing, resolving or choosing between the interest of different stakeholders and setting the overall policy of the organisation.

A synthesis of models

These three models are clearly contradictory (although, of course, in real life none of them exists in its pure form). In practice, the governance model that a voluntary organisation uses will depend on many factors, include the management culture of the organisation, the area of voluntary activity it is engaged in, and the stage it has reached in its life cycle. At any given time, the governance of the organisation may incorporate elements from the stewardship, partnership or political models, depending on the needs of the management and the board. This could be called the 'contingency model', as it helps to facilitate a particular course of action.

The next section of this chapter will look at how to find the right people to act as trustees, how to train them and assess their performance, and how to deal with potential conflicts of interest.

3. The trustee board

What are you looking for in a board member? Do you want people whose skills, experience and personal qualities could complement those of your current board? Taking the trouble to answer these questions could give you ideas about where to look, and could help to improve the composition of your board. After carrying out a skills audit (see Appendix B), the board should decide on a strategy to attract new trustees and to utilise the range of skills which are already available.

The board may wish to set up a nominating committee with the specific task of recruiting new trustees (as well as implementing board development/induction programmes). It is important to write a job description and person specification for trustees: these not only help the organisation to clarify the role of its trustees, but also serve as useful aids for people thinking about becoming trustees, and help those considering nominating others for trusteeship to put forward suitable candidates. It may also be useful to draw up a code of conduct, spelling out the relationship between trustees and the organisation; this can help to clarify expectations on both sides, making their obligations plain to potential trustees. The code should state, for example, that expenses may be claimed, and should give an honest estimate of the amount of support the organisation can give new trustees and the time commitment required of them.

Finding new trustees
Here are some ideas:

- Consider your volunteers, supporters, donors, service users/beneficiaries and colleagues in partner organisations or those involved in related areas of work.
- Organise an event that will enable people to learn about your organisation.
- Do any local firms have employee volunteering schemes? If not, why not encourage them to start one? Contact your local Chamber of Commerce for ideas on who to contact.
- Use a newsworthy event as a lever to obtain free publicity in the media.
- Advertise in national or local newspapers, professional journals, community centres or libraries.
- Try using a trustee brokerage service. These draw their potential trustees from a

variety of different sources – retired people, professionals, business people, black and minority ethnic people etc – and offer levels of services varying from basic introductions to full recruitment.

INDUCTION OF TRUSTEES

In order to be effective, trustees must be given all the information they need to understand the organisation – its aims, who it benefits, the boundaries within which it works – and their own role as trustees.

An induction pack should be compiled containing information about the organisation and the role and responsibilities of trustees. Here are some suggestions about what it should include:

- A brief history of the organisation.
- The governing document.
- Standing orders.
- Roles and responsibilities of trustees, including trustee job descriptions.
- The annual report and accounts for the previous three years.
- Sets of recent board papers and minutes, including management accounts.
- Board and committee structure.
- Terms of reference for the board of trustees and all committees.
- Dates of forthcoming meetings.
- Names, addresses, telephone and fax numbers of trustees.
- Major policy documents.
- If staff are employed, the organisation's staff structure and the Chief Executive Officer's job description.
- A manual (such as NCVO's *Good Trustee Guide*).
- A self assessment form to enable recruits to indicate their support needs: for example, pairing, debriefing meetings.

An effective induction should not only prevent new trustees from getting disillusioned and leaving, but should also mean that they quickly become a useful member of your board.

THE GOVERNING STRUCTURE

Recruits will need to know whether the main board of trustees has any sub-committees, and if so, what their terms of reference are. If the trustees have powers to delegate work to sub-committees, all decisions of those sub-committees should be reported to the full board of trustees, who must take ultimate responsibility for them. Recruits must also be told whether there are any advisory groups and how they fit into the governing structure and whether there are any additional working parties or ad hoc committees.

THE STRUCTURE OF THE ORGANISATION

An organisation chart, together with a list of the names of key staff with their job titles and their responsibilities, will provide a useful overview of the structure of

Figure 1.1: Specimen governing structure

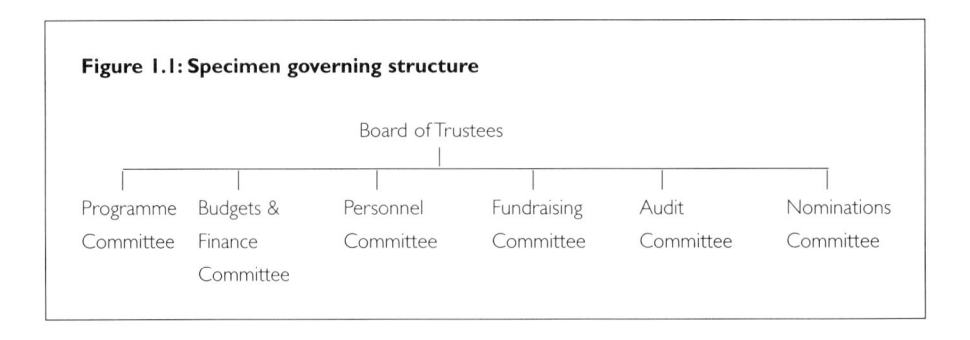

```
                        Board of Trustees
        ┌───────────┬───────────┬───────────┬───────────┬───────────┐
   Programme    Budgets &    Personnel   Fundraising    Audit     Nominations
   Committee    Finance      Committee   Committee    Committee    Committee
                Committee
```

the organisation. Staff are normally accountable through a line management structure to the chief executive, who is in turn answerable to the trustees. To avoid blurring these lines of accountability, trustees may need guidance on when it is appropriate to contact a member of staff directly and when they should go through the chair or chief executive.

ANNUAL REPORTS AND ACCOUNTS

Each year trustees should be given a copy of the organisation's annual report and accounts. They should keep these copies for at least three years.

CONFLICT OF INTEREST

Conflicts of interest arise when the personal or professional interest of a board member is potentially at odds with the best interest of the organisation: for example, when a board member performs professional services for an organisation, or suggests that a friend or relative be considered for a staff position. These decisions are perfectly acceptable if the board made them in an objective and informed manner and they benefit the organisation. Even if they do not meet these criteria, such decisions are not usually illegal – but they are vulnerable to legal challenges and public misunderstanding.

A damaged reputation is the most likely result of a poorly-managed conflict of interest. Because public confidence is so important to voluntary organisations, boards should take steps to avoid even the appearance of impropriety. These steps may include:

- Adopting a conflict of interest policy that prohibits or limits business transactions with board members and requires board members to disclose potential conflicts.
- Disclosing conflicts when they occur so that board members who are voting on a decision are aware that another member's interests are being affected.
- Requiring board members to withdraw from decisions that present a potential conflict.
- Establishing procedures, such as competitive bids, that ensure that the organisation is receiving best value in the transaction.

> **Figure 1.2: An example of a conflict of interest declaration form**
>
> CONFLICTS OF INTEREST
>
> As a trustee, you have to act in the best interests of [name of organisation], but inevitably trustees will have a wide range of interests in private, public and professional life. On occasions, these interests might conflict: for example, when a director is also a supplier or consultant. We are obliged to review any possible conflicts of interest when preparing our annual report, so could I ask you to supply the following details:
>
> | | | |
> |---|---|---|
> | Has [name of organisation] made any loans to you? | No ☐ | Yes ☐ |
> | Have you, or people connected with you through family, business or another charity, an interest in a contract or transaction with [name of organisation]? | No ☐ | Yes ☐ |
> | Have you or any person connected with you derived any pecuniary benefit or gain from [name of organisation]? | No ☐ | Yes ☐ |
>
> Signed: _____   Date: _____
>
> Company Secretary

What is the definition of 'connected persons'? The Charities Act 1993 states that: 'Connected persons' are persons who at any time during the relevant accounting period, or the previous accounting period, are or were:
(a) trustees of the charity;
(b) persons who hold or held the title to property or investments of the charity;
(c) donors of material assets to the charity (whether the gift was made on or after the establishment of the charity);
(d) any child, parent, grandchild, grandparent, brother or sister of any person mentioned in (a) to (c);
(e) any officer, employee or agent of the charity (which would include an organisation which provides management services);
(f) the spouse of any person mentioned in (a) to (e);
(g) any firm or institution controlled by any one or more persons mentioned in (a) to (f), or in which any such person is a partner;
(h) any corporate body in which any 'connected person' mentioned in (a) to (g) has a substantial interest, or in which two or more such persons taken together have a substantial interest.

'Connected person' includes a trustee for, or partner, or nominee of, any such person and 'child', 'spouse', 'controlled' and 'substantial' have the same meanings as in Schedule 5 of the Charities Act 1993. 'Person' includes real persons and bodies corporate.

Self-assessment for the board

Evaluation is a central function of any board. The trustees must assess whether the organisation is carrying out its mission effectively. In addition, they should carry out an annual evaluation of the chief executive. Unfortunately, most voluntary sector boards pay too little attention to these types of evaluation.

At least once a year the board should also review its own performance. Trustees should stand back and ask themselves what role the board is playing in the governance of the organisation and what its strengths and weaknesses have been, and use this evidence to plan for the years ahead. This review can strengthen the board by:

- Identifying the criteria for an effective board.
- Identifying important areas where improvement is needed.
- Measuring progress towards the goals set by the board.
- Shaping the future make-up and structure of the board.
- Building trust and enabling members to work more effectively as a team.

A self evaluation by individual trustees is also helpful. This can identify areas of strength and weakness; support needs; and those board programmes to which the trustee feels best able to contribute. This exercise can also lead a trustee to conclude that it is time for him or her to leave the board!

Another useful part of the learning process could be a one-to-one discussion with the chair of the organisation on the role a trustee has played on the board.

4. THE FINANCIAL MANAGEMENT ROLE OF TRUSTEE BOARDS

The financial management role of a trustee board is quite unlike that of the board of a commercial entity. Most voluntary organisations are financially accountable to a far greater number of stakeholders, because they are funded by a combination of tax concessions and money from the general public, local government and charitable trusts.

The goal of maximising shareholder value – which can be measured objectively – is not relevant to voluntary organisations. Instead, the whole trustee board (not just the treasurer) must demonstrate value for money and effectiveness, which by their nature are more subjective criteria.

This section of the guide examines the three main financial management functions of the board: financial monitoring; financial procedures; and financial management. In doing so, it examines typical weaknesses and introduces various techniques that will be studied in more detail in later sections.

Appendix C is a checklist for identifying the financial governance issues that may affect the voluntary organisation. It helps to emphasise the fact that financial management is the responsibility of the whole trustee board.

FINANCIAL MONITORING

In practice, the financial monitoring carried out by boards is typified by:

- The comparing of budgets for income and expenditure with actual results.
- The consideration of projected sources and level of income and expenditure.
- The need to report to funders.
- The lack of any value added, instead seen as a compliance function.
- Information which is too detailed and conforming to accounting regulations.
- Totally reactive responses conditioned by when information is presented.

Ideally, however, financial monitoring should be characterised by:

- The use of key financial ratio analysis (which can, for example, highlight financial stability).
- The inclusion of financial performance information against predetermined financial policies (for example, income reserves).
- A committee that is adequately empowered in its role by proper induction, an understanding of cost structures and its relationship with management.
- The provision of information that is understandable, timely and accurate.

Financial procedures
These procedures are designed to ensure the propriety and efficiency of the organisation's activities. They typically include policies for the proper accounting, control and protection of the income, expenditure and assets of the organisation.

By means of delegation the board must ensure that financial procedures appropriate to the size and complexity of the organisation exist. This could be achieved by compiling and distributing a financial procedures manual, and/or by responding to reports on areas of weakness by external auditors.

Appendix D gives a typical financial procedures manual for a membership organisation; however, this will have to be tailored to the needs and structure of individual organisations.

The external auditor may discover weaknesses in the internal control procedures that will affect the accounts. The auditor should report these weaknesses to the trustees.

The principal purposes of this report to management are:

- To enable the auditor to comment on the accounting records, systems and controls he or she has examined during the course of the audit: for example, weaknesses in credit control, the reconciliation of ledgers and the maintenance of grant approvals.
- To provide management and trustees with financial statistics that can be used to judge the performance of a charity: for example, the number of weeks' expenditure in reserves, or total staff costs expressed as a ratio of total resources expended.
- To communicate any matter that might affect future audits: for example, new accounting standards.

The report to trustees and management should recommend what changes need to be made to systems in situations where there are no other compensatory controls. The auditor must ensure that the recommended changes have in fact been made.

Financial management procedures

These are the procedures that help management to decide overall strategy and make the best use of resources. Too often, however, the board lacks the expertise to carry out these procedures, or is reluctant to 'step on the chief executive's toes'. As a result, financial management is often seen as a luxury, since the funding does not allow for it; if done at all, it tends to be restricted to budget construction, with little or no consideration of resource inputs, outputs and outcomes.

This guide will enable more informed decision-making by management and a greater financial management role for trustee boards.

The role of the treasurer

The financial management team for a voluntary organisation might comprise the honorary treasurer, a chief finance officer, internal audit function (for the larger charity), external auditors/accountants, investment advisers and bankers. Each is a specialist function in its own right, and together they can do much to ensure that the organisation is managed efficiently and effectively.

The treasurer's role can best be understood by looking at a job description and person specification for a typical treasurer's post (see appendix E).

IN CONCLUSION

This chapter has examined how the governance debate is forcing through changes that will help voluntary organisations to clarify relationships between the executive management and the non-executive trustee board, and to establish codes of conduct that are value based.

It was concluded that a contingency model of governance, combining the best of the stewardship and partnership models, is most likely to prevail within the voluntary sector. The trend towards recruiting more professionally-skilled trustees on to boards will certainly add credibility to the contingency model.

The importance of having the 'right' trustees is increasingly evident as more emphasis is being placed on the proper induction, training and assessment of trustee boards. All this strengthens the role of trustees boards, enabling them to contribute in a way which adds value to the aims of the organisation. What remains is to provide trustee boards with the financial management skills that will allow them to examine objectively, and perhaps critically, the issues presented to them by management. Armed with these techniques, trustee boards can help to ensure that charitable objectives are met in a way that is demonstrably efficient and effective in the eyes of all key stakeholders.

FURTHER READING AND RESOURCES

Are you sitting comfortably? A code of practice for local authority members and officers serving on the boards of voluntary organisations. NCVO 1998.

NCVO Research Quarterly, Issue 1. 'Blurred vision: Public trust in charities'. A quarterly research bulletin published by NCVO Research Team. NCVO 1998.

NCVO Trustee Board Development Programme. This three-year programme, developed by NCVO for trustee board members, chairs, staff and chief executives, provides participants with the latest information, access to various networks of trustee boards, and strategic tools for honing skills and developing efficiency. Contact NCVO HelpDesk for more details.

Meeting the challenge of change: Voluntary action into the 21st century. The report of the Commission on the Future of the Voluntary Sector. NCVO 1996.

Codes of practice for the voluntary sector. Joseph Rowntree Foundation.

*Getting it right together. Compact on relations between government and the voluntary and community sector in Englan*d. HMSO 1998.

The Good Trustee Guide: A resource organiser for members of governing bodies of unincorporated charities and charitable companies. NCVO 1994–9

Trustee Advice Service Information Sheets. A range of information sheets on issues of concern to trustees and potential trustees. Contact NCVO HelpDesk for details.

Standards in Public Life: Local public spending bodies. NCVO analysis of the second report of the Nolan Committee. NCVO June 1996.

NCVO submission to the Committee on Standards in Public Life. Inquiry into aspects of management and propriety in local government in England, Scotland and Wales. NCVO October 1996.

NCVO Review of the Nolan Committee's Third Report on Standards in Public Life. Review of the Nolan III Report on Standards of Conduct in Local Government and Advice on the Review of Responses to the Nolan II Report on Local Public Spending Bodies. NCVO August 1997.

The governance and management of charities, by Andrew Hind. Voluntary Sector Press (out of print).

Board focus: the governance debate. A current view of international corporate governance and the responsibilities of directors and boards, by Sir Adrian Cadbury.

Good governance. Developing effective board-management relations in public and voluntary organisations, by Cornforth and Edwards. CIMA Publishing 1998.

Appendix A: Case studies

Managing conflicts of interest

From time to time every board faces a period of conflict. Sometimes these conflicts are between individual board members, sometimes between factions within the board, and sometimes between the board and the staff. The first thing to note is that conflict is not inherently bad; some tension can be productive. Indeed, many community organisations function as a forum in which conflict can be resolved. But there is a difference between healthy conflict, where differences of opinion are expressed and debated, and unhealthy conflict, which simply hinders the organisation from fulfilling its mission.

These case studies illustrate the different kinds of conflict that may arise and the lessons that can be learned from them.

1. Conflicts between the board and staff

Case study

A chief executive of a thriving community centre had been in post for many years. She had extensive management experience and had recently taken a higher degree in management. The trustees, by contrast, were largely unwaged local people, including a large proportion of young mothers and retired people. Few had much experience of modern management, and the chief executive consequently held them in contempt. In her eyes, they did not 'add value'; for their part, they found the endless papers the chief executive presented on topics such as performance indicators, strategic planning, benchmarking, quality standards and appraisal systems almost incomprehensible. The trustees' solution was to recruit an able chair who was familiar with the current management and governance agenda and could consequently begin to wrest control of the organisation back from the chief executive.

The lessons

The management committee and the chief executive must work together, if not in partnership then at least in a mutually beneficial way. Each must respect the role of the other – which means that the chief executive must respect the governance role of the trustees. Even though they may not have the professional and business skills a manager needs, they are still the custodians of the charity. It is easy enough for a high-powered chief executive to marginalise a management committee of ordinary people. But a skilful chief executive draws on the skills the management committee does possess, and empowers them to do better by providing sympathetic trustee development programmes, encouraging trustees to seek outside professional advice, and presenting information clearly and concisely, if necessary via presentations and question and answer sessions. By contrast, a marginalised trustee board may feel they have no alternative but to recruit a chair tough enough to take back control of the organisation from a domineering chief executive.

Case study
The newly-recruited chief executive of a small counselling organisation had previously been a senior manager in a large statutory agency. He had been accustomed to regular structured supervision, to the informal support provided by colleagues, and to calling in experts from elsewhere in the agency to help with difficult cases. He soon began to feel isolated in his new post, and blamed the trustees for failing to provide adequate support.

The lessons
The chief executive is at the top of the management ladder, no matter how small the organisation. The role therefore calls for leadership and an acceptance that the line management provided in a large bureaucracy is neither appropriate nor possible. Trying to force the trustees (or the chair) to take on a line management role will overburden them – it is, after all, an unpaid, part-time job – and could generate yet more conflict: the chairs of small voluntary organisations are not necessarily familiar with the concept of supervision as practised in large statutory agencies.

The chief executive can reasonably expect the trustees to set out the strategy and direction of the organisation in policies and plans. The chair and chief executive should aim to develop a good working relationship; that will in practice mean contact at least once a week, probably by phone or fax.

Chief executives who feel they need more support than the trustees can give should explore other avenues, such as peer networks and action learning sets. Part of their new leadership role is to show initiative!

2. CONFLICT WITH AN INDIVIDUAL BOARD MEMBER
Case study
A new trustee who had previously been a volunteer has been upsetting people by coming into the office unannounced, bossing staff around, countermanding the director's orders, demanding confidential information and generally meddling in day-to-day affairs.

The lessons
This is a classic example of someone who is confused about which hat they are wearing. Organise a development session for the board and do the 'hats' exercise. Remind them that trustees must act jointly; they have no power individually except that which is specifically given to them by the board.

3. Conflicts between competing factions
Case study
A prominent member (and disgruntled ex-employee) of a community project recruited family, friends and supporters to stand at the next AGM in an attempt to stage a coup. The coup was only 50 per cent successful, leaving the trustee board evenly split. Most of the following year was spent in stalemate, as each half manoeuvred to get a majority at meetings. Each side tried to gain support by

spreading disinformation about the other. As a result, morale among staff and users collapsed, and the planning for the project did not get done, thus jeopardising funding.

The lessons
The values of the organisation need some attention; an attempted coup usually involves subterfuge and is therefore contrary to the principle of openness – as is spreading rumour and disinformation. The leader of the coup is unlikely to be acting from selfless motives, and thus sets a poor example of leadership. The trustee board must act jointly, reasonably and in the best interests of the organisation and its beneficiaries. The welfare of the organisation comes first; trustees who act contrary to its best interests are in breach of trust.

Trustees and potential trustees should be asked to fill in a statement of interests that lists any family, business and political relationships they have with staff and other actual or potential trustees. This statement will help to avoid conflicts of interest that may bring the organisation into disrepute, and should enable members to recognise when apparently unrelated individuals standing for election form a faction.

4. CONFLICTS WITH FOUNDERS
Case study
The founder of a prominent charity effectively runs the organisation by chairing the executive committee which takes all the important decisions. Few people know the precise remit of this committee; it was entered in the minute book, but no one is quite sure where. The remit apparently contains the phrase 'an open door to trustees who wish to attend' – although none of the trustees feels obliged to attend, nor do they feel particularly welcome when they do attend. Consequently the founder, as chair of the committee, is the only trustee to attend regularly; the chief executive and the senior manager are also present. The chair was selected by the founder, and is a busy person who was given to understand that the role was almost that of a president who merely chaired the once or twice yearly trustee board meetings and the AGM. The other trustees chosen were similarly busy people who understood their role to be largely figureheads.

The lessons
Such situations are difficult to tackle. The chief executive could put an update session on the agenda of the next trustee board meeting or AGM, during which trustees could be sensitively but firmly reminded that they have a duty to be active, and that they must act jointly, reasonably and in accordance with the constitution. A governance audit would reveal the true remit of the executive committee and the lack of involvement of the other trustees; it would also provide a timely opportunity to examine the values of the organisation.

General principles

Ensure that new trustees and staff are properly selected and adequately inducted.

Make sure that the boundaries between different roles are clearly defined and clearly understood by everyone.

Put the interests of the organisation first. Staff, volunteers and trustees work together to help the organisation fulfil its mission; the only justification for prolonging conflict is where the long-term benefits will outweigh the short-term disruption.

Consider the values that inform your organisation. Trustees and staff may have competing or incompatible values.

Consider Nolan's Seven Principles of Public Life:

Selflessness	Openness
Integrity	Honesty
Objectivity	Leadership
Accountability	

Appendix B
Skills audit questionnaire

Name:_____ Date:_____

1. What kind of expertise do you consider you bring to the Board?

☐	Administration	☐	History of the sector
☐	Campaigning	☐	Human resources/training
☐	Change Management/ restructuring	☐	Information technology
☐	Consultancy	☐	Legal
☐	Customer care	☐	Management/management systems
☐	Development	☐	Marketing
☐	Disability	☐	Media/PR
☐	Equal Opportunities	☐	Networks/alliances
☐	Financial	☐	Policy implementation
☐	Fundraising	☐	Research
☐	General	☐	Risk management
☐	Governance	☐	Strategic planning and training

Comments:

2. What other experience or skills do you feel you offer?

3. Are there any particular areas of the work of [name of organisation] in which you would like to be involved?

Thank you

APPENDIX C

FINANCIAL GOVERNANCE FRAMEWORK

		YES	NO
1	Does your charity have a clearly defined organisational structure, and has this been effectively communicated throughout the charity?		
2	Does it incorporate all levels within the charity, not just senior management?		
3	Do you know what the greatest threats, both internal and external, to your charity are?		
4	Has any kind of risk analysis or risk awareness programme been conducted within the charity?		
5	Does the charity have a planning cycle that fits with its overall objectives?		
6	Does that planning cycle require departments or functions to evaluate the previous year's performance against plans?		
7	Are explanations provided where planned objectives have not been met?		
8	Do employees understand the significance of controls and what they are designed to ensure?		
9	Do written procedures exist for all key areas of the charity's business?		
10	Aside from internal audit, are the results of any other independent, objective reviews disseminated throughout the charity?		
11	Are the trustees assured of the effectiveness of any controls, plans or procedures in place? If so, how?		
12	Is there a process for reporting discrepancies to the trustees? If so, what form does it take?		

Appendix D
Suggested contents of a financial procedures manual

Trustees' financial responsibilities
- The executive committee.
- The annual plan.
- Approval of the budget.
- Reserves policy.
- Conflicts of interest.
- Staff financial responsibilities.
- Controls on income.
- Grants.
- Legacies.
- Publication sales.
- Decentralised sales invoicing.
- Credit control.
- Bad debts.

Controls on expenditure
- Estimates and tendering.
- Purchase orders and invoices.
- Bank mandates and cheque signatories.
- Credit cards.
- Petty cash.

Controls on the financial assets
- Reconciling cash book to bank.
- Reconciling purchase ledger.
- Reconciling sales ledger.
- Reconciling stock accounts.
- Reconciling publications stock.
- VAT.
- Inland Revenue.
- Reconciling payroll control.
- Treasury management.
- Investment portfolio.

Exercising budgetary control
- Virement.

Controls on human resources
- Staff complement.
- Staff salaries.
- Staff regrading.

- Extra responsibility allowance.
- Starters and leavers.
- Contracts of employment.
- Travel and subsistence.
- The Probity Book.
- Season ticket loans.

Controls on physical assets
- Computer equipment.
- Computer software and data.

Appendix E

Job description for treasurer

This specimen job description and person specification for a treasurer can be adapted to meet an organisation's particular needs. It is also advisable to provide job descriptions for trustees[2] and honorary officers. In addition to clarifying roles, these descriptions are useful for people thinking about becoming trustees or honorary officers, and for those who are considering nominating others.

Job title: Treasurer of [name of organisation]

The role of a treasurer is to maintain an overview of the organisation's affairs to ensure that it is financially viable and proper financial records and procedures are maintained. The responsibilities of the treasurer will include:

- Overseeing, approving and presenting budgets, accounts and financial statements.
- Making sure that the financial resources of the organisation meet its present and future needs.
- Ensuring that the charity has an appropriate reserves policy.
- Preparing and presenting financial reports to the board.
- Ensuring that appropriate accounting procedures and controls are in place.
- Liaising with any paid staff and volunteers about financial matters.
- Advising on the financial implications of the organisation's strategic plans.
- Ensuring that the charity has an appropriate investment policy.
- Ensuring that there is no conflict between any investment held and the aims and objects of the charity.
- Monitoring the organisation's investment activity and ensuring its consistency with the organisation's policies and legal responsibilities.
- Ensuring that the accounts are prepared and disclosed in the form required by funders and the relevant statutory bodies: for example, the Charity Commission and/or the Registrar of Companies.
- If an audit is required, ensuring that the accounts are audited in the manner required, and any recommendations of the auditors implemented.
- Keeping the board informed about its financial duties and responsibilities.
- Contributing to the fundraising strategy of the organisation.
- Making a formal presentation of the accounts at the annual general meeting and drawing attention to important points in a coherent and comprehensible way.
- Sitting on appraisal, recruitment and disciplinary panels as required.

---

[2] In this information sheet the term trustee is used to refer to someone who has ultimate responsibility in a voluntary organisation, and what the top supervisory body trustees belong to is called the board; your own organisation may use the term management committee member, governor or some other term.

Person specification
In addition to the qualities needed by all trustees, the treasurer should ideally also possess the following:

- Fnancial qualifications and experience.
- Some experience of charity finance, fundraising and pension schemes.
- She skills to analyse proposals and examine their financial consequences.
- A readiness to make unpopular recommendations to the board.
- A willingness to be available to staff for advice and enquiries on an ad hoc basis.

2.
Financing the mission

---

1. Defining your mission
2. The necessity of planning
3. The language of planning
4. The process of planning
5. Planning within a quality framework
6. Programme resource assessment
7. Organisation resource analysis

This chapter begins by examining the conflict that often exists between those responsible for carrying out the charitable mission and those responsible for ensuring the financial stability of the organisation.

The chapter will introduce techniques that can be used to improve strategic planning, at the same time showing how voluntary organisations can maintain the balance between developing strategy and meeting financial objectives. The chapter concludes with a demonstration of how the Excellence Model can be used to help planning.

All voluntary organisations must first define precisely why they exist and how they plan to fulfil their mission. Only when this has been done can discussions on preparing a budget begin.

1. Defining your mission

Voluntary organisations usually exist because they have a mission: to cure the sick, to advance a profession, to discover new technologies, to educate the public.

Meeting financial goals is essential to fulfilling this mission, but is not the top priority. Managers must ask a 'chicken and egg' question: Which comes first, the programmes to fulfil the mission or the income (earned and voluntary) to finance the programmes? It is important to recognise that aspirations and financial resources are related, and that it is management's task to co-ordinate the two.

The planning process for voluntary organisations is complex, as they must not only accomplish their mission but also meet their financial goals. Financial planning for voluntary organisations can therefore be thought of as a cycle of related charitable and financial concerns, as shown in figure 2.1 below:

Figure 2.1: Charity programme planning cycle

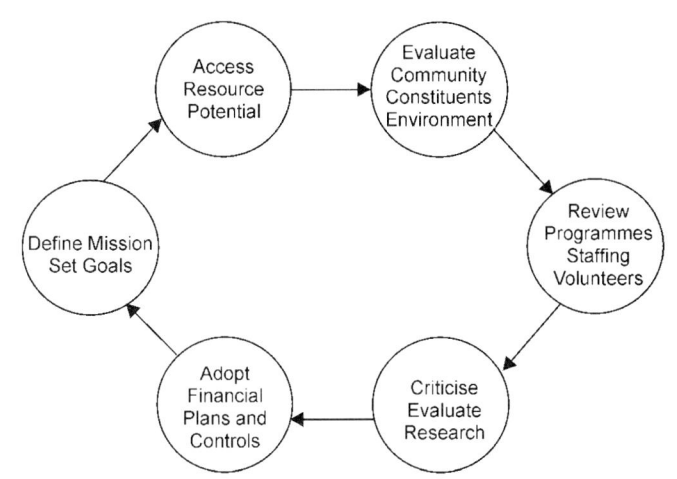

```
         Access Resource          Evaluate Community
         Potential         →      Constituents Environment
            ↑                              ↓
    Define Mission                    Review Programmes
    Set Goals                         Staffing Volunteers
            ↑                              ↓
         Adopt Financial         ←   Criticise Evaluate
         Plans and Controls           Research
```

Source: Financial Planning for Non Profit Organisations, Jody Blazek

An organisation's mission and its financial goals can also be viewed as parallel objectives that complement each other. Certainly, vigorous demand for the services of an organisation is an indication of success. But if financial management is neglected, it will not be long before the whole organisation begins to run on a deficit budget. Once in this situation, the organisation will find it hard to secure extra funding. Similarly, the provision of services for which there is no need – irrespective of the level of finance – will not enable the organisation to accomplish its mission.

2. THE NECESSITY OF PLANNING

Voluntary organisations need to plan effectively. For too many organisations, however, this process merely consists of adding 5 per cent to last year's budgets – which can only be valid in a world where nothing ever changes. For most voluntary organisations, moreover, planning is usually short term, typically in one to three-year cycles, corresponding to funding. This planning also tends to happen in a vacuum, cut off from what is happening in the outside world.

The short-term nature of most funding and the uncertainty caused by constant change are often given as reasons for not planning. But they are very good reasons why voluntary organisations *should* plan, and in a robust way at that.

Although it is beyond the scope of this guide to give detailed guidelines on

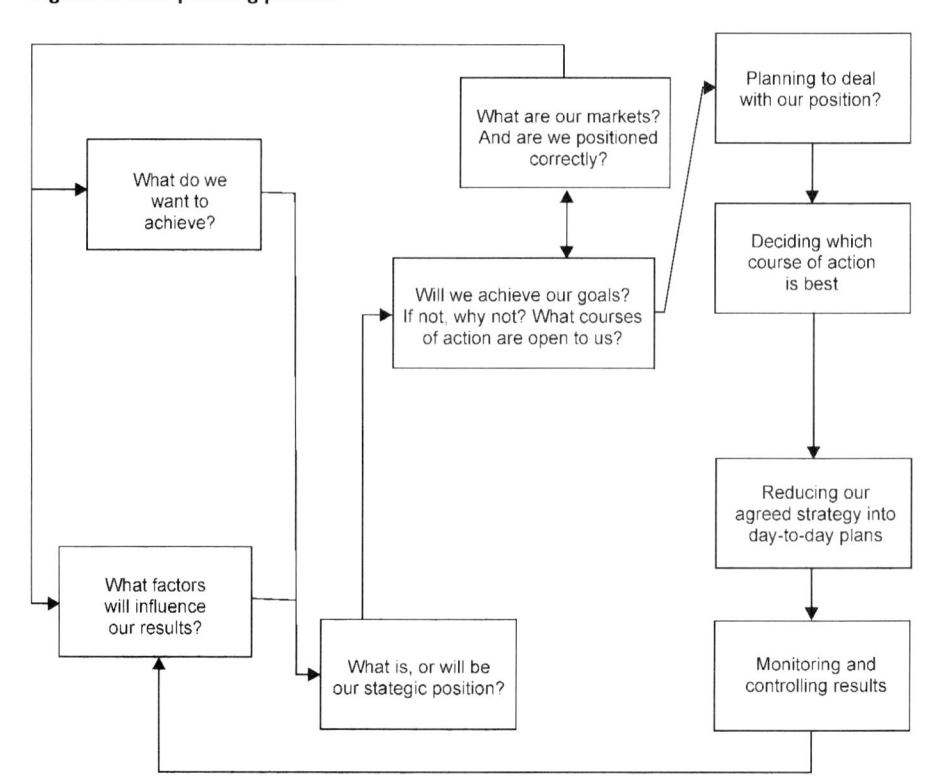

Figure 2.2: The planning process

```
                    ┌──────────────────┐         ┌──────────────────┐
                    │ What are our     │         │ Planning to deal │
                    │ markets?         │         │ with our position?│
                    │ And are we       │         └──────────────────┘
                    │ positioned       │                  │
┌──────────────┐    │ correctly?       │                  ▼
│ What do we   │    └──────────────────┘         ┌──────────────────┐
│ want to      │             ▲                   │ Deciding which   │
│ achieve?     │             ▼                   │ course of action │
└──────────────┘    ┌──────────────────┐         │ is best          │
                    │ Will we achieve  │         └──────────────────┘
                    │ our goals?       │                  │
                    │ If not, why not? │                  ▼
                    │ What courses of  │         ┌──────────────────┐
                    │ action are open  │         │ Reducing our     │
                    │ to us?           │         │ agreed strategy  │
                    └──────────────────┘         │ into day-to-day  │
                                                 │ plans            │
┌──────────────┐                                 └──────────────────┘
│ What factors │                                          │
│ will influence│                                         ▼
│ our results? │    ┌──────────────────┐         ┌──────────────────┐
└──────────────┘    │ What is, or will │         │ Monitoring and   │
                    │ be our stategic  │         │ controlling      │
                    │ position?        │         │ results          │
                    └──────────────────┘         └──────────────────┘
```

strategic planning (comprehensive signposting is given at the end of this chapter), this chapter will provide a general outline that sets the context for the later sections on financial planning.

For any organisation, planning is a continuous process which seeks, in essence, to describe what the organisation aims to achieve; where it currently stands in relation to those aims; what future actions will be required to achieve those aims; and how the organisation will know when it has achieved them. This continuous process is illustrated in figure 2.2.

3. THE LANGUAGE OF PLANNING

The mission
This is a brief statement of an organisation's purpose and values; it is the reason why it exists. The mission says little about what an organisation will do, or how or when it will do it. Missions should be a long-term statement of intent deriving from the vision that originally inspired the organisation.

Example 1: *Our vision is to reduce substantially the incidence and effect of toxoplasmosis (an infection harmful to the unborn child) and ultimately to eradicate congenital toxoplasmosis in the UK.*
The Toxoplasmosis Trust

Example 2: *The Weston Spirit works in the inner city areas of Britain offering young people, who may be experiencing feelings of isolation and hopelessness, a real alternative to problems such as unemployment, drug use, alcohol misuse, homelessness and abuse.*
The Weston Spirit

Strategic goals
These set out the direction of the organisation; they are a statement of its priorities in the medium to long term. Everything the organisation does should be related back to a strategic goal.

Example 1: The Toxoplasmosis Trust
- To raise awareness of toxoplasmosis.
- To support people affected by toxoplasmosis.
- To campaign to raise the profile of toxoplasmosis amongst government, health carers and the public.
- To ensure better prevention and management of toxoplasmosis.

Example 2: The Weston Spirit
- Have a presence in each major city in the UK.
- Influence policy formulation by and within major organisations and institutions affecting young people.
- Network with other organisations providing high quality youth work.
- Increase our annual membership numbers,

The operational objectives
These are detailed, costed and timed plans of what the organisation will do to meet each strategic goal. They set out a work plan for the organisation, typically over a twelve-month period.

Example 1: The Toxoplasmosis Trust
- Organising four pilot study days on toxoplasmosis for midwives around the country.
- Developing a midwives' education pack.
- Sending out a toxoplasmosis newsletter to local and hospital laboratories.
- Developing a new fact sheet for parents of children with retinochoroiditis.

4. The process of planning

What is, or will be, our strategic position?

To answer this question, a voluntary organisation must gather information. As part of this process, the organisation needs to identify the factors that will influence its results, both in terms of outputs and outcomes. To identify these factors will require a review of the external environment in which the organisation operates and of the internal structure of the organisation.

Analysing the external environment is important because without it, changes in, say, funding and government healthcare policy that present opportunities for extra financial support may be missed.

Despite its importance, this analysis of the external environment tends in practice to be constrained by two factors:

1. In many voluntary organisations, the demands of the moment – fire-fighting, meeting income targets and controlling expenditure – leave little time for strategic analysis.
2. Too little is known about how complex external factors affect voluntary organisations.

The effects of these constraints are decreasing, however, as more and more 'professionals' take part in the governance and management of voluntary organisations. In response to the second constraint, NCVO has combined its knowledge of the voluntary sector with the Henley Centre's expertise in forecasting to set up the Third Sector Foresight project, which seeks to understand these external factors and how they impact on the sector.

A conceptual model of how the external environment affects the voluntary sector economy is shown as Figure 2.3.

Figure 2.3: The voluntary sector economy

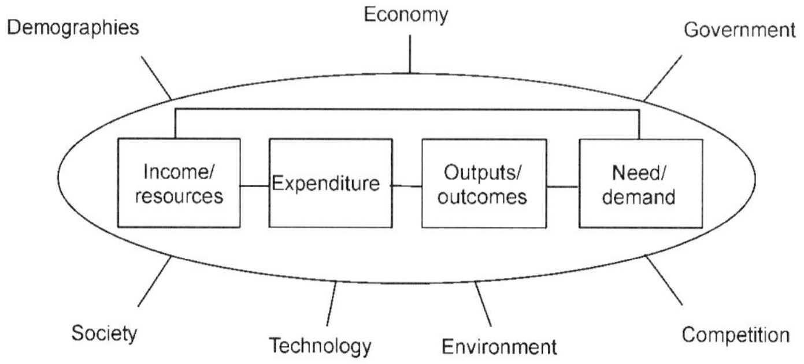

Source: NCVO

Outside the ellipse the key factors in the wider environment that affect voluntary organisations and the voluntary sector as a whole are shown; what they most commonly affect is shown within the ellipse. The ability of the sector to measure these effects is increasing all the time, and it is clear that it is a case of the traditional market linkage of supply and demand. The resources of the organisation lead to expenditure, which in turn lead to outputs and outcomes that satisfy need and demand.

Here are some brief examples of how external factors can affect voluntary organisations:

- *Economy*. The economic growth forecast for 1999 is likely to increase the disposable income of individuals. However, expenditure on housing and personal pension provision, plus the effect of the higher interest rates imposed by a newly-independent Bank of England to curb consumer expenditure, will mean that individuals have less 'free' income to donate to charitable causes.
- *Government*. The voluntary sector, particularly social welfare organisations, will be considerably affected if more community care services are transferred to the independent sector.
- *Society*. There is evidence of a shift of public confidence away from traditional institutions, such as political parties, and towards more voluntary forms of association.
- *Technology*. The increasing flexibility of people's work patterns will affect their ability to volunteer their time.

In short, analysing the external environment in which a voluntary organisation works should make it possible to identify opportunities or threats: for example, levels of economic activity, together with society's attitudes towards volunteering, may affect the organisation's income and other resources, and thus its ability to deliver the desired level of services.

Internal review
As mentioned earlier, an internal review should also be carried out as part of the information-gathering process. The aim of this review is to identify weaknesses that must be addressed and strengths that are not being exploited. A list of the areas that should be covered is given below, followed by a description of the tools that can be used to conduct the review.

Leadership:
- Trustee board characteristics and balance.
- Trustee board focus: core activities and other decision-making systems.
- Skills experience and balance.
- Management training.

Culture:
- Power groupings.

- Power sources: authority, control over resources, ability.
- Social norms.
- Attitudes.

Structure:
- Reporting lines.
- Level of integration.
- Resources balance.
- Information systems.

Functional analysis (this will depend on the type of voluntary activity – the example used is a women's HIV charity):
- Programme services.
- Community development.
- Information, training and education.
- Fundraising.
- Finance and administration.

Control systems:
- Planning systems.
- Budget systems.
- Performance appraisal.
- Internal audit (where appropriate).

Tools to use

Management audit. This sets out to assess the effectiveness of the trustee board, management team and organisational structure in achieving charitable objectives. It will therefore be looking at leadership, culture and structure to identify existing and potential weaknesses and recommend ways to rectify them.

Ratio analysis. Key ratios – such as liquidity, fundraising performance, cost ratios and trading profitability (for trading groups) – can, when analysed over time and compared with those of other voluntary organisations offering comparable services, provide a valuable indication of trends and highlight key relationships.

Contribution analysis. This identifies the absolute or percentage amount that a particular programme contributes to the general overheads (after deducting direct programme costs from any earned or unearned income for that programme). The aim is to ensure that each programme makes a contribution to these overheads.

The position audit

Combining the results of the review of the external environment with those of the internal review and comparing them with the organisation's strategic goals makes it possible to carry out a 'position audit'. This shows where the organisation currently stands in relation to its goals, by identifying what opportunities or threats exist externally, what internal strengths need to be exploited and what internal weaknesses need to be addressed.

The above assessment will help to identify the strategic choices open to the organisation. These may include the following:

- Should the organisation grow, stay the same, reduce its size – or is a recovery programme necessary?
- Should the organisation remain within its existing market, expand into different geographical locations or enter entirely new markets?
- Does the organisation need to modify the services it provides or develop new ones, or can it maintain the existing portfolio of services?
- Should the organisation become a more specialist or more general provider of services?

Choosing a course of action
Once the choices available to the organisation have been identified, there will have to be an evaluation, since it is unlikely that all options will be feasible with the available resources. The choices could be evaluated in terms of their acceptability, suitability and feasibility:

The criterion for acceptability would be whether the chosen strategy fits in well with existing resources, competencies and culture.

The criterion for suitability would be whether the chosen strategy maximises the strengths or reduces the weaknesses of the organisation, and whether it seizes the opportunities or averts the threats offered by the external environment.

Testing for feasibility requires the following questions to be asked:

- Is the leadership suitable?
- Is the culture capable?
- Is the organisational structure appropriate?
- Are the functional policies appropriate?
- Are the resources available?
- Is this strategy an improvement on not changing at all?
- Are there procedures for implementation and monitoring?

Each chosen strategy needs to satisfy all these points. If it fails on any, the organisation must assess whether remedial action is possible.

Preparing day-to-day plans
Once the strategic goals have been identified – in practice there are seldom more than six – they must be translated into day-to-day activities. The Toxoplasmosis Trust, for example, identifies its strategic goals as:

- To raise awareness of toxoplasmosis.
- To support people affected by toxoplasmosis.
- To campaign to raise the profile of toxoplasmosis amongst government, health carers and the public.

- To ensure better prevention and management of toxoplasmosis.

Based on these four goals, a set of operational objectives or action plans has been formulated:

- Organising four pilot study days on toxoplasmosis for midwives around the country.
- Developing a midwives' education pack.
- Sending out a toxoplasmosis newsletter to local and hospital laboratories.
- Developing a new fact sheet for parents of children with retinochoroiditis.

For each of these operational objectives, a detailed plan is drafted which is SMART: Specific (detailed), Measurable (both financially and otherwise), Attainable, Realistic and Timed.

For example, developing a midwives' education pack might be further broken down as follows:

- Identify major issues, medical and otherwise, of which midwives need to be aware.
- Identify main contributors to educational pack.
- Prepare draft, check accuracy of content and design.
- Conduct a limited testing with readers'/users' panel.
- Print.
- Market and promote pack to midwives through hospitals.

The persons responsible for each of these tasks, and the time allotted, should be identified, so as to provide a basis for performance appraisal.

5. Planning within a quality framework

A quality framework makes possible a rigorous and consistent approach to quality throughout an organisation. There is no reason why voluntary organisations should not carry out their planning within such a framework; the pursuit of quality, the commitment to deliver the best possible services to users, has always been a major preoccupation for them.

As will be seen in Chapter Three, the Quality Standards Task Group has concluded that the Excellence Model is the best quality framework and that it is suitable for the entire voluntary sector.

The proposed quality principles for voluntary organisations state that such organisations:

- Strive for continuous improvement in all they do.
- Use recognised standards or models as a means to continuous improvement and not as an end.

- Agree requirements with stakeholders and endeavour to meet or exceed these first time and every time.
- Promote equality of opportunity through their internal and external conduct.
- Are accountable to stakeholders.
- Add value to their end users and beneficiaries.

Many voluntary organisations may already follow these principles, but in a less structured way.

The Excellence Model depends on self-assessment. For this purpose, it provides a framework of general criteria that can be applied to any organisation and is based on the following premise: 'Customer satisfaction, people satisfaction and impact on society are achieved through leadership driving policy and strategy, people management, resources and processes leading ultimately to excellence in business results.'

The framework is depicted diagrammatically in figure 2.4:

Figure 2.4: The Excellence Model Framework

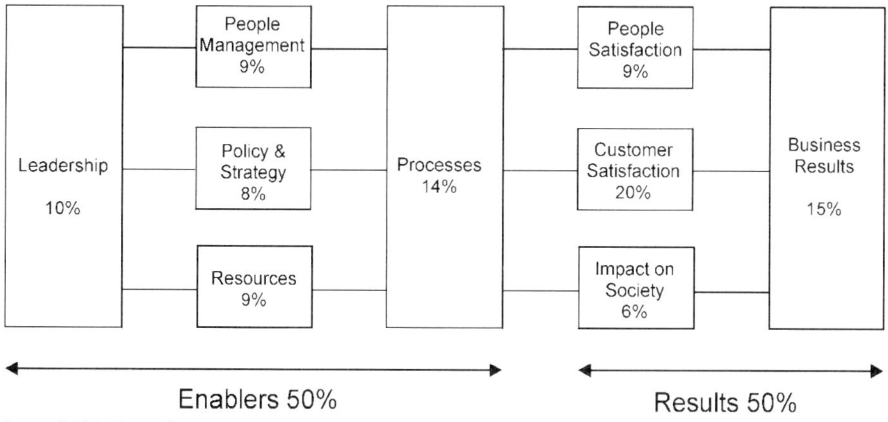

```
                 People                          People
                 Management                      Satisfaction
                 9%                              9%

                 Policy &                        Customer        Business
    Leadership   Strategy       Processes        Satisfaction    Results
    10%          8%             14%              20%             15%

                 Resources                       Impact on
                 9%                              Society
                                                 6%
```

←——— Enablers 50% ———→   ←——— Results 50% ———→

Source: British Quality Foundation

Each of the nine criteria in the Excellence Model can be used to assess the organisation's progress towards excellence. The percentage given for each criterion indicates its relative importance to the overall excellence of the organisation. The guide to self-assessment indicates how each of the nine criteria should be defined and what self-assessment should demonstrate.

Here are the criteria and, where appropriate, the requirements for self-assessment.

1. Leadership

How the behaviour and actions of the executive team and all other leaders inspire, support and promote excellence as the best way to achieve the organisation's objectives.

2. Policy and strategy
How the organisation formulates, deploys, reviews and turns policy and strategy into plans and actions.
Self-assessment should demonstrate:

- How policy and strategy are based on information which is relevant and comprehensive.
- How policy and strategy are developed.
- How policy and strategy are communicated and implemented.
- How policy and strategy are regularly updated and improved.

3. People management
How the organisation releases the full potential of its people.

4. Resources
How the organisation manages its resources effectively and efficiently.

5. Processes
The management of all value-adding activities within the organisation. How the organisation identifies, manages, reviews and improves its processes.

6. Customer satisfaction
What the organisation is achieving in relation to the satisfaction of its external customers.

7. People satisfaction
What the organisation is achieving in relation to the satisfaction of its people.

8. Impact on society
What the organisation is achieving in satisfying the needs and expectations of the community at large.

9. Business results
What the organisation is achieving in relation to its planned objectives and in satisfying the needs and expectations of everyone with an interest or other stake in the organisation. Self-assessment should demonstrate:

- Financial measures of the organisation's performance.
- Additional measures of the organisation's performance.

The approach to strategic planning outlined above should also satisfy the self-assessment criteria of the Excellence Model. For example, under the Excellence Model, a quality voluntary organisation should develop policy and strategy using information relating to:

- Customers and suppliers.
- Social, environmental and legal issues.
- Internal performance.

The strategic planning process of reviewing the external environment and appraising internal strength and weaknesses should achieve the same results.

The Excellence Model can be used by voluntary organisations of all sizes to demonstrate the quality of the services and products they provide and to enhance the effectiveness of their use of resources.

6. Programme resource assessment

At the beginning of this chapter it was emphasised that mission-orientated goals and financial goals are interdependent; and later, when discussing choice of strategies, it was stated that one of the three main criteria is acceptability in terms of fit (with existing strategies), resources (both financial and otherwise), competence (ability and skills) and culture (leadership style). Any changes that give a new strategic direction to charitable programmes require a parallel adjustment to the financial resources devoted to that programme. This section will look at the financial adjustments needed when expansion (or contraction) of services is planned.

Figure 2.5 shows the kind of connections that should be made between mission-orientated goals and financial goals.

It may be useful here to consider a situation where a voluntary organisation is faced with the need to reduce expenditure. The finance committee might prepare a list of possible solutions, and committee members would rate each solution as V for viable or U for unacceptable as shown in figure 2.6.

Figure 2.5: Connecting mission with financial goals

Mission	Financial resource
Feed more children to relieve the suffering of the poor	Get donations of food from supermarkets
Double the congregation to spread the church's spiritual message	Market the church through weekly gospel programmes on the public radio
Publish more training manuals to better educate our league members	Recruit skilled writers to update and expand manuals

Source: Financial Planning for Non Profit Organisations, Jody Blazek

Figure 2.6 Example of worksheet for rating financial solutions

Solution	V or U
Research public perception of accomplishments; interview recipients of services to evaluate their needs and suggestions	
Employ a development officer to increase contributor base	
Raise membership rates, service fees, publication prices	
Charge for services now offered free	
Eliminate programmes or downsize staff	
Merge with, or take over, another organisation	
Sell off under-utilised assets	
Improve marketing, publish magazine, sponsor public events	
Reallocate resources to realign strengths and weaknesses	
Establish new measurement systems to evaluate performance	

Source: Financial Planning for Non Profit Organisations, Jody Blazek

7. ORGANISATION RESOURCE ANALYSIS

Another part of the planning process is a critical look at the organisation's wider financial situation, which provides an opportunity to evaluate its long-term financial stability. The key ratio and financial indicators from the annual financial statements, as discussed in Chapter Five, can be used for this.

Depending on the results of this analysis, the voluntary organisation might adopt certain steps to improve its financial situation; see the model balance sheet of a church in figure 2.7.

At first sight, the church's financial situation may seem healthy. It has £108,510 of unrestricted net assets on its balance sheet, total assets of £390,000 and only £281,490 of debt. This indicates that the church has accumulated assets well in excess of the money it owes.

However, a closer examination of the balance sheet reveals that the church does not have the money to pay the bills that will soon fall due. Compare the liquid assets of £20,000 – that is, the assets currently available to pay bills – with the current liabilities of £81,490. In other words, the debts becoming due in the next year amount to four times the current assets.

The first glance at the bottom line of a financial statement can also be misleading. The church's unrestricted net assets of more than £100,000 might seem reasonable for an organisation of its size. But it is noticeable that the fund balance consists of non-cash assets: that is, the church's equipment and buildings. Because these assets are used every day, they cannot be sold to pay bills. In this condition, the church is

Figure 2.7: Holy Spirit Church – summary balance sheet

	£
Building	250,000
Equipment and furnishings	120,000
Current (liquid) assets	20,000
Total assets	390,000
Current liabilities	81,490
Long term debt	200,000
Total liabilities	281,490
Net assets	108,510
Unrestricted Funds	108,510

Figure 2.8: Prioritising macro resource goals

Priority Level 1-10		Macro resource goal
	A	Establish working capital base
	B	Maintain three (or more) months operating cash balance (improve cash flow)
	C	Retire debt or reduce accounts payable
	D	Seek endowment funding to provide investment income to offset annual fluctuations in grant funding.
	E	Buy or build permanent facilities
	F	Establish branches
	G	Conduct marketing campaign
	H	Raise salaries or increase personnel
	I	Improve employee benefits, e.g. pensions
	J	Hire Chief Financial Officer to improve financial reporting, planning and management

Source: Financial Planning for Non Profit Organisations, Jody Blazek

vulnerable: a delay of a few weeks in funding can cause havoc, as creditors become increasingly demanding, pay cheques bounce and overdue taxes begin to cause embarrassment.

Once the church's management recognise the financial problem, however, they can devise solutions. Over the next two or three years the church might focus on financial goals A, B, C and D in figure 2.8. To enable these goals to be realised, the church must also take steps to balance its mission and financial goals.

The church would have to introduce formal financial planning. First, it would prepare a budget for the coming year, following the guidelines in Chapter Three. Next, it would convert the budget into a monthly cash flow projection. The church's financial managers would review the accounting systems to ensure that accurate and up to date information is available to assess the financial position at any give time. Lastly, the church might consider using ratio analysis (see Chapter Five) to improve its current funding position.

FURTHER READING AND RESOURCES

The Complete Guide to Business and Strategic Planning by Alan Lawrie. Directory of Social Change 1994.

The UK Voluntary Sector Almanac 1998/99. NCVO Publications.

Third Sector Foresight Conference: A report on the Third Sector Foresight Conference. NCVO 1998.

Quality standards in the voluntary sector. Quality Standards Task Group 1998.

A 'White Paper' on quality in the voluntary sector. Quality Standards Task Group 1998.

Guide to the business Excellence Model. British Quality Foundation 1998.

Voluntary interpretation of the business Excellence Model. British Quality Foundation 1998.

Financial Planning for Non Profit Organisations by Jody Blazek, Wiley Nonprofit Series, 1996.

Appendix A: Case studies

1. Rett Syndrome Association

This case study examines the importance of having explicit organisational aims and objectives which are clearly linked with them. The link between aims and objectives helps to ensure that day-to-day activities help to meet a stated aim – a perhaps obvious point that is often overlooked when dealing with mature organisations. The case study also highlights the need to have at least one aim to do with organisational development. The traditional emphasis on service provision means that this too is often overlooked.

Background
The trustees, staff, volunteers and a selection of users of the Rett Syndrome Association recently had a planning 'awayday' at which a number of organisational priorities were identified.

Aims of the Rett Syndrome Association
- To promote the welfare, treatment and advancement of the girls and women suffering from Rett syndrome.
- To support, sustain and assist those caring for Rett syndrome sufferers, whether they be parents, carers or professionals.
- To promote greater understanding and awareness of the syndrome.
- To promote research into causes and effects of Rett syndrome and to disseminate or publish the useful results of such research.

Structure and staffing
Rett Syndrome Association is a registered charity managed by a board of trustees comprised of parents and grandparents of Rett syndrome sufferers and non-parents. The association has a national office staffed by three full-time employees: Office Manager, Development Manager and Fundraising Manager. There is a part-time secretary. There are self-support groups of parents and carers around the country; and there are many volunteers who help either in the office or around the country.

Services provided
- Support for parents and carers.
- Self-support groups of parents and carers and a network of contact parents.
- Written and video information about all aspects of the disorder, including management and therapeutic help.
- A quarterly magazine, *Rett News*.
- An annual Family Weekend giving support, information and respite care.
- Diagnostic and management clinics.
- Work in association with a multidisciplinary team of experts who conduct half day assessments and provide help and advice.

- Presentation and workshops to and by professionals.
- Funding and encouragement of research.
- Provision of reduced price holidays in a specially adapted caravan.
- Contacts with similar associations throughout the world.

Organisational priorities

The trustees have identified six priorities that must be addressed if the future of the organisation is to be secured:

1. *Service planning and development*: we will consolidate and develop the provision of support, guidance and information to parents, carers and professionals.
2. *Human resource development*: we will ensure that the trustees, staff and volunteers are recruited, trained, supported and valued.
3. *Management*: we will ensure that our management arrangements and systems are effective and efficient.
4. *Promotion and marketing*: we aim to ensure that Rett Syndrome and the existence of the RSAUK, its services and contribution, will be recognised by relevant professionals throughout Great Britain and Northern Ireland.
5. *Fundraising and financial management*: we will seek to maximise all potential funding sources to ensure that the strategic targets are resourced.
6. *Campaigning and lobbying*.

The objectives that expand upon the above organisational priorities are shown in figure 2.9.

The findings of the 'awayday' make the following observations possible:

Firstly, in terms of strategic planning, each objective needs to fit very clearly into an organisational aim. For each of the aims, a short statement could be devised that neatly encapsulates the vision for the future. This would involve reassembling the objectives already outlined.

Secondly, each objective should be linked with an aim so that it can be demonstrated that the organisation is addressing each of its aims within the strategic plan. Every objective should be addressed, but not necessarily in an equal amount of detail (though this should be a deliberate decision, rather than one taken by default). Some aims may require a lot of time and little money, some the reverse; this needs to be taken into account when assessing the strategic plan. The chart, figure 2.10, identifies some of the objectives not linked to an organisational aim. Thirdly, there should be objectives in the strategic plan that are not directly related to organisational aims but are about organisational development. These are as essential as externally-directed aims. They are not taking time, energy and resources away from the main task. They ensure that there is personal development of the organisation's staff; these are the people who are being paid to develop the organisation and the organisation has to act responsibly towards them as their employer. Also, if the skills, experience and qualities of staff are developed, they

Fiigure 2.9: Rett Syndrome organisation objections

Service planning and development: Year One

Objectives	Performance	Responsibility
To review current clinic structure and implement a new structure	The needs of potential users have been identified, new consultants have been identified and decisions made and implemented	Chairman
To revise the *What is RS?* booklet	A new booklet is printed	Trustee
To monitor and identify information relevant to the needs of service users	The needs of services users have been identified and an evaluation report produced	Office manager
To plan the collation of research articles	A plan is produced which will outline the structure for cataloguing research papers and resources are secured for implementation of the plan	Trustee
To plan the provision of regional Rett days and run a pilot day	A plan is produced for structuring regular regional meetings, resources are secured for a pilot regional day, and it has happened.	Development Manager
To develop support groups	To have established three additional support groups	Development Manager

Human resource development: Year One

Objectives	Performance	Responsibility
To review the contact parent network	A plan is produced	Chairman
To select and train new contact parents	Resources have been secured and the selection and training of new contact parents has started	Chairman
To identify areas in which staff need training	Individual and office training needs are identified and funding secured	Office Manager
To identify the need for and plan the future use of volunteers	A plan is produced	Office Manager

Figure 2.9—continued

To review the development of roles and responsibilities of staff, officers and trustees	A plan is produced	Chairman

Management: Year One

Objectives	Performance	Responsibility
To clarify respective roles and responsibilities of trustees, contact parents, support groups and staff	Evidence exists of consultation and agreement by key players on roles and responsibilities	Chairman
To introduce induction of new trustees	An induction pack and programme is available for all new trustees	Chairman
To identify areas which need to have policies and procedures	The areas are identified	Chairman
To agree policy and procedure for research applications to the RSAUK	A policy and procedure is produced	Trustee
To keep accurate statistics of services	Monitoring forms have been produced and are being used	Office Manager
To evaluate the current databases and ensure they meet our needs	A written evaluation is produced	Office Manager

Promotion and marketing: Year One

Objectives	Performance	Responsibility
To produce a comprehensive public relations and marketing plan	Resources have been secured to purchase external assistance with the production of a plan	Development Manager

Fundraising and finance

Objectives	Performance	Responsibility
To secure funding for core activities as per planned budget	Funding had been secured for: • Office expenses. • Annual family weekend. • *Rett News*. • Sending out information. • Clinics.	Fundraising Manager

Figure 2.9—continued

To secure funding for the objectives in service planning and development as per planned budget	Resources have been secured for: • New clinic structure. • Pilot Rett day. • Cataloguing research papers. • Service user information.	Fundraising Manager
To secure funding for the objectives in human resource development as per budget	Funding has been secured for: • Training of new contact parents. • Staff training..	Fundraising Manager
To secure funding for a PR and marketing plan	Funding has been secured to implement the plan	Fundraising Manager

provide a better service, because they are more motivated about doing it. Two additional aims could therefore be included into the chart to deal with management and finance. For example:

- Management: 'To ensure that the Rett Syndrome is managed efficiently and effectively in achieving organisational aims'.
- Finance: 'to diversify Rett Syndrome funding sources while retaining financial stability'.

Fourthly, the plans now need to be broken down even further. This is the final step that takes them from the printed page into action. Objectives should be prioritised, the resources they need allocated to each of them, and a realistic time scale set. The lead person for each objective must make a real commitment to meeting the deadline and should be prepared to justify any delays.

This is not to say that there cannot be flexibility, simply that unless everyone commits themselves to the plan, it will not happen. Each deadline has to be realistic for the individual concerned; sufficient time needs to be left in their work plan for their ongoing work as well as any unplanned work – crises will happen, or unexpected opportunities may present themselves.

Fifthly, ensure that the plan is monitored on a regular basis. This can be achieved through committee meetings and through supervision. Each person should have a work plan – which is simply a list of things for them to do – that prioritises activities and shows deadlines clearly. This enables everyone to manage their work to meet deadlines, rather than be surprised when a deadline appears. For this purpose, each objective needs to be broken down into manageable tasks: one objective might require seven or eight actions that have to happen one after the other, so sufficient time needs to be allocated. For example, in a recruitment process the start date for the new person has to be calculated ahead to allow for advertising, shortlisting, interview, notice etc and can then be estimated accurately.

Figure 2.10: Linking organisational objectives to aims.

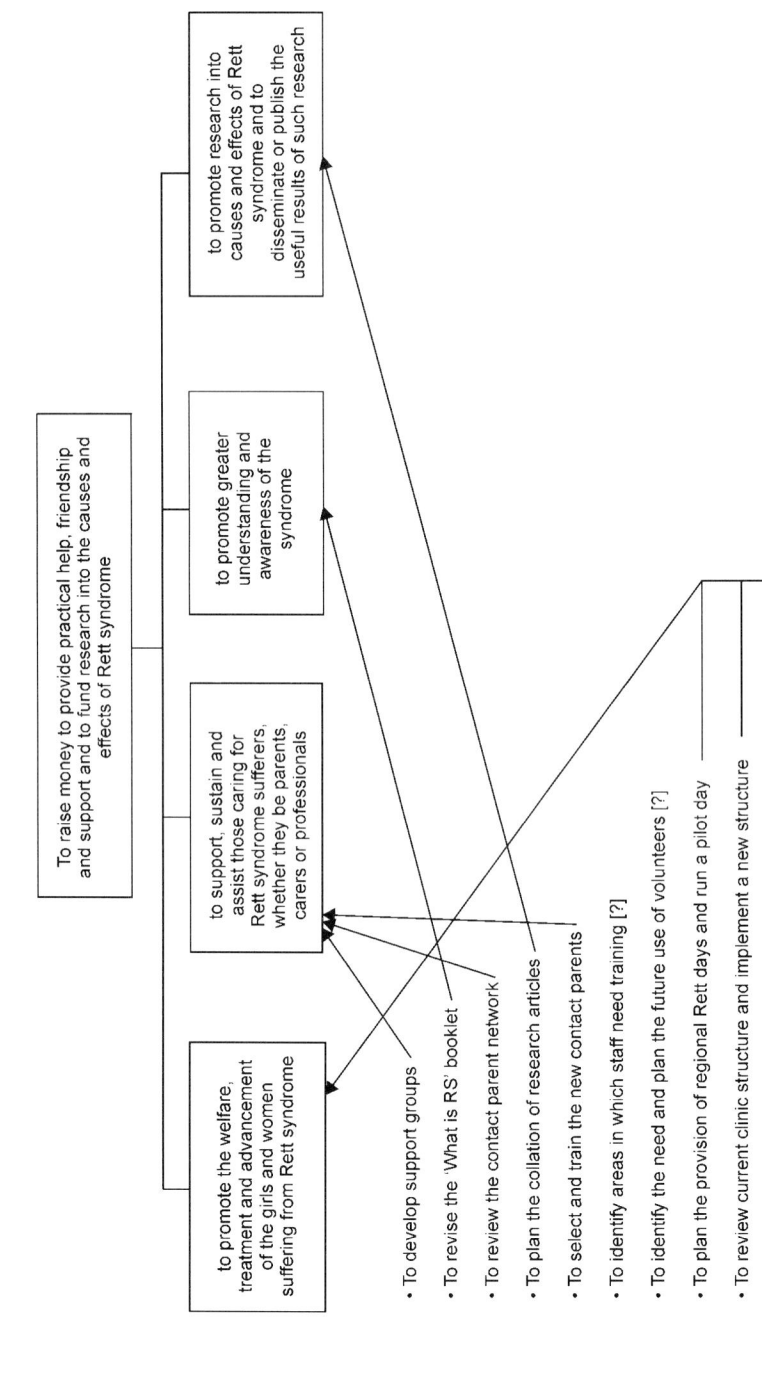

To raise money to provide practical help, friendship and support and to fund research into the causes and effects of Rett syndrome

- to promote the welfare, treatment and advancement of the girls and women suffering from Rett syndrome
- to support, sustain and assist those caring for Rett syndrome sufferers, whether they be parents, carers or professionals
- to promote greater understanding and awareness of the syndrome
- to promote research into causes and effects of Rett syndrome and to disseminate or publish the useful results of such research

• To develop support groups
• To revise the 'What is RS' booklet
• To review the contact parent network
• To plan the collation of research articles
• To select and train the new contact parents
• To identify areas in which staff need training [?]
• To identify the need and plan the future use of volunteers [?]
• To plan the provision of regional Rett days and run a pilot day
• To review current clinic structure and implement a new structure
• To monitor and identify information relevant to the needs of service users
• To review the development of roles and responsibilities of staff, officers and trustees [?]

2. Language Line

This case study demonstrates the usefulness of an environmental analysis.

BACKGROUND

Language Line was set up in January 1990 to provide a telephone interpreting service in seven minority ethnic languages. Remarkably, as director Marc Kiddle observed, 'although similar services were long established in Australia, the United States and Holland, this was the first telephone interpreting service in Britain. It was, then, truly innovative.' At the outset, however, Language Line did not know of the existence of any similar services and so had nowhere to turn for advice or experience. The initial objective was to offer the service to health organisations in the Tower Hamlets area of London, with plans to extend the scheme to other users and areas.

The project received initial support for a pilot from a government task force, British Telecom and a charitable trust. The pilot was judged a success, and in early 1991 it was decided to conduct research to establish whether the project could find alternative sources of income when the initial grants ended. An analysis of how interested potential users might be was therefore needed.

Types of information

Five main types of information should be collected as part of an environmental analysis:

1. Information about the needs and opinions of current and potential users of the services of your organisation. The views of past users of the service will also be valuable in assessing your strengths and weaknesses.
2. Information on important trends and influences in the organisation's environment.
3. The criteria used by grant makers and other funders in deciding whether to support funding applications.
4. Existing patterns of service in areas of activity you wish to become involved in.
5. The activities of organisations with similar services to those of your own.

The director of Language Line and its five permanent interpreters knew that there had been a steady increase in demand from existing users. They believed, from discussions with local officials, that the separation of purchaser and provider roles resulting from reforms of the health service was leading to a new emphasis on access to services for minority language speakers. They also knew that there were other concentrations of minority language speakers who made demands on the statutory services – such as the police force and health service – that might also become users.

In other areas, however, staff were largely in the dark. Until 1991 the service had been provided free: would new customers be willing to pay for the service?

What were the decision making procedures? Staff were unaware of any direct competitors and did not know how successful their limited public relations activity had been in creating awareness of Language Line.

On the basis of this assessment of the information gaps, the project decided that it needed to acquire information on the following:

- Existing provision of interpreting services for minority language speakers (if any) by potential purchasers.
- Plans of potential purchasers for improvements in interpreting services.
- The decision making procedures of potential new users.
- The awareness potential users had of Language Line and their interest in its services.

Figure 2.11: Collecting information – sources and methods

Internal sources	External: secondary	External: primary
Analysis and discussion	Publications	User surveys
Information on service usage	Material from other organisations e.g. annual reports	Discussion or focus groups
Published information	Library searches	Visits to other organisations
Contacts and networking		Exhibitions

Source: NCVO

The information collection methods used by Language Line also vary according to whether the environmental analysis is external or internal (see figure 2.11). Specifically:

- *External.* Review of census data to pinpoint geographical areas with highest concentration of minority language speakers.
- *Internal.* Telephone questionnaire to local authorities, health authorities and police stations in the target area.

Interpreting and presenting the information

In presenting the findings of your environmental analysis, you need to:

- Demonstrate a clear understanding of the needs and expectations of different groups of current and potential users of your organisation's services;
- Identify the opportunities for, and threats to, your organisation as a result of developments in its environment;
- Summarise the management actions you intend to take to maximise the opportunities and minimise the treats you have identified.

3. 'ELEVEN OTHER WINNERS IF WE BEAT THE POLES'

This case study examines the effect of social change upon organisations.

BACKGROUND
Social change affects organisations in a number of ways: it is easy to become blinkered and to only consider fashion, buying patterns and attitudes. Certainly these factors affect some industries, but there are many others that can have a drastic impact on a small industry or individual organisation. Taking advantage of such short-term environmental changes requires a highly adaptive strategy model. As an example, read this article by Sean Rayment published in the *Sun* on 8 September 1993:

'ELEVEN OTHER WINNERS IF WE BEAT THE POLES'
As you read this, think of the forthcoming World Cup and Olympics. There is much more than our national pride at stake when England face Poland at Wembley tonight. Lucrative business deals rest on Graham Taylor's men proving they are fit to join the best in next year's World Cup in the USA.

A win tonight will keep our qualification hopes alive and will raise the spirits of companies, big and small, some of whom have already spent millions in anticipation of England making it to the finals. Here Sean Rayment presents the other England 11, from airline boss to T-shirt maker, who will also be winners if we triumph tonight.

Bookies
Bookmakers William Hill expect to add £5 million to their turnover next year if England win tonight. But the firm's media boss Graham Sharpe said, 'If England don't compete in the World Cup, we face losing a lot. We make and lose money from our turnover. If there's no turnover, we can't make anything. Tonight will be a very tense moment.'

Sponsors
Electronic giants Panasonic have signed a £4 million deal to have their logo displayed on ITV screens before, during and after every World Cup game. They expect 17 million viewers to see their name if England reach the finals. Panasonic advertising boss Russell Simpkins said, 'Of course we are hoping for an England victory tonight.'

TV rentals
Granada UK hope to rent out an extra 30,000 sets next summer if England reach the finals. There was a 50 per cent rise in rentals during the 1990 campaign. Planning boss Graham Packman said, 'We rented out more than 30,000 tellies during the last World Cup directly due to England's success. If we lose tonight we will be lucky if we rent out an extra 10,000.'

Sports shops

Store boss Adrian Pointer, 34, who runs two Simply Sports shops in Kent and Surrey said, 'I will be looking for an increase in business for boots, shirts, footballs and other sportswear of up to 50 per cent. If we were to win the World Cup, that would really be big business. Kit sales would go up 100 per cent without doubt. But first we have to beat the Poles.'

Souvenirs

Leisurewear firm Kick Sportswear have already spent £25,000 on a trial range of England World Cup souvenir sweatshirts and T-shirts. They hope to see sales soar by 20 per cent to more than £1 million next year – but that depends on England's success. Sales boss Stephen Ray said, 'During the last World Cup sales went through the roof. It was fantastic.'

Satellite TV

Dish sales have already soared to more than 20,000 a week. A Sky Sports spokesman said, 'Sales are booming because the football season has just started. If England get to the World Cup, we expect even more interest. Another benefit is that we have a summer of exciting football involving England that will fire up enthusiasm for the next season.'

Travel firms

Sportsworld Travel, one of the few official World Cup travel companies, hopes to generate up to £1 million from an England victory tonight. Marketing boss Mike Norris said, 'We expect that up to 2,000 fans would want to travel to follow the team in America. A win tonight would obviously be good news for us on a patriotic and business front.'

TV advertising

ITV's advertising rates during an England World Cup match would double to about £60,000 for a 30-second slot. But up to £600,000 could be lost during the half-time break of the World Cup semi-final if England were not involved. Derek Hement, sales controller for London Weekend Television, said, 'If England get through to the last eight, audience sizes will double.'

Soccer mags

Thousands more copies of *Shoot!* magazine will be sold each week if England win. When England reached the semi-finals of the World Cup, *Shoot!* sales soared 10,000 a week to 169,000. Editor Dave Smith said, 'To say that *Shoot!* needs England to qualify is an understatement. When England win our magazine sells – it's that simple.'

Airlines

American Airlines, one of the England squad sponsors, have paid £100,000 to be the official airline of the Football Association. They hope for a major share of trade when 5,000 to 10,000 England fans buy tickets to the States for the finals. Spokesman Iain Burns said, 'We want to be associated with the team so that when fans plan their trip they will look at us.'

Strip makers

Umbro are the official sponsor of the England kit. Spokesman Simon Marsh said, 'There will be a dramatic rise in sales if England go through – 30 per cent at least. Fans will want the official tracksuit, the kit bag, everything. We currently have 500 people in manufacturing. If England succeed it will mean 12 hour shifts for our staff.'

3.
Budgeting

1. Budget planning	4. Communicating financial information
2. Preparing forecasts	5. Budgets and IT solutions
3. Structuring the budget	6. Computerising the accounts

After the organisation has examined its priorities and refined its mission in accordance with the financial resources available, it is time to prepare the budget. This is a tool for allocating resources and implementing strategic plans. It charts a way of allocating and maximising the use of resources, and ideally identifies financial problems that could arise in the coming year. The budget provides indicators for evaluating employee performance and gives the staff goals to reach and steps to achieve them.

1. Budget planning

As a financial measure of the voluntary organisation's goals, a budget compiles programmes planned for the coming year in some detail based upon certain assumptions: for example, how many students the voluntary organisation expects to enrol; how much it plans to spend on saving which endangered species; the amount of money it plans to raise; or the number of new fee-paying members that will join. The scope and size of the voluntary organisation's programmes and asset base will dictate the complexity of its budgets.

It is important to distinguish between the portion of the budget that can be readily calculated and that which has to be estimated. The budget planner needs both scepticism and optimism. The process necessarily involves uncertainty; decisions are made about a future that the organisation cannot control. Should the financial planner assume that existing programmes will continue? Which (if any) programmes are essential? Before developing the budgets, the planners must make the specific policy decisions outlined below.

Balancing

The organisation must decide whether the budget is to be balanced. The question of the level of reserves required must also be addressed at this stage. Should the budget reflect sufficient revenue to pay expenses? An organisation that needs to build up working capital might want to project a budget imbalance of revenue and expenses (a surplus). Alternatively, a deficit budget may be acceptable if it arises from investment in future restructuring, for example. However, the organisation will in most cases cease to be viable if there are recurring operating deficits. One exception may be where a policy decision has been made to rely on income from investments, for example, to finance deficits incurred on charitable programmes. An effective budget also balances programme priorities: the organisation's capabilities and resources are allocated to impact on the maximum number of beneficiaries.

There might be other, more detailed parameters affecting the budget, for example:

- No additional posts unless fully funded.
- 2.5 per cent growth in non-salaried expenditure, to account for inflation.
- Any new programmes must be fully funded (direct and indirect costs).

Timing

Budgets must be completed by a deadline that allows time for planning in advance of the period to which the budget applies. The lead time required for grant requests and multi-year projects also make it imperative that the budget process is properly timed. Realistic target dates for the completion of planning should be established for all to follow.

Evolution

Although it is not common practice, some organisations use the original budget as a base from which to forecast changes throughout the year, as indicated by current or future activities. Monitoring the budget establishes criteria that signal the need for change or identify the need to refine or alter the course of action. Although it may be difficult to modify once it is adopted, an original budget that is found to be unrealistic or inaccurate can be changed. In its original or unaltered state, it continues to signal a problem even though the issue has been addressed and changes have been made to correct it.

A budget updated in accordance with the new situation might serve as a better monitoring system, as it is tailored to respond to unforeseen conditions. Most voluntary organisations, particularly small ones, continue to compare current financial information with the originally approved budget and provide footnotes explaining the circumstances that have caused the results to be better or worse than originally expected. The original budget will continue to provide valuable information for trustees, but would be ineffective for monitoring purposes.

Accountability

The people expected to accomplish the programmes and the financial goals expressed in the budget must be actively involved in the budgeting process. Without the active participation of the people who actually carry out the activities, a budget's usefulness is diminished. A budget developed, monitored and revised in the accounts office is of little value to the programme staff.

Zero basis versus incremental

Those responsible for budgeting may adopt either a zero-based system or an incremental methodology for preparing the budget for the coming year. Zero-based budgeting incorporates within itself the process for setting organisational objectives. Starting from a zero base, the financial planners assume that no programme is necessary and no money need be spent. To be accepted, the programmes will have to be proven worthwhile, as well as financially sound, after an evaluation of all elements of revenue and spending. Each programme is examined in order to justify its existence, and is compared to alternative programmes. Priorities are established and each cost centre is challenged to prove its necessity. This can make programme managers feel threatened, so budget setters should exercise sensitivity when using the zero-based method.

An incremental budget, on the other hand, treats existing programmes and departments as already approved, subject only to increases or decreases in the financial resources allocated. The organisation's historical costs are the base from which budget planning starts. The focus of the budgeting process is on the changes anticipated in last year's figures; the planning process has already been completed and the programme priorities established. But there are dangers in using last year's figures. Basing the budget on these figures can, if not properly challenged, introduce an element of 'creeping' costs year on year. Basing the budget on the actual results can encourage the practice of spending up to the budget in the last few months, to prevent future cuts. Despite these dangers, incremental budgeting is often less time-consuming than the zero-based method, and is also felt to be less threatening to programme managers.

TYPES OF BUDGET

Before the budget process begins, the organisation should decide upon which type of budget is best suited to its planning and monitoring needs. The basic budget is a comprehensive look at the entire organisation's projections of income or financial support and its expected expenditures. An endless number of supplementary budgets can be created to meet specific planning and assessment needs.

The options might include at least the following:

- Annual, quarterly and/or monthly projections of income and expenditure for the entire organisation, as well as for each of its departments and branches.
- Receipts and payments budget.
- Revenue projections by type, such as contributors or student tuition.

- Individual project, department, branch or other cost centre projections.
- Service delivery costs by patient, by student, by member or other client.
- Capital additions (buildings or equipment acquisition).
- Investment income (and/or total return).
- Cash flow (short and long term).
- Fundraising event revenue and expenses.
- Retail shop sales.
- Personnel projections.

Advantages and disadvantages

In addition to its value in allocating resources and implementing strategic plans, the budget can produce a wide range of beneficial results. Programme personnel directly involved in carrying out activities can use it to measure their accomplishments numerically and to respond to unexpected changes. Management can use it to evaluate staff performance. But like any tool, the budget can produce good or bad results, depending on the skill and diligence with which it is used. The chief advantages of effective budgeting include:

- A thoroughly planned and implemented budget increases the likelihood of a voluntary organisation being financially successful.
- A budget translates abstract goals into determinable bites: it sets performance goals.
- The planning and preparation of a budget forces the organisation to look at itself, set priorities and narrow its choices.
- A budget facilitates co-ordination and co-operation between the various programmes and financial departments.
- Periodic comparisons between the budget and actual financial performance can signal trouble and allow time for an appropriate response.
- A budget measures how far financial performance meets an organisation's expectations.

The chief disadvantages of the budgeting process include:

- The presence of controls may stifle creativity.
- Because there are so many unknowns at the time when the budget is prepared, the natural tendency is to emphasise cost control.
- A budget based on historical information alone cannot always keep up with a rapidly-changing environment.
- Non-financial staff do not often participate in the budgeting process, resulting in operational blueprints that have been approved without the input of programme staff.
- A budget is not easy to implement and may not always be accepted as useful by the management staff.

WHO PARTICIPATES IN BUDGETING?

A budget cannot guarantee its own success: it is no substitute for responsible management. Almost everyone involved with a voluntary organisation may appropriately participate in planning its budget: at the very least, the top administrators, programme heads and board members or trustees. A budget should be a compilation of information furnished by all the senior programme and administrative personnel, who have in turn taken account of contributions from the people with whom they work. No one person should be responsible for preparing the budget: the organisation's accounts department should compile and monitor it. How far down the organisational ladder the leaders solicit contributions will depend on the organisation's circumstances, but the further the better.

The ideal budget is participatory, involving input from all the programme staff and volunteers who work to accomplish the organisation's goals. There will be a broad range of interested stakeholders, ranging from funders and supporters to employees and the trustee board. Outside funders can sometimes exert considerable influence on the budget: they may want to know if the organisation plans to provide services that are already provided by another organisation in the community; they may try to influence grant recipients to conduct programmes that accomplish the funder's goals.

A budget imposed from the top down dampens the enthusiasm of staff and can hamper the realisation of the organisation's goals. During the budget process, there will naturally be compromise and trade-off. If staff participate from the outset, they may be more willing to accept alterations not initiated by them. It may also make them more understanding about changes, including budget cuts that affect them personally. The participation of the board, officers, staff and volunteers in the process of setting goals enhances the organisation's chances of achieving those goals. Preparing the budget should motivate personnel and inspire the organisation's performance. Everyone should be made aware of the budget procedure by means of a chart similar to Figure 3.1 below.

Figure 3.1: Who works on the budget when

What	Who	When
Provide plan and budget worksheets	Finance dept	Sixth month of the year (or before)
Complete first draft plan and budgets	Programme personnel/ department head/directors	Fifth month before the year end
Combine all budgets into one organisational total	Finance dept	Three months before year end
Review and finalise budget	Chief executive and board of Trustees	Two to three months before the year end

The finance department or officer will specify the broad conditions that the organisational or total budget must satisfy, and will provide the necessary budget worksheets. These worksheets are the basic framework into which figures for income and expenditure are entered; they enable the finance department or officer to use standardised documentation to compile the budget.

Selling the budget

As we have seen, the most effective budgets are prepared with informed input from as many of the organisation's staff as possible. During the whole process, all participants should be encouraged to communicate with each other.

Scheduling the budget process

Ideally, budgeting is a continuous process that repeats itself cyclically and is based on the organisation's long range plan. This requires sufficient time for the budget plans to be fully developed.

Figure 3.2 sets out the planning process which begins with the setting of goals, as described in Chapter Two. The programmes that can accomplish those goals are examined and compared. Only when programme planning and development are complete can the accumulation of the financial aspects of a budget begin.

Figure 3.1 suggests that preparation of the budget should begin six months before the beginning of the period to which the budget applies: for example, an organisation whose financial year ends on 31 March should start preparing the budget for the next financial year by September of the current financial year. This allows enough time to gather reliable forecasting information and to go through an orderly approval process.

Figure 3.2: Scheduling the budget

Step 1.	Set goals	Carry out strategic planning
Step 2.	Establish objectives	Identify programmes and activities to accomplish goals
Step 3.	Design programmes	Describe method of putting the goals into practice
Step 4.	Budget preparation and approval	Quantify revenue and expenditures based upon forecasts and programme accomplishments
Step 5.	Monitor progress	Compile reports comparing budget to actual

BUDGET POLICY MANUAL

To document the budgeting process, a manual containing written procedures and guidelines, budget models, checklists and other aids to preparation is desirable. At the very least, the organisation should prepare a budget policy statement specifying the following:

- *Philosophy.* A description of how the voluntary organisation uses the budget is given, in order to encourage staff participation. Employees should be told how the organisation plans to respond to variations and whether the budget evolves or changes during the year.
- *Responsible persons.* Who does what and when during the budget process (see figure 3.1).
- *Time frame.* A schedule of the expected stages in the process.
- *Forecast guidelines:* These can indicate the economic assumptions to be applied, the methodology for making projections, and the independent sources of information.
- *Report design.* A standard (or suggested) form is given on which programmes or departments can make their input; there are clear instructions about the amount of detail required, and an explanation of assumptions.
- *Follow-up.* A description of the budget monitoring system and its recurring schedule.

Use of budgets

Budgets can be used for a variety of purposes, but this guide will focus on how they can form part of funding applications, project appraisal and project monitoring.

When budgets are used as part of funding applications, their format and construction will be guided by the funder's requirements. Typically, a funder will require costs to be split between capital and revenue items, and where applicable, over the term of the project life (maximum three years). There are likely to be restrictions on the percentage (if any) of apportioned overheads that will be funded (see chapter 4, section 8).

Changing budgets mid-year

The astute project manager is alert to any external factors that will affect the financial performance of the organisation, and will regularly catalogue new information that might be useful in preparing the next year's budget. Some organisations may find a 'living' budget, which changes throughout the year as circumstances change, to be preferable to a fixed and unchanging budget – so long as the bottom line remains the same.

The reasons why a budget needs to change are endless. It may prove inaccurate because of inadequate information or circumstances beyond the organisation's control: an expected grant renewal is denied; a major funder defaults on a pledge; a natural disaster increases the demand for aid; a member of staff leaves.

When unforeseen events occur, should the approved budget be updated to reflect the changes? Or should the monthly management reports use footnotes to explain any significant variations from the approved budget? The attributes of a 'living' or constantly changing budget compared to those of a static budget are given in Figure 3.3.

Figure 3.3: Static versus living budgets

Static Budget	Living Budget
Compares dreams at a point in time to the reality of current situation	Presents realistic statistics based on changing circumstances
No time spent on revisions	Requires continual updating
Wastes funds expended on programmes that are discontinued or found to be ineffective	Constant maximisation of resources
Encourages unreasonable expectations	Positive context for accomplishment

Source: Financial Planning for Non Profit Organisations, Jody Blazek

2. Preparing forecasts

Voluntary organisations face particular problems in forecasting their income flow, particularly those supported by contributions and grants. Voluntary donations depend upon the giver's support for the organisation's mission, but the public's concern about particular social problem – AIDS, for example – may wane. Other intangible factors, such as changes in legislation, can compound the difficulty of making projections: for example, the National Minimum Wage will add an estimated £51 million to the cost of wages in the voluntary sector.

A service-providing voluntary organisation, such as a school or a professional association, may have a slightly easier task in forecasting future income. People will pay for services if they feel that they are useful. As long as the services are of high quality and meet the needs of users, the organisation can reasonably assume that they will continue to pay for them.

The forecaster first studies current income and spending and asks if they can be sustained at present levels:

- If unusual events have occurred in the past year or two, are they likely to recur?
- Otherwise, is it reasonable to expect an increase in revenue?
- What increase does the organisation expect as the result of an action taken in the past, such as last year's setting up of a development department?
- What increases in revenue might result if some new marketing scheme is added to the expense side of the budget?

Demographic information about the voluntary organisation's user community is factored into the forecasts. Information about trends in the voluntary sector economy as a whole can be derived from the findings of the review of the external environment and, in particular, from the findings of Third Sector Foresight. Information of a more local nature can be obtained from a variety of sources, such as reports on local economic activity (consult the local library).

Donations and membership

Forecasting the income from voluntary contributions and membership fees becomes easier as an organisation matures. In these circumstances, the best guide to predicting the future is the organisation's own history, and in particular, tables showing several years of revenue. Some voluntary organisations enjoy considerable goodwill generated during years of operation, but new or young organisations may need to be more cautious about forecasting the success of their development plans.

Using information about donors generated internally (for example, their age, frequency of giving, average amount of gift) in conjunction with an examination of significant trends in the voluntary sector economy can greatly enhance the reliability of forecasts.

According to NCVO's *Voluntary Sector Almanac*, the main factors affecting this type of income are:

- Voluntary income is often described as 'free' income, as it is not tied to a particular outcome; increasingly, however, donors seem more inclined to give if there is a specific project.
- Organisations that appeal to the philanthropic motives of individuals are heavily dependent on the trust that has been developed.
- Public confidence in all types of public institutions continues to decline.
- There is increasing competition, not only among voluntary organisations but with other types of activity, for the disposable income of individuals.
- The voluntary sector is experiencing a decline in charitable giving, particularly organisations with an annual income of £1–10 million.

A SWOT (strengths, weaknesses, opportunities and threats) analysis showing the main characteristics of voluntary income is given in Figure 3.4.

Service delivery fees

The age of an organisation is also significant when forecasting revenue. The mature organisation will know the average number of student places, research reports or other services delivered in the past few years. The needs of these services, and any policy decisions about their delivery, have already been reviewed as a part of the strategic planning process. The financial planner's job may simply be to express those strategic goals in a financial format: for example, the number of people to be served and the expected price. In some cases, however, this price may not reflect the full cost of the service; a subsidy may have to come from voluntary income and/or investment income.

Grants and contracts

Predicting whether grants from local authorities, charitable trusts and business sponsors will be renewed is full of uncertainty. Have the local authority's funding priorities changed? Has the value of the charitable trust's assets fallen, reducing the amount available for grants?

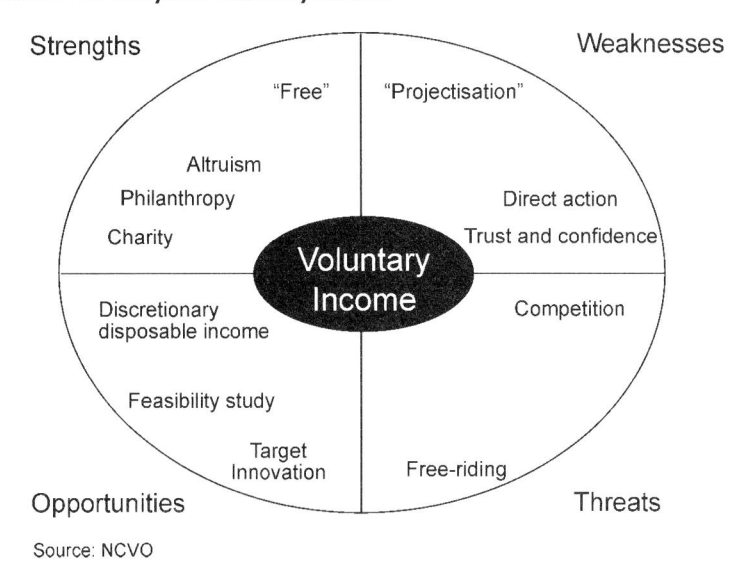

Figure 3.4: SWOT analysis of voluntary income

```
        Strengths                           Weaknesses
                    "Free"    "Projectisation"
              Altruism
           Philanthropy              Direct action
         Charity                    Trust and confidence
                       Voluntary
                        Income
         Discretionary              Competition
         disposable income
         Feasibility study
                    Target
                   Innovation    Free-riding
        Opportunities                       Threats
```
Source: NCVO

Corporate sponsorship is usually tied to the sponsor's profit level – which is usually unknown at budget preparation time. Furthermore, the funding of research often has to be based upon incomplete data, which makes prediction equally impossible.

If an organisation's operating overheads or administrative costs are paid for out of grants, very cautious forecasting is needed. Think about the consequences when the grant that funds half the executive director's salary is not renewed! If there is a good possibility of grants not being renewed, a flexible or evolving budget (as discussed in the previous section) may be sensible; the budget should also specify alternative courses of action.

Conditions of employment for staff members funded by a grant (and the corresponding expenses budget) should recognise the possibility that the funds may cease.

Here are the main characteristics of earned income:

- If an organisation enters into a variety of service contracts, there is a risk that it might lose sight of its mission and become financially dependent on contracts.
- Contracts for services – such as providing health care – often lead to significant growth in infrastructure.
- Loss of a contract can have a devastating effect on service delivery organisations, as they typically employ a large staff.
- There is considerable competition in certain areas of earned income activities, such as health care, particularly when for-profit companies are also providing the same services.

A SWOT analysis showing the main characteristics of earned income is given in Figure 3.5.

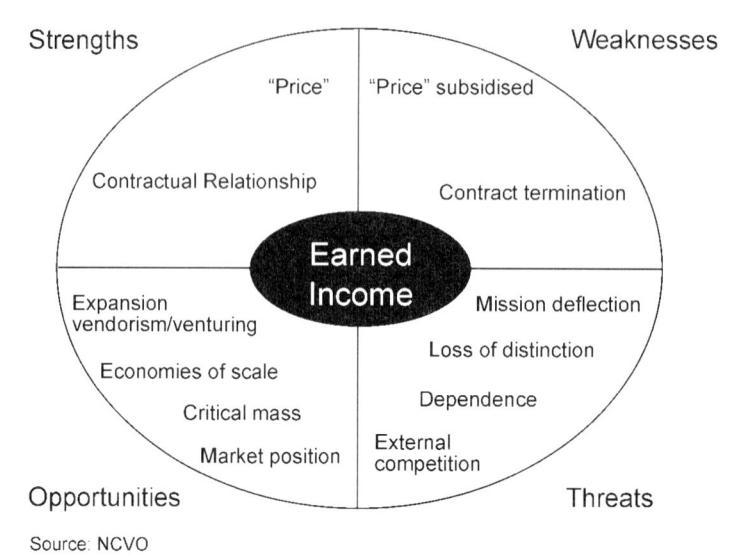

Figure 3.5: SWOT analysis of earned income

```
        Strengths                              Weaknesses
                    "Price"    |   "Price" subsidised
        Contractual Relationship |   Contract termination
                           ┌─────────┐
        Expansion          │ Earned  │   Mission deflection
        vendorism/venturing│ Income  │
                           └─────────┘   Loss of distinction
           Economies of scale
                 Critical mass            Dependence
                                   External
                   Market position  competition
        Opportunities                          Threats
```

Source: NCVO

Investment income

The caution required when forecasting investment income depends upon what proportion of its income the organisation expects to derive from investments; for many voluntary groups, this will be modest. But for an endowed grant-making trust, all of whose income comes from investment, this forecast is vital in establishing funding levels for the coming year.

Forecasting becomes particularly difficult for organisations with long term investment funds. If the funds are administered by a professional investment manager, he or she should provide projections of investment income. However, despite several short-term 'corrections' in recent years, the underlying trend for long-term funds is steady growth.

A SWOT analysis showing the main characteristics of investment income is given in Figure 3.6.

Expenses

Most voluntary organisations can predict their expenditure with some certainty, as they have more control over expenditure than income: for example, the cost of salaries and the lease/mortgage on premises will be relatively stable. Historical expenses are therefore the basis for the expense budget, subject to adjustments for inflation: for example, last year's figures plus 3 per cent.

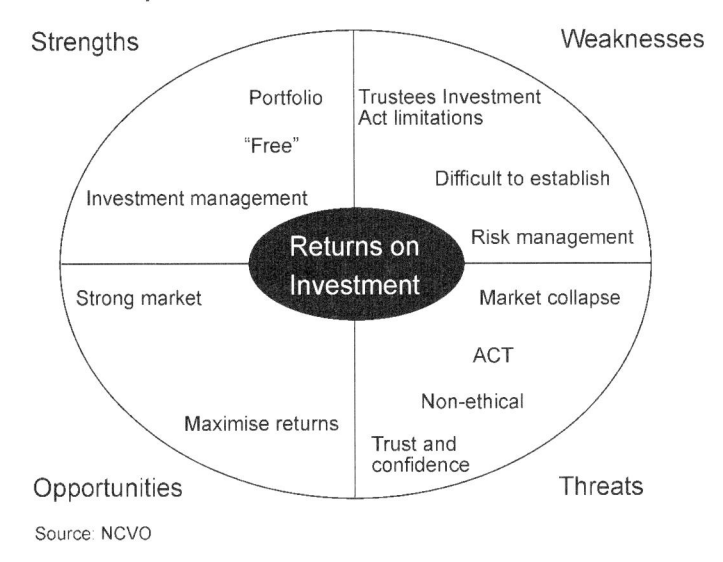

Figure 3.6: SWOT analysis of investment income

```
        Strengths                           Weaknesses
                    Portfolio    Trustees Investment
                                 Act limitations
                      "Free"
                                      Difficult to establish
         Investment management
                                      Risk management
                            Returns on
                            Investment
          Strong market                    Market collapse

                                       ACT
                                       Non-ethical
                   Maximise returns
                              Trust and
                              confidence
        Opportunities                          Threats
```
Source: NCVO

One major challenge in forecasting costs is to identify those that are unpredictable: for example, a disaster relief agency may know how much it costs to clothe and house flood victims, but it cannot know when the storms will occur. Again, historical records may be useful.

Demand for an organisation's services is often difficult to predict, so it is essential to acknowledge this uncertainty and submit a flexible budget. The prudent budget planner uses the best possible information to hand, but submits forecasts that are subject to change. Another way is to distinguish clearly between costs that are controllable and those that are uncontrollable.

If expected costs are too high, the financial planner must consider cheaper alternatives. For example, a voluntary organisation may need skilled people to supervise a specialised project, but the salary such people would expect might skew the organisation's overall pay scale. In such a situation, the organisation has several options:

- Outsource the job to another company.
- Hire skilled people on a part-time or hourly basis to run the project and train in-house staff.
- Eliminate the project, reduce its size or run it jointly with another voluntary organisation.

Phasing the budget

When preparing an income and expenditure budget for a project, it is important to identify when in a twelve-month period the income and expenditure items are likely to arise. For example, costs such as insurance and rates are not incurred regularly throughout the period. Similarly, grants might be paid quarterly in advance or in arrears, and income from events will arise just before an event.

This phasing of the budget is important, because without it, useful comparisons between actual and budgeted income and expenditure will not be possible. A blank template for phasing a budget is given in Appendix B, and also forms the basis of the sample project budget in figure 3.11; this template allows for the budget to be phased either across the budget period or by individual organisational aims.

Statistical operational data
A voluntary organisation must regularly gather statistics and information relevant to the budgeting and planning process. Each organisation needs a method of measuring its own effectiveness: Are its goals being met? What are the results of its efforts? Successes and failures, weaknesses and strengths, should be regularly evaluated and the results used as a basis for making decisions. The sophistication and scope of the self-assessment process will vary according to the organisation, but to be effective not only the performance of the organisation itself but also that of staff, volunteers, managers and trustees should be measured.

3. STRUCTURING THE BUDGET

A voluntary organisation should have a structure that will ensure the efficient fulfilment of its strategic aims: in practice, this means setting up departments or appointing project managers with the responsibility for providing products or services. In most voluntary organisations, budgetary control and budget reports reflect the hierarchy of the organisation. The reporting – from the project manager responsible for delivering services to the board of trustees responsible for the financial health of the whole organisation – will be less detailed the higher up the organisation.

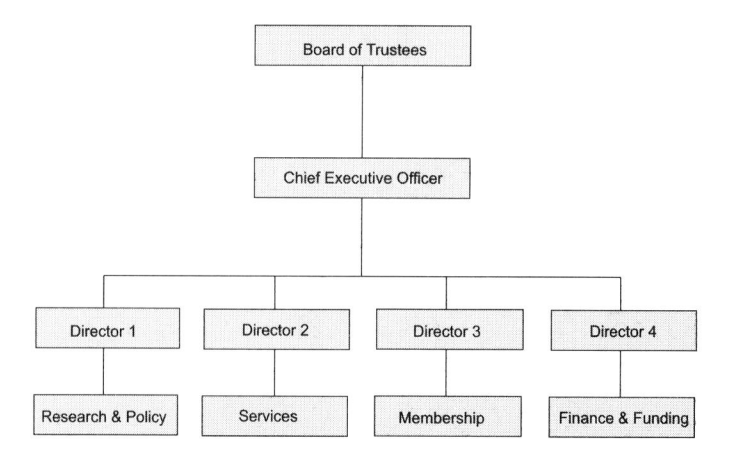

Table 3.7: Organisational structure of Environ Alliance Trust

Figure 3.7 is a typical organisational structure: Environ Alliance Trust works to ensure that environmental issues are taken into account by the decision-making processes of government and other organisations.

The budget reports should reflect this structure, so detailed individual budgets should be prepared for the Chief Executive's Office, Research and Policy, Best Practice Development and Membership departments and for Fundraising, Finance and Administration. The directors will receive summarised budget reports for each department, and the trustee board will receive a further summarised budget report for the whole organisation.

Model budgets

Using the above example, the following model budgets might be prepared. At board of trustees level, the concern will be to ensure that the organisation meets its financial goals: for example, to achieve a balanced budget of income and expenditure to the end of the year, or to plan for a surplus. A further concern will be to ensure that the organisation has sufficient incoming cash resources to meet its obligations as they fall due.

The income and expenditure budget shown in figure 3.8 will have the totals for rows A to D and a balance shown in row E. Staff costs have been separately disclosed because for many voluntary organisations they represent up to 60 per cent of total expenditure and thus warrant careful monitoring. Total running costs (C) will include both direct costs of projects and an element of organisation-wide costs.

The budgeted surplus or deficit should correspond to the target identified at the initial planning stages.

The headings for each of the columns can be explained as follows:

- *Full year budget (1)*. This represents the original budget or plan, which the organisation's staff and management would have started to compile some six months before the start of the year, and which was approved by the board approximately two months before the start of the year.
- *This month actual (2), this month budget (3), variance (4)*: These columns taken together represent the difference from the original budget or plan for the current month as identified by the variance column. This set of figures allows for the examination of current month activities in income and expenditure terms.
- *Year to date actual (5), year to date budget (6), variance (7)*. Taken together, these columns represent the accumulated difference from the original plan or budget, as identified by the variance column. They enable the examination of six-month figures for income and expenditure, and therefore serve as a guide to the feasibility of the year-end financial goals.
- *Last forecast (8), this forecast (9), variance to last forecast (10)*. These columns allow amendments to be made to the original budget, to reflect changing circumstances since it was approved. The *variance to budget (11)* column enables the effect of changing assumptions on the original plan or budget to be monitored.

The six-month income and expenditure budget for the Environ Alliance Trust delivers key messages that should concern the trustee board:

- The original budget planned for a surplus of £23,122 (column 1) to be taken to reserves. At the end of the six-month period the organisation is forecast to make a reduced surplus of £14,255 (column 9).
- The reduction occurs because the current forecast for total income to the end of the year is £511,777, compared with the original budget of £547,270.
- In response to the revised income forecast, the organisation has been cutting non-salary costs, as is evident in the reduction of the running costs budget from the original £256,655 to £226,258.
- The trustee board should examine the possibility that income will further decline and the effect this might have on the work programme of the charity.
- The trustee board should investigate the reasons why income has declined. Have earned income targets been met? Has a grant application fallen through?

The cash flow forecast will be another important document for trustees. This identifies the total receipts and payments, and is primarily used to ensure that the organisation has sufficient incoming resources to meet its obligations as they fall due. The example presented in figure 3.9 is a six-month forecast with the accumulated results to August rolled up into the first column, and a separate column for September. The cash flow statement is produced by reference to the Income and Expenditure budgets, which serve as a basis for adjusting the individual entries to reflect amounts accrued or prepaid for each month. For example, since membership subscriptions are invoiced on a monthly basis, the amounts shown in the income and expenditure account will reflect the total invoiced for membership in a particular month. However, the amount shown in the cash flow statement reflects the actual receipt of cash credited to the bank for membership subcriptions in the month. Previous experience will inform management what proportion of subscriptions invoiced in any month will be paid in the following and subsequent months.The six-month cash flow forecast for the Environ Alliance Trust delivers certain key messages that should concern the trustee board:

- From month to month there is a net cash outflow from the organisation of averaging £5,000, which is currently being met from the accumulated balance at the bank.
- Although this net cash outflow may be sustainable in the short term, the trustee board must consider whether additional finance should be sought or must examine the feasibility of reducing the cash outflow by making additional savings.
- The 'project charges' row in both the cash inflow and cash outflow sections recognises that projects which cannot be directly attributed should be charged for general overheads. Since these charges are internal movements of cash, there is no impact on the cash flow of the voluntary organisation.
- It is important to appreciate that the cash flow statement will be different from

BUDGETING   71

Figure 3.8: Total income and expenditure budget for Environ Alliance Trust for six months to September 19X9

DESCRIPTION	FULL YEAR BUDGET (1)	This month ACTUAL (2)	This month BUDGET (3)	VARIANCE (4) (3) – (2)	Year to date ACTUAL (5)	Year to date BUDGET (6)	VARIANCE (7) (6) – (5)	Last FORECAST (8)	This FORECAST (9)	VARIANCE to last F/C (10) (8) – (9)	VARIANCE to budget (11) (1) – (9)
TOTAL INCOME (A)	547,270	31,331	27,418	3,913	188,761	234,130	(45,369)	519,838	511,777	(8,061)	(35,493)
TOTAL STAFF COSTS (B)	267,493	21,047	21,828	781	111,966	110,775	(1,191)	269,498	271,264	(1,766)	(3,771)
TOTAL RUNNING COSTS (C)	256,655	8,581	16,995	8,414	65,835	100,820	34,985	231,741	226,258	5,483	30,397
TOTAL EXPENDITURE (D) (B) + (C)	524,148	29,628	38,823	9,195	177,801	211,595	33,794	501,239	497,522	3,717	26,626
SURPLUS / (DEFICIT) (E) (A) – (D)	23,122	1,703	(11,405)	13,108	10,960	22,535	(11,575)	18,599	14,255	(4,344)	(8,867)

the income and expenditure figures. The cash flow statement represents movements in cash held at the bank, whilst the income and expenditure statements reflect amounts which are due to the organisation (income) and amounts payable by the organisation (expenditure).
- The cash flow statement will also need to include the effects of value added tax (VAT). This may result in a cash outflow (representing payments to Customs) or a cash inflow (representing a refund from Customs). The impact of VAT on the organisation will depend upon its business activities (see Chapter 7).

The trustee board should ask the following key questions of management:

- If income projections decline further, what effect will this have on the organisation's ability to carry on with its projects?
- Are there any contingency plans to safeguard projects? (For example, borrowing or bridging-type loans).
- Is it feasible to launch an immediate fundraising appeal?

To answer the above questions, the trustee board may need to be supplied with more detailed budget sheets on which each department's income and expenditure will be monitored.

As mentioned above, the trustee board may wish to seek further explanations of the income and expenditure position of Environ Alliance Trust, and for this purpose should be provided with the detailed departmental breakdown (figure 3.10). This report would be provided as a matter of course to the director and departmental managers.

The format of the report remains the same, making it easier to prepare. The main highlights from this report are:

- The Chief Executive's Office, Research and Policy and Services departments currently run on a deficit budget, being financed through membership subscriptions (see column 1, row D). This may be based on management's policy of allowing members' subscriptions to pay for policy and research activity and members' services. However, as is evident from the detailed report, such an arrangement requires careful cost management, as it may not be possible to pass on increasing costs to members through increased subscriptions.
- The income from the Research and Services Department is significantly below that budgeted at the end of six months. The variances in column 7 under year to date income clearly show this. There may be many reasons for this decline in income: for example, the original budget was not phased for income and therefore meaningless variances are being generated; income generation activities have not been undertaken; or loss of funding has resulted in the shortfall.

It is important to recognise that, when profiling the budget, the budget holder will need to consider the timing of when income and expenditure may arise within the

BUDGETING 73

Figure 3.9: Environ Alliance Trust cash flow forecast 19X9

	Year to Aug. actuals	September actuals	October budget	November budget	December budget	January budget	February budget	March budget	Total
RECEIPTS									
Membership subscriptions	34,560	10,588	12,500	12,500	12,500	12,500	12,500	12,500	120,148
Grant income	30,000	2,500	0	0	2,500	0	0	2,500	37,500
Publications	11,024	1,051	920	920	1,990	2,500	920	1,070	20,395
Conferences	13,762	936	1,188	1,938	1,988	1,838	1,738	1,988	25,376
Fees and other income	55,316	14,675	3,500	5,000	5,000	5,000	5,000	5,000	98,491
Project charges	0	0	0	0	0	0	0	0	0
TOTAL CASH FLOW	**144,662**	**29,750**	**18,108**	**20,358**	**23,978**	**21,838**	**20,158**	**23,058**	**301,910**
PAYMENTS									
Staff costs	92,250	17,235	17,218	17,237	17,237	17,166	17,166	17,167	212,676
Premises costs	6,669	1,350	1,500	1,205	1,205	1,205	1,305	1,305	15,744
Publication costs	4,877	1,565	1,220	3,000	1,000	1,000	1,000	2,000	15,662
Conference costs	6,358	1,458	1,500	2,500	2,500	2,000	1,500	1,500	19,316
Other running costs	32,974	6,859	5,000	5,000	5,000	5,000	5,000	5,000	69,833
Project charges	0	0	0	0	0	0	0	0	0
TOTAL CASH FLOW	**143,128**	**28,467**	**26,438**	**28,942**	**26,942**	**26,371**	**25,971**	**26,972**	**333,231**
Net cash inflow/(outflow)	1,534	1,283	(8,330)	(8,584)	(2,964)	(4,533)	(5,813)	(3,914)	(31,321)
Bank balances at beginning of period	42,344	43,878	45,161	36,831	28,247	25,283	20,750	14,937	42,344
Bank balances at end of period	43,878	45,161	36,831	28,247	25,283	20,750	14,937	11,023	11,023

Figure 3.10: Departmental budget report for Environ Alliance Trust

DESCRIPTION	FULL YEAR BUDGET (1)	This month ACTUAL (2)	This month BUDGET (3)	VARIANCE (4) (3) – (2)	Year to date ACTUAL (5)	Year to date BUDGET (6)	VARIANCE (7) (6) – (5)	Last FORE-CAST (8)	This FORE-CAST (9)	VARIANCE to last F/C (10) (8)-(9)	VARIANCE to budget (11) (1) – (9)
INCOME											
Chief Executive	100	0	83	(83)	210	415	(205)	100	100	0	0
Research and Policy	101,050	3,668	5,391	(1,723)	25,948	46,677	(20,729)	97,655	93,912	(3,743)	(7,138)
Services Development	129,690	1,685	4,556	(2,871)	18,206	41,638	(23,432)	104,783	99,785	(4,998)	(29,905)
Membership	120,000	11,998	8,698	3,300	60,209	57,730	2,479	121,000	121,000	0	1,000
Non Team	196,430	13,980	8,690	5,290	84,188	87,670	(3,482)	196,300	196,980	680	550
TOTAL INCOME (A)	**547,270**	**31,331**	**27,418**	**3,913**	**188,761**	**234,130**	**(45,369)**	**519,838**	**511,777**	**(8,061)**	**(35,493)**
EXPENDITURE											
Chief Executive	45,000	3,700	3,750	50	18,750	18,700	(50)	45,000	45,000	0	0
Research and Policy	72,758	6,239	6,062	(177)	33,405	31,628	(1,777)	77,610	77,011	599	(4,253)
Services Development	122,887	8,915	9,779	864	47,878	49,260	1,382	120,532	121,940	(1,408)	947
Membership	11,173	878	931	53	4,398	4,656	258	10,681	10,638	43	535
Non Team	15,675	1,315	1,306	(9)	7,535	6,531	(1,004)	15,675	16,675	(1,000)	(1,000)
TOTAL STAFF COSTS (B)	**267,493**	**21,047**	**21,828**	**781**	**111,966**	**110,775**	**(1,191)**	**269,498**	**271,264**	**(1,766)**	**(3,771)**
Chief Executive	5,930	2,150	494	(1,656)	4,126	2,471	(1,655)	5,930	7,930	(2,000)	(2,000)
Research and Policy	71,991	1,249	5,471	4,222	13,527	29,035	15,508	67,080	62,731	4,349	9,260

Figure 3.10—continued

DESCRIPTION	FULL YEAR BUDGET (1)	This month ACTUAL (2)	This month BUDGET (3)	VARIANCE (4) (3) – (2)	Year to date ACTUAL (5)	Year to date BUDGET (6)	VARIANCE (7) (6) – (5)	Last FORE-CAST (8)	This FORE-CAST (9)	VARIANCE to last F/C (10) (8)-(9)	VARIANCE to budget (11) (1) – (9)
Services Development	112,051	1,899	5,857	3,958	19,080	42,665	23,585	91,394	88,060	3,334	23,991
Membership	36,308	1,252	2,173	921	14,452	13,993	(459)	36,962	37,162	(200)	(854)
Non Team	30,375	2,031	3,000	969	14,650	12,656	(1,994)	30,375	30,375	0	0
TOTAL RUNNING COSTS (C)	**256,655**	**8,581**	**16,995**	**8,414**	**65,835**	**100,820**	**34,985**	**231,741**	**226,258**	**5,483**	**30,397**
Chief Executive	(50,830)	(5,850)	(4,161)	(1,689)	(22,666)	(20,756)	(1,910)	(50,830)	(52,830)	(2,000)	(2,000)
Research and Policy	(43,699)	(3,820)	(6,142)	2,322	(20,984)	(13,986)	(6,998)	(47,035)	(45,830)	1,205	(2,131)
Services Development	(105,248)	(9,129)	(11,080)	1,951	(48,752)	(50,287)	1,535	(107,143)	(110,215)	(3,072)	(4,967)
Membership	72,519	9,868	5,594	4,274	41,359	39,081	2,278	73,357	73,200	(157)	681
Non Team	150,380	10,634	4,384	6,250	62,003	68,483	(6,480)	150,250	149,930	(320)	(450)
SURPLUS / (DEFICIT) (D) (A) – (B) – (C)	**23,122**	**1,703**	**(11,405)**	**13,108**	**10,960**	**22,535**	**(11,575)**	**18,599**	**14,255**	**(4,344)**	**(8,867)**

year. Although it is reasonable to assume that certain expenses, such as rent, are incurred evenly over twelve months, this is not always the case: for other items, the budget holder will need to consider when in the year a particular activity will give rise to income being earned or expenditure incurred. In the absence of such profiling, large variances can occur, rendering the budget practically useless as a management tool.

- In response to the identified shortfall in income, Environ has made significant savings in the running costs of both the Research and Services departments, as demonstrated by the variances identified in column 7 under running costs (row C).
- As a result of the identified shortfall in income, Environ has decided to reforecast its total income, as is shown by the latest forecast figures for income, column 9. Column 11 reveals the total effect of these revisions on the original budget: total income is now forecast at £511,777, compared with the original budget of £547,270, a variance of £35,493.
- Because of the revised total income figures, Environ had decided to defer or cancel programmes and expenditure in the Research and Services departments.

Our final example of a budget for an individual project is given (in figure 3.11). This uses the same basic format as the previous reports, but the income and expenditure will be particular to this project. The format allows for the close monitoring of income and expenditure against budgets and latest forecasts.

The budget bids worksheet, shown in figure 3.12, demonstrates how a budget for a project is phased over a twelve-month period. This worksheet can also be used to phase a budget by aim or activity; when used in this way, it links up with the planning process discussed in Chapter 2.

Both income and expenditure have been phased according to when a particular item is receivable or payable. So, for example, the income from conferences follows closely on from when the conferences are held; and salaries can be phased evenly throughout the twelve months.

The actual budget report prepared for the project follows the same format as the budget bids worksheet, which makes it easier to put together. The budgeted figures for the current month shown in column 3 correspond to the figures for month six in the budget bids worksheet. When budgets are used in this way, the variances are likely to be more meaningful than when all the income and expenditure is simply distributed over twelve months.

Budgets and budgetary control

When used properly, budgets can enable effective financial control of a voluntary organisation. Since they often reflect the organisational structure and are typically assigned to departments, projects and individuals, budgets are a way of assigning specific responsibility for the resources that have been allocated according to a plan of activities. It should be possible to trace back each of these activities to the

BUDGETING

Figure 3.11: Project Budget – Environ Alliance Trust

DESCRIPTION	FULL YEAR BUDGET (1)	This month ACTUAL (2)	This month BUDGET (3)	VARIANCE (4) (3) – (2)	Year to date ACTUAL (5)	Year to date BUDGET (6)	VARIANCE (7) (6) – (5)	Last FORE-CAST (8)	This FORE-CAST (9)	VARIANCE to last F/C (10) (8)-(9)	VARIANCE to budget (11) (1) – (9)
INCOME											
Grants	5,000	0	0	0	5,000	5,000	0	5,000	5,000	0	0
Income from conferences	15,500	0	1,625	(1,625)	3,250	3,250	0	18,500	19,500	1,000	4,000
Fees for services provided	41,000	3,756	3,500	256	21,587	20,500	1,087	39,000	38,500	(500)	(2,500)
Other income	5,000	287	417	(130)	3,043	2,500	543	4,000	3,750	(250)	(1,250)
TOTAL INCOME (A)	**66,500**	**4,043**	**5,542**	**(1,499)**	**32,880**	**31,250**	**1,630**	**66,500**	**66,750**	**250**	**250**
EXPENDITURE											
Salaries	33,190	2,505	2,765	260	16,595	16,595	0	33,190	33,190	0	0
Temporary staff costs	500	0	40	40	155	250	95	500	650	(150)	(150)
Training received	1,000	1,000	1,000	0	1,000	1,000	0	1,000	1,000	0	0
TOTAL STAFF COSTS (B)	**34,690**	**3,505**	**3,805**	**300**	**17,750**	**17,845**	**95**	**34,690**	**34,840**	**(150)**	**(150)**
Travel & subsistence	800	0	65	65	247	400	153	600	600	0	200
Telephone & fax	500	37	40	3	256	250	(6)	550	550	0	(50)
Printing	14,000	0	0	0	7,590	7,000	(590)	14,000	14,200	(200)	(200)
Photocopying	500	52	40	(12)	213	250	37	650	650	0	(150)
Stationery	800	10	65	55	456	400	(56)	600	600	0	200

78   THE GOOD FINANCIAL MANAGEMENT GUIDE

Figure 3.11—continued

DESCRIPTION	FULL YEAR BUDGET (1)	This month ACTUAL (2)	This month BUDGET (3)	VARIANCE (4) (3) – (2)	Year to date ACTUAL (5)	Year to date BUDGET (6)	VARIANCE (7) (6) – (5)	Last FORE-CAST (8)	This FORE-CAST (9)	VARIANCE to last F/C (10) (8)–(9)	VARIANCE to budget (11) (1) – (9)
Postage	1,500	25	125	100	358	750	392	1,500	1,500	0	0
Books & Periodicals	400	0	35	35	197	200	3	400	400	0	0
Catering	2,200	0	200	200	400	400	0	2,350	2,350	0	(150)
Subscriptions	200	200	200	0	200	200	0	200	200	0	0
Conferences organised	2,000	400	400	0	800	800	0	2,000	2,000	0	0
Accommodation charge	5,600	1,400	1,400	0	2,800	2,800	0	5,600	5,600	0	0
Central services charge	8,140	2,035	2,035	0	4,070	4,070	0	8,140	8,140	0	0
TOTAL RUNNING COSTS (C)	**36,640**	**4,159**	**4,605**	**446**	**17,587**	**17,520**	**(67)**	**36,590**	**36,790**	**(200)**	**(150)**
TOTAL EXPENDITURE (D) (B) + (C)	**71,330**	**7,664**	**8,410**	**746**	**35,337**	**35,365**	**28**	**71,280**	**71,630**	**(350)**	**(300)**
SURPLUS / (DEFICIT) (E) (A) – (D)	**(4,830)**	**(3,621)**	**(2,868)**	**(753)**	**(2,457)**	**(4,115)**	**1,658**	**(4,780)**	**(4,880)**	**(100)**	**(50)**

BUDGETING 79

Figure 3.12: Budget bids by team aims/month

DESCRIPTION & CODES	BUDGET BID	AIM/MONTH 1	AIM/MONTH 2	AIM/MONTH 3	AIM/MONTH 4	AIM/MONTH 5	AIM/MONTH 6	AIM/MONTH 7	AIM/MONTH 8	AIM/MONTH 9	AIM/MONTH 10	AIM/MONTH 11	AIM/MONTH 12	TOTALS
ACCOUNT INCOME CODE														
Grants	5,000			5,000										5,000
Income from conferences	15,500			1,625			1,625			6,250			6,000	15,500
Fees for services provided	41,000	2,750	4,750	2,750	4,000	2,750	3,500	3,500	3,500	4,000	2,750	3,500	4,000	41,000
Other income	5,000	416	416	417	417	417	417	417	416	417	417	417	417	5,000
TOTAL INCOME	**66,500**	**3,166**	**5,166**	**9,792**	**4,417**	**3,167**	**5,542**	**3,166**	**3,916**	**10,667**	**3,167**	**3,917**	**10,417**	**66,500**
STAFF COSTS														
Salaries	33,190	2,766	2,766	2,766	2,766	2,766	2,765	2,766	2,766	2,766	2,766	2,766	2,765	33,190
Temporary staff costs	500	42	42	42	42	42	40	42	42	42	42	42	40	500
Training received	1,000						1,000							1,000
TOTAL STAFF COSTS	**34,690**	**2,808**	**2,808**	**2,808**	**2,808**	**2,808**	**3,805**	**2,808**	**2,808**	**2,808**	**2,808**	**2,808**	**2,805**	**34,690**

Figure 3.12:—continued

TEAM/SUBTEAM

DESCRIPTION & CODES	BUDGET BID	AIM/ MONTH 1	AIM/ MONTH 2	AIM/ MONTH 3	AIM/ MONTH 4	AIM/ MONTH 5	AIM/ MONTH 6	AIM/ MONTH 7	AIM/ MONTH 8	AIM/ MONTH 9	AIM/ MONTH 10	AIM/ MONTH 11	AIM/ MONTH 12	TOTALS
ACCOUNT CODE														
RUNNING COSTS														
Travel & subsistence	800	67	67	67	67	67	65	67	67	67	67	67	65	800
Telephone & fax	500	42	42	42	42	42	40	42	42	42	42	42	40	500
Printing	14,000	2,000		2,000		3,000		2,500		1,500		3,000		14,000
Photocopying	500	42	42	42	42	42	40	42	42	42	42	42	40	500
Stationery	800	67	67	67	67	67	65	67	67	67	67	67	65	800
Postage	1,500	125	125	125	125	125	125	125	125	125	125	125	125	1,500
Books & Periodicals	400	33	33	33	33	33	35	33	33	33	33	33	35	400
Catering	2,200			200			200			1,000			800	2,200
Subscriptions	200						200							200
Conferences organised	2,000			400			400			600			600	2,000

Figure 3.12:—continued

TEAM/SUBTEAM

DESCRIPTION & CODES	BUDGET BID	AIM/ MONTH 1	AIM/ MONTH 2	AIM/ MONTH 3	AIM/ MONTH 4	AIM/ MONTH 5	AIM/ MONTH 6	AIM/ MONTH 7	AIM/ MONTH 8	AIM/ MONTH 9	AIM/ MONTH 10	AIM/ MONTH 11	AIM/ MONTH 12	TOTALS
ACCOUNT CODE														
Accommodation charge	5,600			1,400			1,400			1,400			1,400	5,600
Central services charge	8,140			2,035			2,035			2,035			2,035	8,140
TOTAL RUNNING COSTS	**36,640**	**2,376**	**376**	**6,411**	**376**	**3,376**	**4,605**	**2,876**	**376**	**6,911**	**376**	**3,376**	**5,205**	**36,640**
TOTAL EXPENDITURE	**71,330**	**5,184**	**3,184**	**9,219**	**3,184**	**6,184**	**8,410**	**5,684**	**3,184**	**9,719**	**3,184**	**6,184**	**8,010**	**71,330**
SURPLUS / (DEFICIT)	**(4,830)**	**(2,018)**	**1,982**	**573**	**1,233**	**(3,017)**	**(2,868)**	**(2,518)**	**732**	**948**	**(17)**	**(2,267)**	**2,407**	**(4,830)**

strategic aim it seeks to meet. In this way, the organisation can move from its high-level strategic aims to identifying objectives to detailed activity plans that have been costed and approved in the form of a budget.

Budgetary control is the practice of holding departments, projects and individuals to account for allocated resources, by comparing actual results for income and expenditure against the costed plan of activities. This procedure is designed to ensure that the overall financial strategy is realised. Significant variations from the costed plan will require justification, and will, if necessary, lead to changes in the costed plan. In this way, the activities of departments, projects and individuals, and ultimately of the whole organisation, are monitored to ensure financial viability.

Budgets and budgetary control affect the way people behave. Many studies have shown that departmental or programme managers seek to safeguard the level of spending allocated to them. Meeting the budget targets often becomes the primary objective for individual employees, a tendency that is reinforced if that individual's performance and reward are determined by whether the targets have been met. Empire building and manipulating the budget in order to meet targets can rapidly become the order of the day.

This causes the link between strategic aims and actual activity to become blurred, if not lost, and as a result budgets are used to measure organisational performance. The fulfilment of charitable aims ceases to be the primary measure of performance.

To guard against this loss of direction, the management of voluntary organisations should take care to monitor and measure its outcomes and the impact it has on society against its strategic aims.

The management committee and board of trustees need to be informed about both the organisation's financial health and its effectiveness in meeting its strategic aims. As mentioned in chapter 2, programme aims and financial goals are interdependent, and success in one cannot be achieved at the expense of the other. To be able to provide this more balanced reporting, the voluntary organisation needs to monitor and measure performance over a broader range of criteria than simply the financial.

One way of achieving this which is gaining in popularity in the voluntary sector is the Excellence Model. This identifies sets of criteria for the five 'enabling' elements: leadership; policy and strategy; resources; people; processes. Excellence in these enabling elements will allow the organisation to achieve success in the 'results' elements: customer satisfaction; people satisfaction; impact on society; and ultimately the financial stability that all voluntary organisations seek. These results elements also have excellence indicators that allow the organisation to assess how well it is performing. Further details of how the Excellence Model can be used in voluntary organisations are given in Appendix A.

4. Communicating financial information

The responsibility for compiling financial reports often falls on the finance officer or finance department. They are charged with maintaining financial data that is manipulated in a variety of ways to produce reports. These reports set out to inform a wide range of stakeholders, including project managers, the organisation's management and trustee board, funders and regulatory bodies. The design and content of these reports should be determined by the needs of the audience; it is not enough to blindly follow a predetermined template. The internal audience would usually be presented with management accounts consisting of income and expenditure and cash flow reports, whereas for external audiences – such as funders and the Charity Commission – the form and content will often be prescribed beforehand.

For many people in voluntary organisations, 'management accounts' mean reams of paper covered in numbers that are produced by the accounts department and ignored by everyone else. Management accounts are, however, vital for running an organisation effectively – so what should be done to make them more accessible?

The information provided must be relevant
Management accounts must contain the financial information that the reader actually needs to plan and control the financial resources for which he or she is accountable. The finance officer who is preparing the management accounts must therefore be aware of the issues that affect the organisation in general and the reader in particular.

Understanding the organisation's cash flow may be much more important than income and expenditure. How often are balance sheets used, and have restricted funds been used according to the donor's wishes?

The information must be up to date
There is a trade-off between accuracy and speed: the more accurate the information, the longer it will take to produce. The management needs to understand the organisation well enough to determine at what point accuracy ceases to affect the decision being made.

The information must be accurate
Inaccurate information is worse than no information at all. Accuracy here means not only eliminating data handling errors – miscodings, wrong entries, incorrect totals or transfers of figures – but also ensuring that nothing is omitted.

The accounts must be intelligible
However timely and accurate the accounts may be, they are no use if they do not inform the reader. Management accounts frequently contain too many numbers presented in a discouraging format. The finance officer must be clear about who the audience is and what information they need to make the decisions expected of them.

The accounts must be available

Users should have access to management accounts at the times when they need them. This is unlikely to coincide with predetermined deadlines for monthly reporting. For many organisations, however, this flexibility may be impossible, particularly if the accounts are held on a manual system. But it should remain an objective for organisations with computer accounting systems, which could be designed to allow non-accounting staff 'read only' access to information.

The accounts must describe what is actually going on

What do readers understand 'actual' to mean? Expenditure and payments are not the same thing, but do they realise that? What the user of management accounts sees in the 'actuals' column will depend on the method of accounting for transactions that is adopted. If users are not clear about which transactions are included, they can seriously misinterpret the true financial position. The budget manual should therefore explain how to use the management accounts and the meaning of the terms employed. Figure 3.13 below shows that the longer the gap, the greater the risk.

Figure 3.13

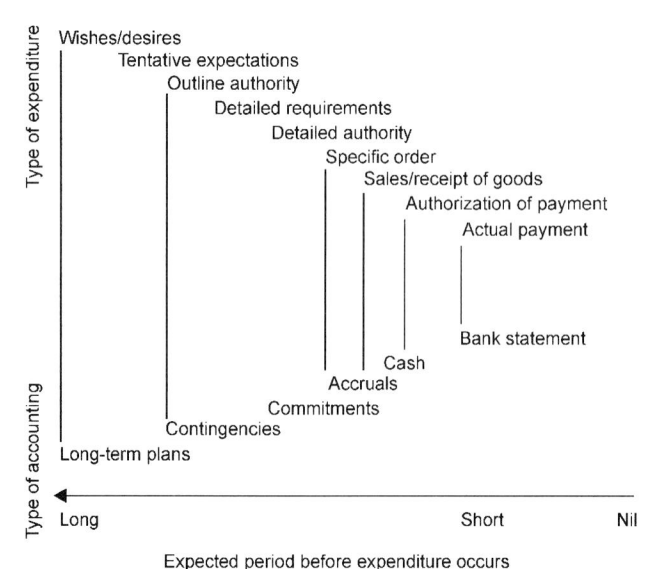

```
Type of expenditure
  | Wishes/desires
  |   Tentative expectations
  |     Outline authority
  |       Detailed requirements
  |         Detailed authority
  |           Specific order
  |             Sales/receipt of goods
  |               Authorization of payment
  |                 Actual payment
  |
  |                     Bank statement
  |               Cash
  |             Accruals
  |           Commitments
  |       Contingencies
  |   Long-term plans
Type of accounting
  <------------------------------------------->
    Long                    Short          Nil
       Expected period before expenditure occurs
```

Source: *Quality in the Finance Function* by David Lynch. CIMA/ Kogan Page 1994.

Using a cash accounting policy, an amount will appear in the actuals column only once a payment has been made: for example, once a cheque has been written. This might be some time after the legal liability has been incurred and well after a commitment has been made to spend the funds. If management accounts only reflect the commitment once the liability has been met, the risk of overstating 'free' funds is considerable.

A first step in rectifying the above position is to move to an accruals accounting policy, by accruing liabilities when they are incurred rather than recognising them only when they are met. This means, for example, charging invoice values as expenditure and coding payments to creditor balances.

An even more advanced move is to switch to commitment accounting, where 'accruals' include commitments made (for example by the placing of an order), even though the goods or service has not yet been provided, and therefore no liability for payment has yet been incurred. Some form of ordering system is required to adopt commitment accounting. Typically, copies of orders made are entered in the accounting system, to be matched against invoices once received. As well as enabling the management accounts to inform the user at the point of commitment that funds have been earmarked, and are therefore not 'free' for other purposes, using orders minimises the risk of payment for an invoice being processed twice.

Even when the user understands what 'actual' means, the information is of limited value unless it has a context. Management accounts that simply tell the user 'you have spent £X on legal costs' do not tell them very much. The information only begins to be useful if the user can compare the figure with a benchmark that provides a financial context. The budget is perhaps the most useful benchmark, as it lists the desired results that staff should work towards. But before they can determine whether it is satisfactory to be where they are, staff must have a clear understanding of the assumptions made in preparing the budget.

Using *previous actuals* has the advantage of showing historical fact. Last year's actuals are a real precedent against which to judge this year's. But is it possible, or even desirable, to repeat last year's results?

Moreover, if last year's actuals are used, the budget becomes more and more dated as the financial year progresses. This can be remedied by amending the budget to reflect the latest forecasts. Although the original budget, as approved by the trustees, will remain as a benchmark, budget-holders can reflect in these forecasts any changes they know to have happened (or expect to happen).

Although the three standards of comparison described above are the most common, there are others that may be useful – particularly if your organisation seeks to be the best in its class. For example, you could compare your fundraising costs with:

- The five most successful UK charity results, suitably adjusted.
- Your best ever performance.
- The average of the Barclays/*NGO Finance* Charity 100 index.
- Any commercial organisations listed as an example of best practice in the DTI Inside UK Enterprise scheme.
- Your closest competitor.

- Your equivalent organisation overseas.

How will the management accounts be communicated?

A typical set of management accounts will show actuals versus budget for both the latest month and, cumulatively, the annual budget, and perhaps the projected full year forecast, but other formats can be considered. For example, graphs are effective in illustrating trends. Management accounts can also be presented orally: for example, in open workshops for staff and management committee members – these have the advantage of allowing for discussion.

Who owns the management accounts?

Because budgets are produced by the accounts department, that department is often seen as owning them. Users need to feel that *they* are the owners of management accounts rather than merely passive recipients. This question of ownership can be resolved by addressing the following issues:

Involvement. The more the user can influence the management accounts, the more likely they are to value them as a decision-making aid. This does, however, require the user to have commitment and the relevant skills. Involvement is more likely when:

- Operating or programme staff (those involved in spending the money) prepare the budgets.
- Programme staff have a detailed understanding of the organisation's priorities.
- Programme staff contribute to the design of reports, albeit within the statutory framework.
- The inputting of data – such as invoice details – is performed by programme staff instead of accounts clerks.
- Users are able to get reports whenever they need them. Why should the accounts department generate management accounts?

Transparency. Organisations should recognise that information is a resource which should be made freely available to all staff (but without compromising privacy). In this way, both good and bad news can be communicated.

Accountability. Those who make decisions about the use of the charity's financial resources should be held accountable for those decisions. Accountability can be achieved by requiring the users of management accounts to:

- Prepare budgets using a zero-based approach where the user has to justify the resources needed.
- Explain variances that arise, so that problem areas are identified and action taken.

- Reforecast year-end results as the year progresses, so that programme staff are encouraged to think about whether they are on track.
- Revise budgets if the resource requirement for the programmes has changed.

Trust. Users of management accounts should feel that they are trusted to manage the resources for which they are accountable. This can be difficult, as it requires the accounts department to strike a balance between wise stewardship of the charity's financial resources and obtrusive policing. In practice, trust means:

- Examining the levels of authority that users exercise, and perhaps increasing them so as to give the users the discretion to spend resources.
- Managing expectations by stressing that the budget is a *plan* based on assumptions that may not hold true – it is not to be used for disciplinary purposes.

5. BUDGETS AND IT SOLUTIONS

Increasingly, voluntary organisations of all sizes are using spreadsheet applications to prepare management accounts. Although the above remarks about accounts apply equally to manual and computerised systems, the approach to the design of spreadsheet-based management accounts will be different. Information technology is often used to produce budgets because of its speed and convenience, but too little thought is generally given to how useful these computer-generated reports actually are.

This section gives guidelines on how to organise, design and implement budgetary control using spreadsheet applications. They will help organisations to use information technology solutions that genuinely assist management rather than hinder it, as is so often the case.

Preplanning

A budgetary control system will require a number of different modules: what these consist of will differ from organisation to organisation and from department to department. However, a typical requirement might be for departmental/project budgets, actuals, variance and year-to-date reports. Selected data from these reports may be required at corporate level to help compile the overall aggregated reports for the organisation.

For anything other than the simplest application, there are key stages to developing a spreadsheet model that should be strictly followed; see Figure 3.14 over page.

Figure 3.14: Stages in the spreadsheet development process

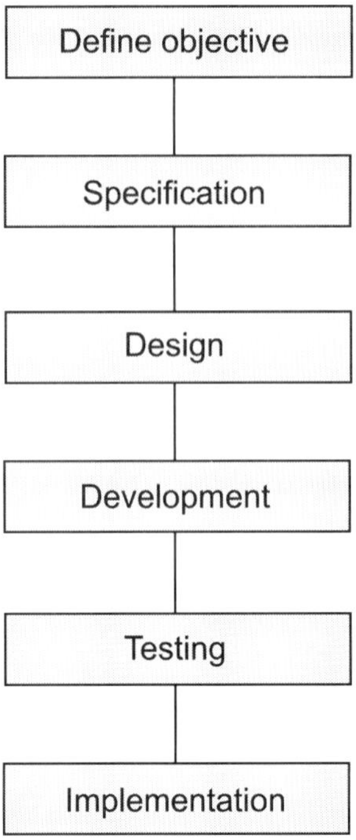

```
Define objective
      │
  Specification
      │
    Design
      │
  Development
      │
    Testing
      │
 Implementation
```

Source: Spreadsheet Skills for Budgeting, S Nugus

Problem definition

Before entering data into the spreadsheet, think carefully about the objective of the spreadsheet system. Talk to the people who might need to extract information from the system when it is complete. It is much more difficult to change the format of a financial plan after it has been committed to the spreadsheet. At this stage, the level of detail required should be decided; many spreadsheets systems include detailed calculations that are irrelevant to the problem or are never used.

Model specification

Next, consider the assumptions on which the system will be based. The overall format of the system – in terms of what information will be kept on which sheet, what data will be stored in separate files etc – should be agreed by everyone who will have to use it.

Spreadsheet design

A detailed breakdown of how the system will be laid out should now be prepared, including how data input forms will be used, how much of the descriptive information can be repeated for different parts of the system, how much documentation will be included in the system etc.

Spreadsheet development
This is the point at which the actual building of the system begins. Too many people ignore the preceding stages and jump straight into spreadsheet development. This usually results in needlessly complex models that take longer than necessary to develop, based on assumptions that were not part of the original brief.

Testing
Even after thorough planning and careful spreadsheet development, it is essential to test all components of a system. This can be done by entering several sets of data and checking the logic; historical data with known results is useful for this purpose.

Implementation
The effort required for implementation will vary according to the complexity of the system, the number of people who will use it and whether training or ongoing support will be needed. However, even if the system has been developed for a single user, it is wise to allow for the fact that someone other than that person might have to use the spreadsheet at some stage.

6. COMPUTERISING THE ACCOUNTS

Most voluntary organisations of any size will have to ask the question: 'Do we need to computerise our accounts?' The reasons usually given for doing so include saving staff time or other resources, obtaining more detailed or more accurate information, and producing reports and answering queries more quickly.

It is usually clear when an accounting system is failing to meet the needs of an organisation, or when the resources it is consuming seem out of proportion to the results. In some cases, improving the existing manual system may be all that is needed. However, every organisation is different; here are some key criteria that should be considered before deciding to computerise:

- Is your annual income or expenditure more than £100,000?
- Do you have three or more different projects that need separate accounting?
- Do you handle a large number of similar transactions?

If the answer to all three is 'no', then your organisation is unlikely to benefit from computerising its accounts; 'yes' to two or more means that it probably would.

If the organisation is small, with a simple financial structure, it should be possible to design an effective manual system for the main accounting records. However, within such a manual system there may be areas of work involving a large number of repetitive transactions – such as subscriptions – that lend themselves to computer assistance.

When to start?

The best arrangement is to close the old system down at the end of one year and start the next year with the new system. Unfortunately, this means that the busy period when annual accounts are being prepared will coincide with any teething troubles in the computer system – although potential problems can be minimised by careful planning and preparation.

Planning should begin well in advance: for an April start, detailed preparation should be under way by September, and it may be necessary to start discussions even earlier to agree on an approach that involves the committee, management and key staff. These early discussions should include a review of the additional resources needed to install the new system: for example, will it be necessary to bring in outside expertise and/or temporary assistance? Are there any sources of funding, or free expertise or assistance, for this investment? Even at this early stage it can be useful to visit similar voluntary organisations in order to learn from their experiences.

What to avoid

Here are some guidelines on what not to do:

- Using 'informal' systems – those that allow entries to be changed at a later stage without a clear record being kept of the amendment.
- Expecting staff without adequate training, supervision or control to enter complex data reliably.
- Becoming over-sophisticated – for example, by trying to provide excessively detailed analysis or automating procedures better left manual.
- Allowing one enthusiastic employee or volunteer to set up a system that only he or she can understand.

Which package?

A package that lends itself to a project-based system would be most useful, as that reflects the structure (and funding pattern) of many voluntary organisations. Unfortunately, most packages have been designed for commercial application and hence are not appropriate for a project-based system. Figure 5.15 shows an alternative solution using a simple, and inexpensive accounting package to do the basic bookkeeping on double-entry principles, with a full audit trail to keep track of every entry or adjustment. Although many such packages offer budgeting and reporting facilities, it is far better to use a separate spreadsheet package – which is much more flexible and user-friendly – to produce reports of actual expenditure against budget.

How to set up?

In the computer package, income and expenditure headings will be represented by codes (a chart of accounts) that will enable you to analyse income and expenditure.

Figure 3.15: Management accounts using spreadsheets

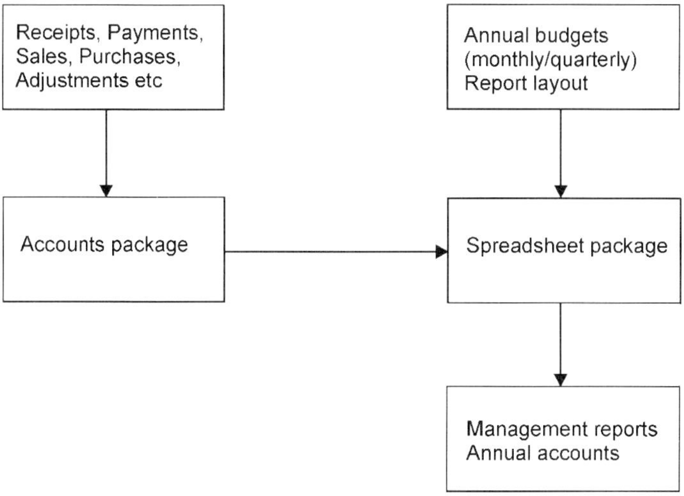

```
┌─────────────────────┐              ┌─────────────────────┐
│ Receipts, Payments, │              │ Annual budgets      │
│ Sales, Purchases,   │              │ (monthly/quarterly) │
│ Adjustments etc     │              │ Report layout       │
└──────────┬──────────┘              └──────────┬──────────┘
           │                                    │
           ▼                                    ▼
┌─────────────────────┐              ┌─────────────────────┐
│ Accounts package    │─────────────▶│ Spreadsheet package │
└─────────────────────┘              └──────────┬──────────┘
                                                │
                                                ▼
                                     ┌─────────────────────┐
                                     │ Management reports  │
                                     │ Annual accounts     │
                                     └─────────────────────┘
```

This needs careful thought, as no two charts of accounts will be the same, but a few general tips may help:

- Work backwards from the reports you want to produce to determine the most convenient structure and sequence of accounts.
- Use different levels of analysis as appropriate, perhaps using a separate code for each individual's training costs, but one code for, say, postage.
- Leave generous gaps between codes to allow for new developments.

Who needs training?

Almost everyone in the organisation, and perhaps a few people outside, should be made aware of the new system. Those with the main training needs will be the people who prepare information for inputting – for example, whoever looks after the petty cash – or who receive output information: for example, the members of the committee who read the final reports.

FURTHER READING AND RESOURCES

The UK Voluntary Sector Almanac 1998/99 NCVO 1998.

Quality in the finance function by David Lynch. CIMA/Kogan Page 1994.

Spreadsheet skills for budgeting by S Nugus. CIMA 1998.

Voluntary interpretation of the business excellence model. British Quality Foundation 1998.

Appendix A: Case studies

1. Giltim Union: a comprehensive examination of a budgeting system

This case study provides a comprehensive examination of a budgeting system. Specifically, it allows the reader to:

- Evaluate the Giltim budget reporting system in terms of design, speed, frequency, clarity, and overall effectiveness for region, division and head office.
- Criticise the design of the report.
- Establish how well the budget system motivates regional secretaries to achieve union objectives.
- Consider how senior management could make the system more effective.

Top management approach to reporting

The general secretary and controller of Giltim insisted upon a rapid and efficient system of reporting monthly operations. They believe in up-to-date reports to enable timely action by head office, division and regional secretaries. However, they believe that regional secretaries should not wait until the month end to deal with critical problems, but should be on top of them daily.

Region reports were reviewed on an 'exception' basis, comparing actual against budget performance. This was felt to be good for morale, and regional secretaries were expected to explain overspending but not under-spending.

Monthly flash reports

On the third business day after the month end, each region faxed key figures for income, gross surplus and net surplus to division and head office, together with the variances from budget. A summary of these figures was studied the next day by senior management, which was concerned about critical variances.

Monthly detailed reports

On the eighth working day the regional operating summary and supporting reports were due at divisional head office. These were consolidated to show the results by region and division, then distributed the next day to senior management.

In addition, at the beginning of each month regional secretaries were expected to submit current re-forecasts of anticipated performance for the month and year end. Such re-forecasts enabled head office to shape financial plans and to get regional secretaries to look at their programmes on a yearly as well as a day-to-day basis.

Dealing with regional problems

When a potential problem became apparent, daily reports on it were required for the division and head office. A specialist team was sometimes sent to the region concerned to make recommendations. It was up to the regional secretary to accept or reject these; but it was generally expected that they would accept such 'advice' gracefully.

Income decline
If a decline in income became evident early in the year, and the regional secretary could convince senior management that the change was permanent, the region budget could be revised to reflect the new circumstances. But if income fell below the predicted level towards the year end, no revision was allowed.

Regional secretaries were expected to go back over the budget with their staff to see where cost reductions could be made that would do the least harm. Specifically, they were expected to consider what could be either eliminated or postponed until next year.

Branch and region co-ordination
Whenever problems arose between regions and branches, local managers were expected to solve the problems themselves. Members' needs always came first. However, if the local programme involved a major regional expense out of line with the budget, this was decided upon by division or head office.

Motivation of regional secretary
Regional secretaries – and indeed, all of their staff – were motivated to meet surplus targets through promotion and pressures from division and head office. In addition, each month the regions were ranked competitively for recruitment efficiency, and the results were published widely throughout the union. Inter-region competitions, with prizes, were also conducted for special cost reduction programmes, improvements in methods etc. Regions were encouraged to stress quality and delivery to meet competitive pressures. All region workers knew that, to survive in the competitive market, Giltim had to produce high-quality services in time and at reasonable cost.

Conclusions
Regional secretaries and other staff were not particularly happy under the system, but they worked hard to achieve targets and were generally successful, despite changes in the market conditions.

Schedule of monthly region report

- *Region operating summary.* Income, costs, other income and expense. Actual against budget for the month and year to date. Percentage analysis on sales and assets employed.
- *Income analysis.* Income by membership bands. Actual, budget and variance analysis for the month and year to date.
- *Region variance cost* of material, labour and variable expense. Actual budget and variance analysis.
- *Recruitment and sales.*
- *Region fixed expense.* Region expense other than variable and special expense. Actual, budget and variance analysis.

Figure 3.16: Giltim Union, No.1 Region Operating Statement, March

	This Month Actual £	This Month Budget £	Last Month Actual £	This Month Last Year Actual £
Recruitment income	170,167.95	294,325.00	162,270.94	289,979.05
Other income	47,132.16	16,000.00	37,420.16	13,111.11
TOTAL INCOME	217,300.11	310,325.00	199,691.10	303,090.16
Variable costs	142,216.99	187,500.00	137,821.26	192,174.72
GROSS MARGIN	75,083.12	122,825.00	61,869.84	100,915.44
Fixed costs	41,211.11	36,400.00	38,174.14	41,117.76
OPERATING INCOME	33,872.01	86,425.00	23,695.70	69,797.68
% income	15.587%	27.849%	11.865%	23.028%
SPECIAL COSTS (SURPLUS):				
Method improvements	(17,426.22)	(21,300.00)	(28,321.89)	(12,174.16)
Standard revisions	24,174.14	9,400.00	7,416.27	6,811.20
Price variances	(12,111.11)	(6,000.00)	3,567.47	4,666.54
Miscellaneous	(8,126.46)	(6,000.00)	(30,100.26)	(22,178.88)
TOTAL	(13,489.64)	(23,900.00)	(47,438.41)	(22,178.88)
REGION SURPLUS	47,361.66	110,325.00	71,134.11	92,672.98
Assets employed	1,816,411.20	1,874,426.00	1,742,111.89	1,052,111.91
% Return	2.6074%	5.8871%	4.0834%	8.8091%

NOTE: Year to date figures on next page *[not provided here]*.

Source: School of Social Entrepreneurs

- *Special costs and surplus.* Special items under the control of the region secretary, including sale of scrap, methods improvement, standard revisions, cost reduction programmes etc. Actual, budget and variance analysis.
- *Region investment.* Stock, capital projects, debtors included in computation of assets employed by the region. Actual, budget, variance and ageing analysis.

Evaluation of reporting system

- *Design.* Reports include actual and target data. Head office requires re-forecasting of activity that deviates from budget. Highlight on excess spending over budget, but no importance attached to under-spending. Concentrates on problem areas with special reports. Report sample is badly designed.

- *Speed*. Flash reporting in three days and full reporting to head office in eight days provides timely data for management. Probably achieved by cut-off of activities before the month end and efficient data processing.
- *Frequency*. Excellent: monthly data on regular operations, weekly or daily for critical problems.
- *Clarity*. Poor layout and lack of graphical presentation.
- *Effectiveness*. Highly effective for head office control of activity against budget. Provides control data to focus manager on target achievement and critical problems. Probably over-emphasises short-term meeting of the budget at the expense of long-term performance.

Performance of Region No 1 and design of Report No 1

It was difficult to evaluate the performance of Region No 1 from this report (figure 3.16) as 'year to date' figures were not provided. However, evaluation of March's performance raised many questions that need investigation:

- Recruitment income is seriously below target: is this a national trend or a regional failure?
- Variable cost of recruitment and sales controlled: is this due to office efficiency?
- Fixed costs seriously above target: why?
- Operating income well below target both in amount and percentage: is this due to failure of income?
- Special costs and surpluses generally consistent with targets, but why did regional secretary fail to cut costs to make up for the lack of activity?
- Region income well below target and return on assets employed unacceptable.

The following improvements are suggested in the design of the report:

- Eliminate 'previous month' and 'last year' columns, since the budget is the real target.
- Show only actual data for the month and the year to date with variance from the budget (not the budget itself).
- Eliminate all data below £1000 to reduce the digits to significant items only; reports should not be too black with figures.
- Design each report page as a complete entity supported by detail on subsequent sheets.
- Design report with graphics sections to emphasise signals.

Motivation of managers

1. System provides highly centralised control by head office and is probably defensive.
2. Extensive interaction in setting the targets probably conditions managers to accept them. Personal contact with head office staff and visit by controller most helpful.

3. Unreasonable to expect regional secretaries to meet surplus budget if recruitment falls off, but quite possible for them to feel bound to do so and to believe that they can and do achieve budget!
4. Regional secretaries probably underspend on maintenance, research, training etc in the early months of the year until income levels indicate that they can 'afford' to spend up to the budget cost levels.
5. Regional secretaries motivated to achieve target by:
Budget preparation process
Senior management interest in and follow-up of reporting
Salaries and bonuses
Competition between regions
Staff assistance and daily reports on critical problems
Requirements to continually re-forecast any expected performance below target
Budget effect on personal promotion in the union
6. Tendency to achieve short-term targets with some loss of long-term potential. However, this loss may not be significant.
7. Long-term planning retained by head office and divisional management (the latter is fairly impotent). Little motivation to think beyond current year at region level. Poor development of regional secretary's potential.
8. Fairly dynamic environment created by the constructive friction between region, head office and division.
9. May achieve a lower level of long-term performance, but all staff are not merely cost orientated but out-turn orientated too.
10. System meets senior management objective of surplus now. Puts surplus responsibility close to operations that achieve surplus. Related to the specific industry sector features of delivery, quality and efficient cost control.

Changes recommended
1. Consider the technical, human and organisational problems that any change would have to overcome. Managers may prefer the devil they know, and may therefore be reluctant to accept any new system.
2. Consider all the alternatives and their implications:
- Make division out-turn orientated: that is, positively seeking opportunities to generate income as a contribution to costs (regions become only cost orientated)?
- All-budget revision when income falls off (managers more motivated to justify revisions than to achieve out-turn budgets)?
3. Proposals:
- Try to assign income and surplus responsibility to one manager in one centre.
- If this is not possible, introduce some flexibility in budget revision when income falls off substantially.
- Expand budget system for a three-year horizon. Plan every year for three years ahead. Let the annual budget targets be developed from the first year of plan.
- Include all managers in short and long-term planning process.

Figure 3.17: Giltim Union, revised regional operating summary, March

REPORT No.1

	This Month Actual £'000	This Month (Under)/Over Budget £'000	Year to date Actual £'000	Year to date (Under)/Over Budget £'000	
Recruitment Income	170	(124)	847	(122)	
Other Income	47	31	84	56	
TOTAL INCOME	217	(93)	763	(66)	
% Gain/ (loss)	–	(30.0%)	–	(7.9%)	See Report 2
Variable costs of recruitment & sales	142	(45)	384	(64)	See Report 3
GROSS MARGIN	75	(48)	379	(2)	
% Income	34.6%	(5.1%)	49.6%	3.6%	
Fixed costs	41	5	211	10	See Report 4
OPERATING INCOME	34	(53)	168	(12)	
% Income	15.7%	(12.4%)	22.0%		
Special costs (surplus)	(13)	(11)	12	11	See Report 5
REGIONAL SURPLUS	47	(64)	156	(1)	
% Income	21.7%	(13.8%)	20.4%		
Assets employed	1,816	(58)	1,816	(58)	See Report 6
% Return	2.6%	(3.3%)	8.6%	8.4%	

Source: School of Social Entrepreneurs

- Introduce a training and development programme for managers to give them an understanding of long-term and short-term planning.
- Discourage the idea that meeting the budget is the same as doing the management job!

Learning points
- Budget reports should be available three to eight days after the month end.
- Achieve fast reporting, day early cut-off and efficient use of IT.
- Design reports for use by managers, not accountants: simple, graphic, exciting.
- Signal the key factors, do not give the complete detail.
- Design reports for local as well as top management.
- Recognise that manager motivation is not automatically achieved by participation, but is a complex phenomenon resulting from the total system.

- Managers may sometimes not be rationally responsible, but may be convinced that they are and act accordingly. Behaviour is not completely rational in logical or economic terms; emotional needs.
- To modify the budget system and motivate the managers is a complex problem. They may not work as effectively under a new and 'better' system.
- Set surplus centres as close to operations (the 'front line') as practicable, to make managers not merely cost orientated but also surplus orientated.
- Head office 'advice' may really be orders.
- Region 'agreement' may really be imposed by head office.
- Technical problems with the budget are fairly easy to solve, but the human problems are not.
- The involvement of senior management in the budget process is vital if it is to motivate managers.
- A three-year horizon involving all managers is more useful than mere budgetary control each year. This provides the underlying data for the annual and monthly budget targets.
- Design the budget system with reference to senior management objectives, industry sector key factors and the organisational structure of the union.
- Measure the effectiveness of the budget system by what the managers do, not by what they say.
- Review and redesign budget reports periodically to meet changing needs.
- Recognise that reports for head office may not necessarily meet local management needs; thus leading to two (or more) reporting systems, formal and informal.

2. THE BUSINESS EXCELLENCE MODEL

In this case study, the quality director of United Response shows how the establishment of quality standards is becoming increasingly relevant for voluntary organisations, because it enables them not only to measure their own performance but also to demonstrate value for money to funders. It is also a good example of how the excellence model has been adapted to fit on top of an existing quality management programme.

United Response was founded in 1973. It is a registered charity and voluntary agency providing community support services to adults with learning disabilities and people with mental health difficulties. Currently it supports over 1200 people, employs 50, has a turnover of £10 million and operates throughout England. Since 1994 they have been developing their own brand of quality management and use the Excellence Model to assess progress and underpin corporate planning. United Response's approach to quality management, and where the Model fits into this, is described below.

Quality management in United Response

In the 1990s and beyond, quality management is on the agenda for voluntary organisations whether it is welcomed or not. As you pick your way through shelves full of established quality standards, such as ISO 9000 and Investors in People, or are confounded by a galaxy of quality gurus, it is difficult to work out what to choose. Meanwhile, funders anxious to demonstrate best value are baying for quantifiable results. A quality system selected off the shelf may offer short-term gains and win approval from stakeholders, but it will not necessarily become established as a vehicle for change and improvement within the organisation. First, you must work out why you are embarking on quality management and what it should look like.

United Response introduced quality management in 1994 for four reasons:

1. It enables them to provide services that are based on their knowledge of what the people they support need and want.
2. The people who use their services, or who have a direct interest in them, know what they can expect.
3. It fosters a culture of continuous improvement.
4. It encouraged all their staff and services to be aware of the impact of their work and to work on ways of developing it.

United Response's approach could be broadly defined as Total Quality Management. They were also keen to establish themselves as a 'learning organisation' by using quality management techniques to learn from their own practice. Finally, they deferred introducing a formal system of external accreditation because they feared it may produce only a form of quality assurance without achieving the substance of organisation-wide ownership and participation.

There are two main components to their quality management system. These are:

1. Setting standards

Using the expertise of service users, staff teams and all those who have a direct interest in their services, they introduced a collaborative method of standard setting, development and maintenance. Story telling, informality and team work are key components, helping to make the standards rigorous and realistic. The goal is for all those involved to own the process and what it achieves. Integration is key, as central services such as payroll and personnel recognise that they are also service providers and need to set standards.

2. Auditing standards

United Response set up a system for auditing standards internally that involved everyone in the organisation. It is a continuous process of self assessment that gradually works through our 30 quality standards; these are divided among the following areas:

- *Who needs what?* This covers areas such as individual planning and setting up a new service.
- *Supporting people.* All the standards necessary to provide a support and care service: for example, referrals, medication, food and cooking.

- *Supporting staff.* Everything connected with staff needs: for example, induction, supervision, learning and development.
- *General activities.* This includes finance, health and safety and property maintenance.

Each month a user-friendly checklist is issued based on one of the standards. Local managers work through it with staff teams to identify good practice and areas for improvement. Administrative staff become involved when auditing a standard relevant to their work (staff supervision, team meetings). The results are reviewed by the management team and follow-up action is agreed and recorded. All staff are briefed on the outcome. This co-ordinated approach helps the company to develop while at the same time highlighting good practice. Furthermore, audit outcomes provide a wealth of management information, a foundation for planning and goals for staff development.

Using the Excellence Model
United Response was introduced to the Model by the Charities Evaluation Service, which had been asked by the British Quality Foundation to find a suitable organisation in which to pilot its use. As they had already begun developing their own style of Total Quality Management, the Excellence Model offered a valuable template for assessing their progress.

The benefits of the Model are its flexibility and the fact that it enabled them to make a quick, but fairly detailed, examination of virtually everything the organisation does. Given United Response's client groups, assessing how their work affects the quality of their lives is a considerable challenge. The value of the Excellence Model is the weight that it gives to 'enablers', the breadth of outcomes it measures, and its encouragement to assess the impact of their work on a wide range of internal and external stakeholders.

Within United Response, the Excellence Model has been used as a self assessment tool in a number of ways:

- For an annual self assessment by the management team in order to identify national quality targets. When this task was undertaken they were assisted by colleagues from the Lloyds TSB quality department.
- As background material for the development of their own quality standards.
- To start the strategic planning cycle.
- By central departments and each of their seven regions as a planning tool and to identify quality targets.
- As an overall aid to identifying organisational learning goals.
- By their sister organisation, United Response Northern Ireland, as a first step towards the introduction of quality management.

Using the Model has meant that their planning has become more precise while goals and targets have been clearly defined.

Effective use of the Model demands a 'driver' at senior level. The task involves selling the Model internally and working on the detail of how it can be made relevant and useful to each region and/or department.

A word of caution: a certain amount of translation is needed to make the Model fit a voluntary organisation's culture and circumstances. Other users must be able to recognise the scope of the Model and not be inhibited by its seemingly formal language. This limitation has been acknowledged by the British Quality Foundation, which is working with Charities Evaluation Service to make the model more user friendly for voluntary organisations.

During the 1997-98 planning cycle, United Response undertook a more detailed self assessment exercise as the first stage in the production of their corporate plan. Last year's results were used, in combination with the outcome of a recent positioning exercise. Organisation-wide feedback was given on the priorities under each element of the Excellence Model. At the end of the exercise they distilled the details of the plan on to a single sheet outlining the key priorities for the organisation and distributed it widely.

United Reponse found that the Excellence Model enabled them to link quality management, corporate planning, performance evaluation and benchmarking in a continuous process. They may eventually go for the award, but the benefits have already been felt in endorsing and developing their own home-grown style of quality management. Above all, they seem to be taking the organisation with them.

Appendix B: Budget bids by team aims

DESCRIPTION & CODES	FIXED TEAM COSTS	AIM / MONTH 1	AIM / MONTH 2	AIM / MONTH 3	AIM / MONTH 4	AIM / MONTH 5	AIM / MONTH 6	AIM / MONTH 7	AIM / MONTH 8	AIM / MONTH 9	AIM / MONTH 10	AIM / MONTH 11	AIM / MONTH 12	TOTALS
ACCOUNT INCOME CODE														
Grants														
Income from Conferences														
Fees for Services Provided														
Other Income														
TOTAL INCOME														
STAFF COSTS														
Salaries														
Temporary Staff Costs														
Training Received														
TOTAL STAFF COSTS														
RUNNING COSTS														
Travel & Subsistence														
Telephone & Fax														
Printing														
Photocopying														

Appendix B:—continued

DESCRIPTION & CODES	FIXED TEAM COSTS	AIM/ MONTH 1	AIM/ MONTH 2	AIM/ MONTH 3	AIM/ MONTH 4	AIM/ MONTH 5	AIM/ MONTH 6	AIM/ MONTH 7	AIM/ MONTH 8	AIM/ MONTH 9	AIM/ MONTH 10	AIM/ MONTH 11	AIM/ MONTH 12	TOTALS
ACCOUNT CODE														
Stationery														
Postage														
Books & Periodicals														
Catering														
Subscriptions														
Cconferences Organised														
Accommodation Charge														
Central services Charge														
TOTAL RUNNING COSTS														
TOTAL EXPENDITURE														
SURPLUS / (DEFICIT)														

Appendix C:

The budgeting process

This list of key questions should be reviewed by the chief finance officer or other person responsible for organising the budget and compiling the information. It could also be reviewed by the board finance committee to establish whether all the appropriate steps in the process have been taken.

1. Why is a budget useful?
a. It outlines in financial terms the goals and policies approved by the board.
b. It is a method of monitoring adherence to, and deviations from, plans throughout the year.
c. Its preparation causes the organisation to focus on planning, evaluation of programmes, and accomplishment of its mission.

2. Is the budgeting process properly timed?
a. Can the proposed staff or project changes realistically be implemented before the financial year end?
b. Is board membership scheduled to change prior to budget approval? (Avoiding making a new board responsible for a budget they didn't approve).
c. If the budget is approved by members, when is the annual meeting?
d. Must major funding requests be submitted in advance of approval of the overall budget? If so, consider the need for a two or three-year plan.

3. What type of budget is appropriate for this organisation?
a. Is a zero-based budget needed for critical evaluation of priorities to force a serious cutback in the level of expenses?
b. Are existing programmes examined as closely as proposed projects?
c. Will a functional or line-item budget allow for proper review of programme goals?
d. Is the budget based on existing operations, with incremental increases or decreases for economic conditions?

4. Who prepares the budget?
a. Is a budget committee needed?
b. Would a budget committee made up of accounting department staff, board members and outside advisers be effective?
c. If each department does the initial preparation, are standard formats and instructions distributed to ensure consistency?
d. Is the final budget comprehensive, including restricted funds, endowments, capital improvements and all financial aspects?

5. What are the stages in budget preparation?
a. Develop goals and objectives for a three to five-year period first (long-range plan, dreams).

b. Quantify long range goals, such as raising an endowment, financing new facilities or increasing staff.
c. Evaluate last year's results:
i. Were objectives achieved?
ii. If not, were they unreasonable?
iii. What caused variances? Were mid-year revisions appropriate?
iv. What changes were indicated by ratio analysis?
d. Establish objectives for the coming year.
e. Prepare programme justification.
f. Prepare estimates of income and expenses of programmes.
g. Compile, evaluate and balance the results.
h. The budget should be approved first by the staff, then by the board (with intervening stages as the nature of the organisation dictates).
i. Amend the budget when the monitoring process shows a need for change.

6. *Evaluate programmes and services rendered*
a. Who are the stakeholders?
b. Is the organisation reaching them?
c. Should promotion be budgeted?
d. Is the cost per person too high?
e. Is a competing organisation providing the same service?

7. *Evaluate the pricing of services*
a. Should changes be made? Price increases or decreases?
b. Would audience/membership etc increase with a decrease in prices, resulting in more revenue?
c. Are funding sources available to cover free or reduced-cost services?

8. *Evaluate fundraising activities*
a. Can board members and other volunteers devote sufficient time to help the organisation reach its fundraising goals? If not, should consultants or new staff be hired?
b. Is an annual special giving campaign necessary in addition to the membership campaign? Would it drain the membership?
c. Can project sponsors or co-sponsors be found?
d. Should a planned giving programme be established?

9. *Evaluate expenses*
a. Could alternative approaches improve efficiency and thus reduce costs?
b. Is the use of volunteers effective?
c. Would 'investing' in a paid development director or volunteer co-ordinator more than pay for itself?
d. Are computers used effectively?
i. To save money, are cheaper but time-consuming or inadequate programmes being used?

ii. Would networking, e-mail or a Web site pay for themselves through savings in time and mailings?
e. Are fixed and variable costs segregated? If so, are they properly allocated to programmes?
f. Are changes in salary level factored into benefit costs?

10. *Consider outside forces*
a. Is funding likely to be cut owing to the depressed state of the economy?
b. Has there been a shift in population? Have plants closed? Are standards in the profession changing?
c. Are accreditation or grant requirements changing?

11. *Before final approval, consider these issues*
a. Is there any doubt about the reliability of projections?
b. Do sufficient cash reserves exist to cover shortfalls?
c. Re-evaluate policy goals if cuts have to be made.
d. Could projects be carried out in co-operation with, or by, another organisation?
e. Would charts or graphs illustrate trends and make decisions clearer?

12. *Prepare supplementary budgets to implement the overall budget*
a. Cash flow projections.
b. Investment objectives.
c. Capital expenditure timing.
d. Restricted fund budgets.

13. *Devise a follow-up system for monitoring the budget*
a. Use timely financial reports to compare actual expenses and income with those budgeted.
b. Revise budget to reflect recurring changes during the year.

With acknowledgement to Jody Blazek.

Appendix D
Quality and budgets

This appendix explains some of the difficulties that arise when organisations use financial budgets as a basis for measuring the performance of charitable programmes and/or the organisation as a whole. The Excellence Model is suggested as a way of resolving these difficulties and providing a more balanced approach to performance. Any quality planning model should identify the objectives, measures, targets and initiatives to be used in successfully implementing the organisation's vision and strategy.

Here are some of the excellence indicators or targets for each of the nine elements used by the Excellence Model.

Leadership
Definition: how the behaviour and actions of the executive team and all other leaders inspire, support and promote excellence as the best way to achieve the organisation's objectives.
Some excellence indicators may be that:
- Leaders (managers, trustees etc) champion the organisation's approach to excellence.
- Organisational values are made explicit.
- Leaders are accessible.
- The organisation is recognised as excellent within the sector.
- Leaders are strongly committed to people satisfaction.
- Leaders focus on customers (recipients or beneficiaries of the activities).
- Leaders act as coaches.

Policy and strategy
Definition: how the organisation formulates, deploys, reviews and turns policy and strategy into plans and actions.
Some excellence indicators may be:
- Customer focus.
- Involvement and empowerment of people and teams.
- Clear, easily remembered values.
- Long-term planning horizon.
- 'Excellence' planning integrated with business planning.

People management
Definition: how the organisation releases the full potential of its people.
Some excellence indicators may be that:
- People's roles are linked with wider local and/or national organisation's aims and mission.
- People are trained in relation to all new initiatives and to understand their impact on the customer.

- The organisation has an integrated approach to volunteer development.

Resources
Definition: how the organisation manages resources effectively and efficiently.
Some excellence indicators may include:
- Resources that are focused to support key processes and policy and strategy.
- Financial decision making that is focused on service delivery.
- Budgets that are effectively and efficiently managed at the lowest organisational level.
- Technology that is used to summarise and present information to enhance customer awareness and satisfaction.

Processes
Definition: How the organisation identifies, manages, reviews and improves its processes.
Some excellence indicators may include:
- Clear definitions of key processes.
- Clear quantitative measures of process effectiveness.
- Setting challenging targets.

Customer satisfaction
Definition: What the organisation is achieving in relation to the satisfaction of its external customers.
Some excellence indicators might be that:
- The main customer/client groups are identified.
- Creative, proactive ways of assessing customer/client satisfaction are used.

People satisfaction
Definition: What the organisation is achieving in relation to the satisfaction of its people.
Excellence indicators might include:
- Regular assessment of the satisfaction of the people of the organisation.
- People satisfaction results are benchmarked.
- Acceptance by the people of organisational culture.

Impact on society
Definition: What the organisation is achieving in satisfying the needs and expectations of the community at large.
Excellence indicators might include:
- Use of measures that directly indicate society's perception of the organisation.
- Significant community support and/or local partnerships.
- The organisation acts as a role model for the community.
- The organisation acts as a 'good neighbour' to its related communities.

Business results

Definition: What the organisation is achieving in relation to its planned objectives and in satisfying the needs and expectations of everyone with an interest or other stake in the organisation.

Excellence indicators might include:
- A broad base of improvement trends in products, services, campaigning, internal operations etc.
- Appropriate financial measures are in place, measured and compared.
- Financial reports demonstrate good stewardship of funds.

With acknowledgement to the British Quality Foundation.

4.
Resource management

1. Maximising resources	6. Prudent investment planning
2. Forming alliances	7. Restricted funding
3. Charity mergers	8. Overhead costs
4. Outsourcing	9. Endowments
5. Cash flow planning	10. Charity reserves

A voluntary organisation's resources, or assets, are best managed from the perspective of a going concern: that is, without assuming any limit on the organisation's existence. Although the finance officer will strive to get the best return on invested assets, he or she must be sure that the organisation has sufficient liquid assets available to finance current operations. The goal, therefore, is to maintain the optimum balance between available assets and invested, or growing, assets. A going concern operates in a financially solvent fashion. Solvency in this context means the ability to pay the organisation's debts in a timely manner or to meet its financial responsibilities – not to dissolve like sugar.

This chapter will consider how a voluntary organisation's resources flow and interact. It examines tools for managing that all-important resource: cash. Issues to consider when accepting and protecting restricted and endowed funds are explored, and reserves policy formulation and types of borrowing.

1. Maximising resources

For a voluntary organisation to be financially solvent and operate as a going concern, its managers must, after the budgets are developed, focus on two more objectives:

1. Smoothly financing current operations by making the most efficient use of current, or liquid, funds.

RESOURCE MANAGEMENT   111

2. Maximising available and obtainable resources to enhance return on the resources or capital.

The task of accomplishing these objectives can be called either asset management or resource allocation. The overall resource flow for a professional association is depicted in Figure 4.1.

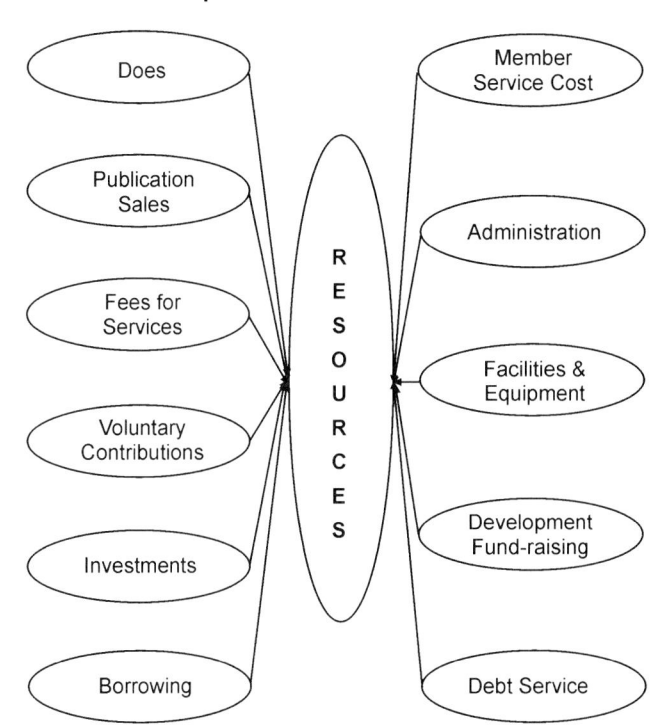

Figure 4.1: Resource flows for a professional association

```
        Does                                  Member Service Cost

    Publication Sales
                                              Administration
                              R
                              E
    Fees for Services         S
                              O
                              U                Facilities & Equipment
                              R
    Voluntary Contributions   C
                              E
                              S                Development Fund-raising
    Investments

    Borrowing                                  Debt Service
```

Source: Financial Planning for Non Profit Organisations, Jody Blazek

The prominent centre labelled Resources represents the funds available to finance or pay bills. Theoretically, the flow of funds coming from the sources on the left side of the chart is sufficient to finance the outflows on the right. Some argue that the successful voluntary organisation focuses first on the left: the sources of funds. They say that it is easy to spend the money; the difficult part is to obtain it. Others reason that excellent programmes draw the support of a voluntary organisation's natural beneficiaries, and should therefore be the focus of the organisation. However, the objective of resource management is to look at the organisation holistically and to capture the benefit of its resources – from sources to programmes and back again – with a balanced perspective.

GETTING RESOURCES

To further examine the resource picture, the organisation's managers consider the choices available for obtaining those resources. A voluntary organisation's funding comes from one or more of the following sources as shown in figure 4.2

Figure 4.2: Income matrix

SOURCES OF INCOME	TRANSACTION TYPE		
	Earned income/sales of goods and services	Voluntary income/grants and donations	Return on investments
General public	• Fees for goods and services (eg. book/product sales, residential home fees, concert tickets) • Membership subscriptions (with significant benefits).	• Street and door to door collections • Convenants and gift aid payments, • Legacies, • Membership subscriptions (no significant benefits).	–
Government	• Local authority community care contracts	• Grants for core funding and project activities from central government and also the European Union.	–
Voluntary organisations	• Services provided under contract.	• Grants from charitable trusts.	–
Business	• Sponsorship, • Research services, • Patent royalties	• Grants from businesses' community affairs departments.	–
Internally generated	–	• Covenanted profits from trading subsidiaries.	• Equities. • British Government • securities. • Common Investment Funds.

Source: NCVO

There is a wealth of published information and advice about fundraising that cannot be summarised here. The intention of this section is to whet the finance officer's appetite by exploring, firstly at a strategic level, ways of maximising the use of resources that might be overlooked and about which there is very little information. At an operational level, there should be policies that maximise the working capital available.

2. FORMING ALLIANCES

Strategic alliances may be formed for any number of reasons, not always financial. Alliances between voluntary organisations can take a variety of forms: from networking groups to funding partnerships, from joint ventures on specific projects to full mergers. Mergers will almost certainly require the advice and permission of the Charity Commission; the others are examples of less formal collaboration. This section of the guide will look at both informal partnerships formed with a view to reducing costs, and at full mergers undertaken for more strategic reasons.

Consortium arrangements
Although a merged organisation may have greater purchasing power, and may therefore be able to secure price reductions on items ranging from insurance premiums to photocopying paper, there are other ways of achieving the same objective. The Charities Consortium has been set up to share information about deals that can be struck with banks, insurance companies and other service providers so that all members can benefit. The whole operation is funded by a percentage of the savings achieved in what is essentially a 'cost reduction partnership'.

The initial cost of establishing a consortium will probably be rapidly overtaken by the cost savings, particularly when a sufficiently large number of organisations come together.

Agency arrangements
These may be an option where a charity's operations have a considerable geographical spread, as it may be inefficient to run small and relatively expensive branches or to have resources tied up in an area where another charity or commercial operator is already well established. The charity may therefore like to consider appointing a separate organisation as its agent to carry on operations on its behalf. The terms of such agency arrangements would need to be negotiated, but the commission or fee payable might be more attractive financially than continuing with the current situation.

Joint ventures
These can be established as a matter of contract between the parties, or by establishing a joint venture company in which the respective interests are reflected at board level. Agreements will typically regulate:

- The nature of the venture undertaken jointly.
- The respective contributions of each party.
- The financing of the venture.
- Matters relating to termination.
- Details of activities which can only be undertaken if jointly agreed.

The advantage of joint ventures is that they do not involve the sharing of liability that characterises a true partnership. They can also contain arrangements for their orderly termination, either because a specific project has been accomplished, or because one of the participants was in breach of its obligations. The opportunities for joint venture are many: for example, Mencap City Insurance Services is a fifty-fifty joint venture by Mencap and an individual to provide insurance brokering services to the voluntary sector.

Mutual support
These are arrangements where charities can see mutual benefit in collaborating but do not wish to set up a formal joint venture: for example, Age Concern and Help the Aged, charities that both pursue their own separate issues, also collaborate on research into matters of mutual concern.

3. Charity mergers

Only if an organisation's resources problem cannot be solved by any of the foregoing solutions should merger be considered, for it implies that the charity has no future as a stand-alone entity. Voluntary sector mergers are quite rare: the largest-known organisation to have resulted from one is Jewish Care, formed in 1990 by the merger of the Jewish Blind Society and the Jewish Welfare Board. Since then, eight other agencies have joined with Jewish Care.

Why charities merge
The most commonly cited reason is to rationalise the use of resources and prevent the overlap of activities. The creation of a single streamlined organisation is seen as a way of maximising resources and achieving significant cost savings.

- Various organisations may be doing the same job, which could cause confusion among clients or the public.
- To develop a unified voice, which helps campaigning and opens up greater networks.
- Improved geographic coverage.
- In certain circumstances, remaining as a single organisation is an obstacle to reaching the greatest possible number of those in need.
- To influence funders: for example, a government department may be confused by two organisations working in the same field and may thus welcome a merger.
- Members may be calling for greater co-operation, and this may develop into pressure to merge with a particular organisation.
- PR reasons: it may be time for an organisational face-lift that can only be brought about by a merger.

Why mergers are successful
Although mergers are rarer in the voluntary sector than they are in the private sector, they are usually highly effective. It is not always clear why this is so; the following reasons *may* be relevant, although it is equally possible to say that the opposites are true (for example, it could be argued that a merger between organisations of equal strength is more likely to be a stumbling block).

- Mergers are most likely to occur between closely related charities; often there is only one logical partner.

- Successful mergers are between bodies of equal strength and determination.
- They should be undertaken willingly, with a shared vision between the partners of what the merger will achieve.
- Cultural differences need to be recognised.
- For a merger to be successful, strong leadership is needed, as is harmony between board and staff; a neutral intermediary was often found to be helpful.

Problems with mergers

- Organisations and individuals may have to abandon cherished parts of their history.
- Within the new organisation the former organisations might still compete with each other. a new corporate identity is therefore needed.
- Each party needs to wield equal political power in the senior management team and the board of trustees.
- There needs to be a will to work together, and the parties need to have a balance of strengths to trade off.
- Mergers as a strategic alliance can achieve economies of scale that maximise a voluntary organisation's existing resources. The attitude at the turn of the century could be characterised as: 'Why should all the arts organisations have individual Web pages? Why not have an ArtSite on the Internet accessible to all?'

4. Outsourcing

Another way of maximising the use of resources is to outsource: to buy in from third parties services and processes that were previously provided in-house. The day-to-day management of the outsourced activity is delegated to the third party.

This option is gaining acceptance as voluntary organisations become more professional. Even small organisations use their local Council for Voluntary Service to provide bookkeeping services. and larger organisations will formally outsource catering and premises management to professional service providers.

The types of activity currently being outsourced in the voluntary sector include:

- Payroll and accountancy services.
- Internal audit.
- Banking and investment services.
- Donor database management.
- Parliamentary campaigning and PR.
- Publications.
- Catering.

It is worth considering the outsourcing of an activity if an external provider can perform that activity for less cost and to a higher standard. For many voluntary organisations, the delivery of services is the first priority, and the organisation's staff have developed skills in this area. The support functions may be seen as a distraction, a use of resources that does not add value. Furthermore, there is constant pressure to reduce the fixed cost base of an organisation in order to attract funding for services.

Benefits of outsourcing
According to voluntary organisations, the main benefits of outsourcing are that it enables them to:

- Focus on core services.
- Improve the quality of services.
- Obtain expertise from outside the organisation.
- Achieve cost reductions.
- Have access to latest technology.

Problems with outsourcing
The most commonly cited drawbacks of outsourcing are:

- Unclear expectations of what performance benefits should accrue from outsourcing.
- Resistance from staff, who may see outsourcing as a form of downsizing unless its benefits have been properly communicated.
- Loss of control over the outsourced process.
- Lack of prior experience of outsourcing.
- Inadequate planning.

The main reason why outsourcing fails is poor planning, particularly when deciding which activity is ripe for outsourcing, when selecting an appropriate service provider and when preparing the outsource contract. It is important to ensure that the service provider:

- Guarantees to meet specific service levels in the contract.
- Has a proven track record in the process or service being outsourced.
- Maintains close contact to prevent loss of control.
- Has experience in the voluntary sector.
- Guarantees specific cost savings in its contract.
- Ensures that there is no conflict of interest with other clients.
- Provides on-going training of staff.

Appendix B is a more detailed checklist of the issues involved in outsourcing.

5. Cash flow planning

Often the most important resource for a voluntary organisation – apart from its staff and volunteers – is its cash. To maintain solvency, the organisation must have sufficient liquid assets. Certain non-cash assets, such as donations receivable, eventually contribute to liquidity and are a part of the non-cash management process. Such assets are commonly called 'current assets' on a financial statement and include those with a potential to become liquid within a short period of time: monthly student tuition fees receivable, bookshop inventory etc. One way to conceptualise the cash management process is to think of the cycles of cash that continually flow through the organisation. To maintain solvency, the cash must flow smoothly and be readily available when it is time to pay creditors and personnel.

Understanding accountants' cash flow statements

The cash flow statements that accompany certain annual accounts are provided because the financial reports that accountants issue may reflect an excess of incoming resources (or income) over resources expended (or expenditure), even when there is no money in the bank. This situation arises, for example, when the organisation spends cash to acquire equipment. On the assumption that the equipment will be useful over a number of years, only part of its purchase price is expensed (depreciated) for the year of purchase, even though the full price was spent. A charitable pledge is reported as income in the year pledged, and it likewise may produce a non-cash profit. On the other hand, the voluntary organisation showing a deficit may have money in the bank from selling obsolete equipment. These apparent contradictions arise because, under the accruals method of accounting, income is recognised when earned as opposed to when received, and expenditure is recognised when incurred as opposed to when paid.

The example of a cash flow report, shown in figure 4.3, is designed to explain the differences in resource flow and cash in the bank. The cash flow report reconciles the impact on the voluntary organisation's resources of its current operations, its borrowing or financing activity, and lastly its investing activity (see figure 4.4). The statement calculates the sources of increase or decrease in cash to arrive at the total change in cash.

Cyclical fluctuations

The other side of cash flow planning addresses timing cycles and cash flow management generally. For most voluntary organisations, cash inflows and outflows fluctuate throughout the year, for many reasons other than the accounting ones illustrated below. Churches, for example, typically receive generous donations during the Christmas season and much scantier ones during the summer vacation. Schools often require parents to pay a full year's tuition before the school year begins. Some membership organisations, such as unions, collect their members' dues once a year. Grants may be received quarterly, or contract money quarterly in arrears.

Table 4.3: Reconciliation of net incoming resources for the year to net cash inflow

	£'000
Net Incoming resources from Statement of Financial Activites	3,100
Adjustments to reconcile change in resources to net cash inflows from operations:	
+ (-) Depreciation	360
+ (-) Gain on disposal of tangible fixed assets	(20)
+ (-) Increase in creditors: Current liabilities	1,200
+ (-) (Decrease) in creditors: long-term	(600)
+ (-) (Increase) in debtors	(1,200)
+ (-) Decrease in stocks	100
= Net cash inflow from operating activities	2,940

Table 4.4: Example of cash flow statement

	£'000	£'000
Net cash inflow from operating activities		2,940
Investing activities		
+ (-) (Purchase) of tangible fixed assets	(1,590)	
+ (-) Proceeds from sale of tangible fixed assets	150	
+ (-) (Purchase) of investments	(1,200)	
+ (-) Proceeds from sale of investments	1,990	
= Net cash outflow from investing activities		(650)
Increase in cash and cash equivalents		**2,290**

For the many voluntary organisations whose funding arrives at irregular intervals throughout the year, cash flow planning is essential. The fluctuations in cash probably cannot be entirely controlled. Instead, the finance officer becomes aware when cash shortfalls are likely to occur, and prepares to bridge the gap with delayed expenditures, borrowing or some new fundraising event. Postponement of payments or acceleration of payment terms for constituent billings are typical ways of solving the problem. However, it is important to appreciate that the organisation may be insolvent, at least technically, if there is insufficient cash to pay bills when due.

Cash management is about achieving maximum effectiveness of cash receipts and disbursement processes, thereby making sure that the money is working for the charity and returning a satisfactory yield, but is still available when needed. Best practice guidelines suggest that voluntary organisations should:

- Streamline the collection processes to reduce the time taken to translate the amounts owing to the organisation into available funds.
- Centralise disbursement accounts and streamline procedures for different functional areas such as accounts payable and payroll, by using (for example) BACS payment methods.
- Develop close partnerships with customers and suppliers to negotiate mutually beneficial payment policies.
- Consolidate banking relationships by choosing lead banks that can offer customised cash management services: for example, handling appeal monies.
- Develop accurate cash flow forecasting techniques and models that are linked to budgets and strategic plans.
- 'Conduct regular cash management reviews to check controls and ensure appropriate use of current technology: for example, telephone/Internet banking;
- Ensure that investing, borrowing, disbursement and other financial transactions are properly authorised.

Much of the above may be self evident, but it is surprising how often voluntary organisations ignore the fundamentals of good cash flow management.

Designing cash flow budgets

Once the annual operating and capital budgets are authorised, they can be converted into a cash flow budget to verify the availability of resources; in other words, to see if the organisation can finance the plan. The cash flow budget is prepared on a monthly basis to pinpoint possible cash shortfalls that do not appear in the annual compilation of numbers. The task is to summarise the projected sources and uses of cash for the coming year, according to the actual months of receipt and payment.

To do so, first estimate when collections of year-end receivables will occur. Next, calculate the normal time lag, if any, between the invoicing or billing for services or pledges (the point at which income is recognised in the accounts under the accrual system) and depositing the money in the bank. Use this statistic to convert the budget to expected inflows of cash from revenue-producing activity on a monthly basis.

Correspondingly, chart the expected expenditure of cash according to when the payment is required. The prediction should be based on past experience and an element of educated guesswork. Expected capital expenditures, sale of assets, borrowing, debt repayment and other financing transactions are then factored in.

In the light of any deficits revealed by the cash flow budget, consider whether there is a need to borrow or to redesign the entire budget. Monitoring the cash flow budget is an continuous process. Especially close attention is needed if cash flows fluctuate widely or if months of deficit funding are expected. Although it is possible to perform this task monthly by hand, cash flow budgets produced on computer spreadsheets save countless calculations.

Figure 4.5: Cash flow projection for the year (version 1)

	January	February	March	April	May	June	July	August	September	October	November	December	Total
RECEIPTS													
Corporate members fees	10,000	40,000	20,000	30,000	10,000	5,000	3,000	2,000	30,000	40,000	30,000	50,000	270,000
Individual members fees	3,000	10,000	8,000	12,000	6,000	2,000	1,000	800	1,200	5,000	11,000	30,000	90,000
Information services	14,000	14,000	12,000	12,000	12,000	10,000	10,000	8,000	16,000	14,000	14,000	14,000	150,000
Publication sales	20,000	20,000	20,000	20,000	20,000	10,000	10,000	10,000	25,000	25,000	25,000	25,000	230,000
Professional training	8,000	8,000	20,000	8,000	8,000	2,000	2,000	2,000	22,000	8,000	16,000	6,000	110,000
Annual meeting	10,000	5,000	5,000										20,000
Royalty income	0	6,000	0	8,000		20,000			8,000				42,000
Interest income	200	200	200	200	200								1,000
Total receipts	65,200	103,200	85,200	90,200	56,200	49,000	26,000	22,800	102,200	92,000	96,000	125,000	913,000
PAYMENTS													
Salaries & payroll taxes	30,000	30,000	30,000	30,000	30,000	30,000	30,000	30,000	30,000	30,000	30,000	30,000	360,000
Pension benefits	2,500	2,500	2,500	2,500	2,500	2,500	2,500	2,500	2,500	2,500	2,500	2,500	30,000
Professional fees	1,000	1,000	12,000	10,000	1,000	1,000	1,000	1,000	1,000	1,000	1,000	1,000	32,000
Supplies	2,200	2,200	2,200	2,200	2,200	2,200	2,200	2,200	2,200	2,200	2,200	2,200	26,400
Telephone	1,667	1,667	1,667	1,667	1,667	1,666	1,667	1,666	1,667	1,666	1,667	1,666	20,000
Postage & shipping	1,667	1,667	1,667	1,667	1,667	1,666	1,667	1,666	1,667	1,666	1,667	1,666	20,000

Figure 4.5—continued

	January	February	March	April	May	June	July	August	September	October	November	December	Total
Building costs	2,000	2,000	12,000	2,000	2,000	2,000	2,000	2,000	2,000	3,000	4,000	3,000	38,000
Equipment repair & insurance	1,100	1,100	1,100	1,100	1,200	1,200	1,200	1,200	1,200	1,200	1,200	1,200	14,000
Printing & publications	12,000	8,000	12,000	9,000	12,000	9,000	11,000	9,000	20,000	9,000	10,000	16,000	137,000
Travel	1,000	1,000	6,000	1,000	3,000	3,000	1,000	1,000	3,000	3,000	3,000	4,000	30,000
Meetings & classes	500	500	18,000	500	2,500	500	0	1,000	2,000	2,000	1,500	3,000	32,000
Information services	4,000	15,000	15,000	9,000	5,000	4,000	4,000	4,000	5,000	5,000	5,000	5,000	80,000
Marketing	11,650	11,650									23,300		46,600
Purchase of equipment	10,000										7,400	10,000	27,400
Total Payments	81,284	78,284	114,134	70,634	64,734	58,732	58,234	57,232	72,234	62,232	71,134	104,532	893,400
Excess (deficit) of cash	(16,084)	24,916	(28,934)	19,566	(8,534)	(9,732)	(32,234)	(34,432)	29,966	29,768	24,866	20,468	19,600
Cash at beginning of month	60,000	43,916	68,832	39,898	59,464	50,930	41,198	8,964	(25,468)	4,498	34,266	59,132	60,000
Cash at end of month	43,916	68,832	39,898	59,464	50,930	41,198	8,964	(25,468)	4,498	34,266	59,132	79,600	79,600

Figure 4:6: Cash flow projection for the year (version 2)

	January	February	March	April	May	June	July	August	September	October	November	December	Total
RECEIPTS													
Corporate members fees	10,000	40,000	20,000	30,000	10,000	5,000	3,000	17,000	15,000	40,000	30,000	50,000	270,000
Individual members fees	3,000	10,000	8,000	12,000	6,000	2,000	1,000	800	1,200	5,000	11,000	30,000	90,000
Information services	14,000	14,000	12,000	12,000	12,000	10,000	10,000	12,000	12,000	14,000	14,000	14,000	150,000
Publication sales	20,000	20,000	20,000	20,000	20,000	10,000	10,000	20,000	15,000	25,000	25,000	25,000	230,000
Professional training	8,000	8,000	20,000	8,000	8,000	2,000	2,000	2,000	22,000	8,000	16,000	6,000	110,000
Annual meeting	10,000	5,000	5,000										20,000
Royalty income	0	6,000	0	8,000		20,000			8,000				42,000
Interest income	200	200	200	200	200								1,000
Total receipts	65,200	103,200	85,200	90,200	56,200	49,000	26,000	51,800	73,200	92,000	96,000	125,000	913,000
PAYMENTS													
Salaries & payroll taxes	30,000	30,000	30,000	30,000	30,000	30,000	30,000	30,000	30,000	30,000	30,000	30,000	360,000
Pension benefits	2,500	2,500	2,500	2,500	2,500	2,500	2,500	2,500	2,500	2,500	2,500	2,500	30,000
Professional fees	1,000		12,000	10,000	1,000	1,000	1,000	1,000	1,000	1,000	1,000	1,000	32,000
Supplies	2,200	2,200	2,200	2,200	2,200	2,200	2,200	2,200	2,200	2,200	2,200	2,200	26,400
Telephone	1,667	1,667	1,667	1,667	1,667	1,666	1,667	1,666	1,667	1,666	1,667	1,666	20,000

Figure 4:6—continued

	January	February	March	April	May	June	July	August	September	October	November	December	Total
Postage & shipping	1,667	1,667	1,667	1,667	1,667	1,666	1,667	1,666	1,667	1,666	1,667	1,666	20,000
Building costs	2,000	2,000	12,000	2,000	2,000	2,000	2,000	2,000	2,000	3,000	4,000	3,000	38,000
Equipment repair & insurance	1,100	1,100	1,100	1,100	1,200	1,200	1,200	1,200	1,200	1,200	1,200	1,200	14,000
Printing & publications	12,000	8,000	12,000	9,000	12,000	9,000	11,000	9,000	20,000	9,000	10,000	16,000	137,000
Travel	1,000	1,000	6,000	1,000	3,000	3,000	1,000	1,000	3,000	3,000	3,000	4,000	30,000
Meetings & classes	500	500	18,000	500	2,500	500	0	1,000	2,000	2,000	1,500	3,000	32,000
Information services	4,000	8,000	8,000	8,000	8,000	8,000	8,000	8,000	5,000	5,000	5,000	5,000	80,000
Marketing		10,000								10,000	13,300	13,300	46,600
Purchase of equipment	10,000										7,400	10,000	27,400
Total Payments	69,634	69,634	107,134	69,634	67,734	62,732	62,234	61,232	72,234	72,232	84,434	94,532	893,400
Excess (deficit) of cash	(4,434)	33,566	(21,934)	20,566	(11,534)	(13,732)	(36,234)	(9,432)	966	19,768	11,566	30,468	19,600
Cash at beginning of month	60,000	55,566	89,132	67,198	87,764	76,230	62,498	26,264	16,832	17,798	37,566	49,132	60,000

The model cash flow statements for a professional business association providing services to both corporate and individual members is shown as figures 4.4 and 4.5. The first version of the cash flow produced a deficit in the month of August. This has been charted and shown as figure 4.7. This illustrates the balance at the bank at the end of each month as a bar chart, which makes it possible to identify clearly the months in which deficits are likely to occur.

Figure 4.7: Cash flow charted (version 1)

Version 1 Cash Flow Charted

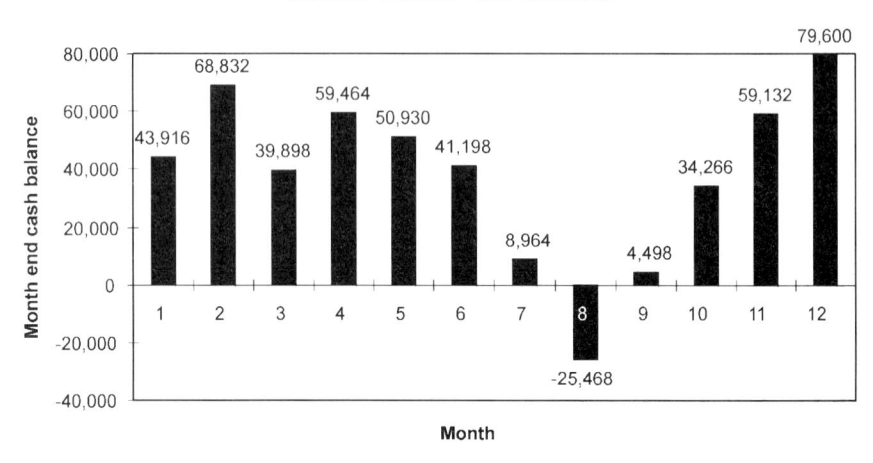

Month	Month end cash balance
1	43,916
2	68,832
3	39,898
4	59,464
5	50,930
6	41,198
7	8,964
8	-25,468
9	4,498
10	34,266
11	59,132
12	79,600

Figure 4.8: Cash flow charted (version 2)

Version 2 Cash Flow Charted

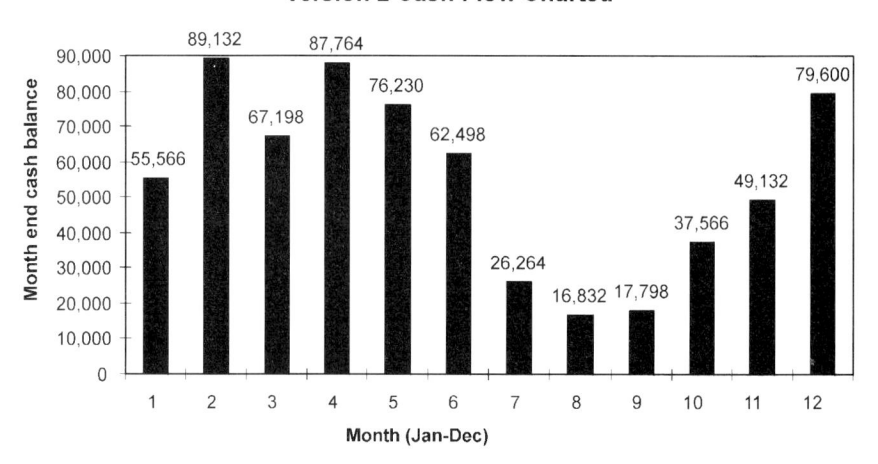

Month (Jan-Dec)	Month end cash balance
1	55,566
2	89,132
3	67,198
4	87,764
5	76,230
6	62,498
7	26,264
8	16,832
9	17,798
10	37,566
11	49,132
12	79,600

The management of the professional business association has then reworked the cash flow to eliminate the deficit balance in August. This has been achieved by rescheduling the timing of membership fees, receipts from information services and publication sales. On the payments side, payments for marketing have been delayed till later in the year and payments for information services spread more evenly throughout the year. By this process, it has been possible to eliminate the deficit in August while at the same time maintaining both the total receipts and payments for the year the same as before, and (as illustrated in figure 4.8) presenting a healthier cash flow position.

The above bar chart, figure 4.7, is based on version 1 of the cash flow projection. By presenting the cash balances at the end of each month in graphic form, it allows trends to be evaluated. In particular, the bar chart highlights the overdrawn position in August (month 8).

A bar chart for the revised cash flow projection, figure 4.8, version 2, is shown above. This shows that the projected overdrawn balance for August (month 8) has now been resolved; the overall effect the changes have had on the cash flow is also visible.

Beyond cash flow imbalances
Ideally, a voluntary organisation always has cash in reserve for unforeseen circumstances. Contingency cash balances can almost never be too high! A new organisation in particular needs to budget for revenue surpluses in its early years until a sufficient level of cash is accumulated. To a young organisation struggling to meet its payroll, building a cash reserve may seem like a luxury it can ill afford. Nevertheless, the financially prudent organisation plans from the very start to build working capital reserves equivalent to several months of operating expenses.

Whenever cash flow budgets indicate excess cash reserves, plans for temporary investment are in order. As much money as possible can be kept in interest bearing accounts to maximise yield. Once cash reserves exceed the current year's need, the opportunity for longer term investment arises. This task of resource management requires complex decision making ideally, by a finance committee with the assistance of professional investment managers. Investment policies must weigh the permissible level of risk to the organisation's resources against the expected return.

More money in the bank
The financially astute voluntary organisation will ensure that its cash balances work in its favour by keeping its money in the bank for as long as possible. Whether the organisation is able to earn interest on the money, or to avoid paying interest on funds it must borrow or bills it pays late, money in the bank is obviously desirable. On the incoming cash side, early settlement discounts are designed to accelerate the receipt of money owed. A voluntary organisation can also charge interest on late payment and offer discounts for early payments.

The accounting system should contain all suitable information and have the capacity to bill promptly for services rendered. Similarly, the membership renewal system should remind members promptly that it is time to send in their support. The submission of quarterly cost reports for grants payable by instalments should never be late. The fundraisers will know the deadlines for submitting grant requests to potential funders well ahead of time. Unfortunately, there are many voluntary organisations with cash flow problems that are slow in sending the renewal notices or grant reports that would provide the funds to pay staff.

On the outgoing side, bills are scheduled to be paid when the terms for purchase require it and not before. A regular cycle can be established – say the first and fifteenth day of the month – for bill payments. These set days are made known to the staff and creditors, so that all can expect to receive their money at the appropriate point in the cycle. Such a simple policy can save considerable effort and earn interest by keeping the money in the bank.

To borrow or not

When the cash flow budget indicates that a deficit in cash will occur during the year, a voluntary organisation faces a tough decision. Does the organisation attempt to borrow the funds, can it find new funding, or does it reduce projected payments? The answer will of course depend on several factors. Is the deficit temporary? Will it reverse itself in a few months? For a new organisation, interim borrowing may not be an option. For a mature one that is, for example, expecting to refurbish old buildings, there may be alternatives. The decision must be based on the facts of the case.

Securing a loan requires good planning. When the need for short term indebtedness is recognised as a part of the budgeting process, solutions can be found. The budget itself probably shows that the situation will reverse itself with money expected to be received later in the year. For an organisation in this situation, preparing a business plan in order to make a formal application to a bank is a useful exercise. If a bank cannot be persuaded to make a loan, the voluntary organisation goes back to the drawing board and revises its budgets and/or finds new funding sources.

A cash deficit created by proposed capital acquisitions may have a simpler solution. The tangible nature of a capital asset makes it suitable as collateral for a loan. Therefore it may be possible, even for a new organisation, to borrow money needed to equip the organisation. Lenders expect to be able to get their security back if the voluntary organisation defaults on payments.

6. Prudent investment planning

Once the voluntary organisation accumulates cash assets beyond its operating needs for the coming year, it can begin to develop permanent investment plans. In managing the organisation's investments, the trustees have a duty to maximise the value of the assets and therefore to obtain a good return. However, the trustees should not risk assets by investing in highly speculative ventures; they must balance risk against return.

The trustees must also balance the future needs of the voluntary organisation against current needs, so they should consider whether the maximisation of income for current consumption is in the best interest of future beneficiaries. Trustees need to balance long-term capital growth against short-term income generation. Capital growth should be, at the very least, sufficient for assets to maintain their value compared to inflation.

Powers to invest
Trustees must familiarise themselves with the investment powers of the voluntary organisation. These should be contained in the trust deed, constitution or Memorandum and Articles of Association. If the governing documents contain no reference to investment powers, then the Trustee Investment Act 1961 will apply. This Act will also apply if the charity was established before 3 August 1961, irrespective of what the governing documents say. The majority of voluntary organisations established after that date will detail express powers of investment for the organisation; in these cases, the express powers will take precedence over the Act.

Trustee Investment Act 1961
The Trustee Investment Act 1961 sets out the duties of charity trustees with regard to investments. Although the Act may be repealed or amended in due course, the duties it specifies are likely to remain the guiding principles for judging whether trustees have acted properly with regard to investment.

The Act requires the trustees to split the assets 25:75 at the outset between two funds: the narrower and wider range (explained below). It is not necessary subsequently to make transfers or to attempt to balance up the two funds, although new money must also be split 25:75 between them. The reason for the split is that the narrower range funds (25 per cent) may only be invested in gilts, whereas the wider range funds may be invested in certain equities where there is some risk that the capital could be lost.

Further details of narrow and wide range investments, together with issues trustees need to consider when formulating an investment policy, are given in Appendix C.

Ethical investment
Ethical investments are those which avoid certain market areas such as defence, tobacco and countries with oppressive regimes. It may also be appropriate for voluntary organisations to avoid such areas if they contradict the charitable objectives of the organisation: for example, a cancer charity may be justified in eliminating tobacco companies from its investment portfolio. However, it is the voluntary organisation's charitable objectives that must determine whether certain market areas are to be avoided rather than the personal convictions of trustees.

Eliminating such company stocks from the investment portfolio may well have an adverse impact on the risk profile of the portfolio, since there is no longer full diversification of risk. The trustees are still bound to act in the interest of beneficiaries by ensuring the maximum level of return for a given acceptable level of risk.

Facing the unknown

Healthy scepticism and an appreciation of the uncertainty that surrounds investments are both important. The financial markets in which a voluntary organisation places its funds are influenced daily by international forces beyond its control. Who knows if the stock market will go up, if a global stock fund will sustain its yield, or if the pound will go up against the US dollar?

Diversification is a very valuable technique for facing the unknown. It says essentially, 'Don't put all your eggs in one basket.' A prudently balanced investment portfolio contains a variety of financial instruments: stocks, bond, real estate and so on. The mixture of investments is based on the assumption that some will go up and some go down, but that in the long run the averages will provide a desirable stream of income.

7. RESTRICTED FUNDING

In the recent past the funding environment of the voluntary sector has changed dramatically. Voluntary organisations are increasingly being funded to deliver specific outputs in return for grant funding, or more formal arrangements under contracts. As a result there has been a rapid increase in funding for the delivery of specific charitable programmes and a consequent decline in funding of a more general nature.

Over the last decade a 'contract culture' has grown up. Instead of receiving grants, a growing number of charities are entering into legally-binding agreements (contracts) with public bodies to provide services to the public on behalf of those bodies. A contract will specify the services to be provided by the charity and what the charity is to be paid for providing them. It will also include provisions, in greater or lesser detail, setting out the legal obligations that each of the parties accepts in order to fulfil the purposes of the contract.

On the positive side, a contract can establish a partnership between the charity and the public body and clarify their relationship by specifying in detail what is expected from each party. A contract can also offer a secure source of funding over the period it covers.

On the other hand, some charities feel that entering into contracts with public bodies would lead to the loss of their independence: their freedom to set their own policies and to decide, within the range of their charitable objects, what services to provide.

Charities must ensure that they take all their costs into account when pricing a service to be provided under contract on behalf of a public body. These costs will comprise direct costs, capital costs and indirect costs (or overheads). Chapter 5 provides details on how projects should be fully costed and priced to prevent the organisation indirectly funding public services from unrestricted funds.

Restricted funding can be defined as funds which have donor-imposed restrictions or where the voluntary organisation raises funds for a specific appeal. The reasons for the growth in restricted project funding are many, but the general scarcity of funding means that charitable trusts and other funders are under increasing pressure to obtain maximum value and impact from the projects they fund. As a result, they are reluctant to provide core funds, for which outputs and impacts are much more difficult to quantify.

Perhaps the most important financial requirement relating to such income is the responsibility to isolate the money. Under trust law, the voluntary organisation owes a fiduciary duty to contributors and grantors to use funds for the purposes for which they are given. Accordingly, before accepting restricted funds, an organisation must have in place a mechanism for tracking the receipt of such funding and the expenditure that can be set off against it.

The restrictions imposed can vary in their tightness. A wildlife conservation charity raising funds by mailshot may work under the very broad restriction that the funds collected 'are to help preserve wildlife.' At the other end of the spectrum, the funding could be restricted to saving a particular type of tree in a certain part of Africa because its wood is used for musical instruments and the supply is dwindling.

By accepting restricted funding, the trustees of the voluntary organisation have accepted the responsibility of ensuring that the restrictions are met. It is important that in their fundraising – for example, public appeals – voluntary organisations should not create restricted funds by the way they advertise. There are, however, some circumstances when the restriction can be removed or made less stringent: for example, where the objective for which the funds were originally raised is no longer relevant, the project has been completed or is deemed impossible to complete. In the first case, it will be necessary to contact the original donors or, if that is no longer possible, to obtain the permission of the Charity Commission.

Exit strategies

Since the majority of funding arrangements are uncertain and are limited to a three-year period at most, the voluntary organisation must ensure, well before the funding comes to an end, that it has strategies to cover the next phase.

If the project is to be continued, this next phase will usually involve finding other sources of income, either from another funder or by income generation. If the original objectives have been met, the closure of the project may involve financial liabilities for staff redundancy.

8. Overhead Costs

In the interests of resource management, it is essential that any funding for projects should cover the general overheads apportioned to those projects. This can be achieved by carefully following the original funding guidelines. There are three common scenarios:

- *The funder says it will not fund any overheads apportioned to a project.* In this case, the funding application should include all costs that will be incurred as a direct result of undertaking the project. These may include additional telephone costs (on calls and rental of new line), recruitment costs and stationery costs, all included under the appropriate budget headings.

- *The funder queries the amount shown for overheads in the funding application.* In this case, the voluntary organisation should explain the rationale for allocating overheads: the staffing, management and premises, and how the organisation works.

- *The funder has a policy of funding a fixed percentage for administration.* In this case, the voluntary organisation must be clear about the definition of administration costs and how the percentage is to be calculated. In most cases, this will be a fixed percentage of direct costs. If this is so, then it will be possible to include certain costs as direct – staff supervision, for example – that otherwise would have been treated as indirect.

Overheads are not merely 'administration' costs that can be dispensed with: they are real costs associated with delivering the project effectively. Without overhead costs, it would be impossible to accomplish the charity's programmes; most funders do accept this!

9. Endowments

There are two types of endowment fund:

1. Permanent endowment funds are donations that have been given to the voluntary organisation to be held as capital with no power to convert the funds to income. These may be cash or other assets.
2. Expendable endowment funds are donations that have been given to a voluntary organisation to be held as capital, but where the trustees do have a discretionary power to use the funds as income.

An endowment gift is usually invested to produce income to fund a specific project – such as scholarships – or unspecified operational costs. Although endowment funding is a highly desirable resource, the terms of the endowment must be thoroughly discussed with the donors before the gift is accepted.

When is an organisation ready to seek endowments? Potential endowment funders must perceive it as sufficiently permanent or stable to survive for a long time; it is for this reason that universities, hospitals, and churches have traditionally attracted such funding.

The other important issue is the terms governing the voluntary organisation's use of the gift. If these are to meet the organisation's needs, the following must be agreed upon:

- *Life span of endowment.* For how many years must the endowment remain restricted? Can the funds be used for another purpose in times of crisis? If so, what type of crisis? What happens to the endowment funds should the organisation cease to exist or the charitable objective be met?
- *Definition of income.* Are realised gains treated as current income? Is the endowment principal – defined as its original sum – certain, or is it the original plus all appreciations less declines in underlying value?
- *Nature of investment.* Do the endowment creators wish the assets originally given to be retained? Can they be sold? Must they be sold in a particular fashion or offered for sale to particular persons first? If sold for cash, is there a restraint on the way in which the cash can be reinvested?

It should be clear by now that endowment funding needs to be carefully considered, as it brings many onerous responsibilities.

10. CHARITY RESERVES

Charity reserves have been a controversial issue for some time. The media have criticised many large national charities for apparently accumulating large reserves while at the same time conducting additional fundraising appeals. Furthermore, many funders automatically look at the fund balances shown in annual accounts when deciding whether to approve applications for funding.

It is generally assumed that voluntary organisations should not hold on to charitable funds for long periods of time, since the organisation was granted those funds to provide services. This may well be true, but it is also necessary to consider the question of reserves from the point of view of resource management. From this point of view, the existence of reserves is a sign of good financial management. Any organisation requires a minimum level of reserves to fund working capital requirements and/or contingencies identified at the planning stage as being necessary to safeguard the continuing activities of the organisation.

What are charity reserves?

The Charity Commission in its publication CC19 defines reserves as income that becomes available to the charity and is to be expended at the trustees' discretion in furtherance of any of the charity's objectives (sometimes referred to as 'general purpose' income), but which is not yet spent, committed or designated (i.e. is 'free'). This excludes the following (as defined by CC19):

- Permanent endowment.
- Expendable endowment.
- Restricted funds.
- Designated funds.
- Income funds that could only be realised by disposing of fixed assets held for charity use.

The Charity Commission now takes the view that voluntary organisations should 'explain and justify' the level of reserves they hold. In order to meet this requirement, even the smallest of organisations that aspire to financial security must have a reserves policy.

Reserve policy

The policy should cover:

- The reasons why the charity needs reserves.
- The level (or range) of reserves the trustees believe the charity needs.
- What steps the charity is going to take to establish or maintain the reserves at the agreed level (or range).
- Arrangements for monitoring and reviewing the policy.

The essential steps in developing a reserves policy are shown in Figure 4.9. Table 4.10 shows the reserves policy within the context of the planning process.

Figure 4.9: Developing a reserves policy

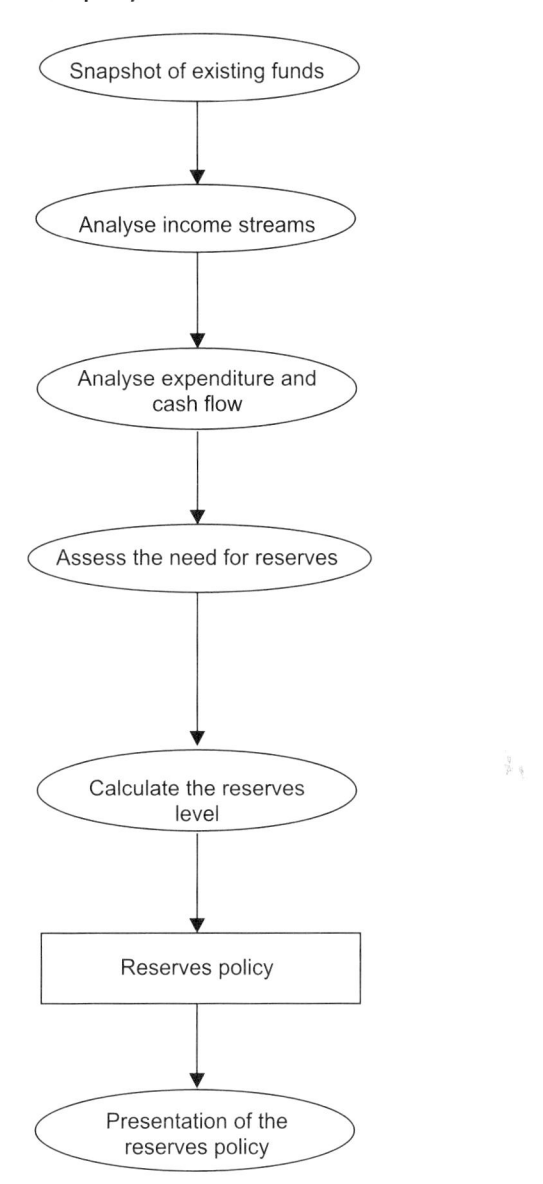

- Snapshot of existing funds
- Analyse income streams
- Analyse expenditure and cash flow
- Assess the need for reserves
- Calculate the reserves level
- Reserves policy
- Presentation of the reserves policy

Source: NCVO

Table 4.10: Reserves policy and the planning process

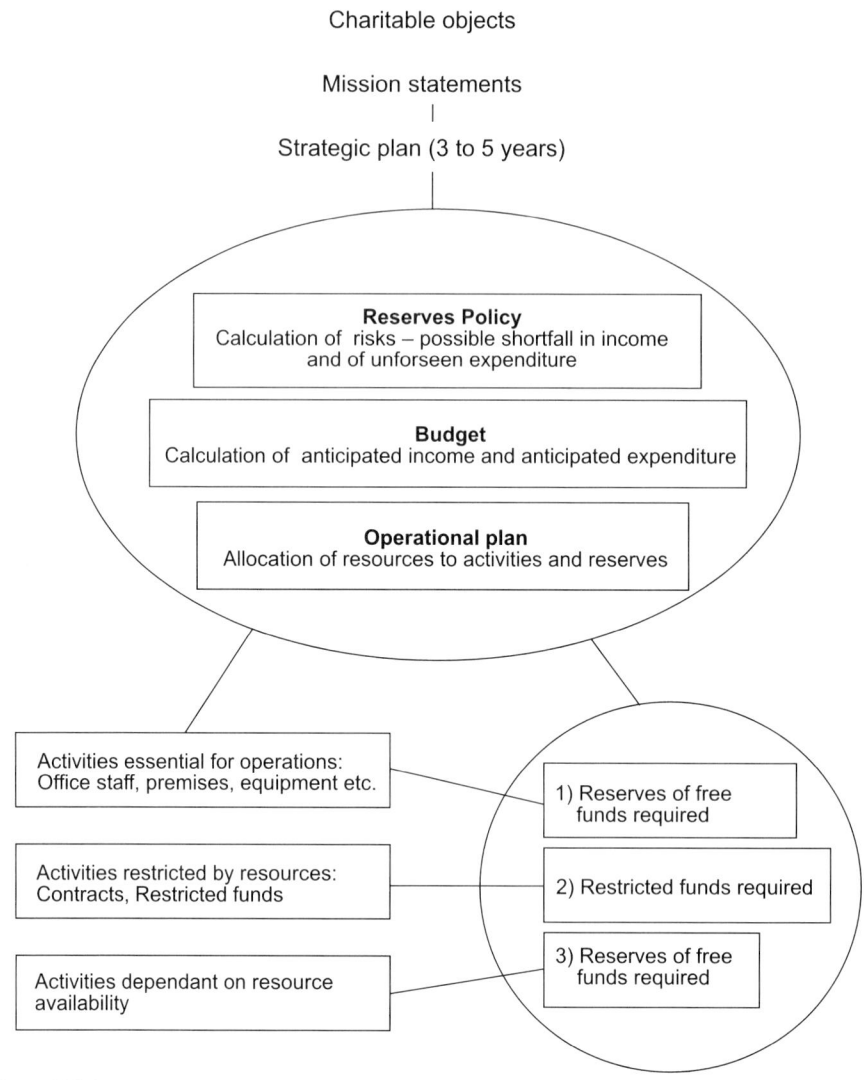

Charitable objects

Mission statements
|
Strategic plan (3 to 5 years)

Reserves Policy
Calculation of risks – possible shortfall in income and of unforseen expenditure

Budget
Calculation of anticipated income and anticipated expenditure

Operational plan
Allocation of resources to activities and reserves

Activities essential for operations: Office staff, premises, equipment etc. — 1) Reserves of free funds required

Activities restricted by resources: Contracts, Restricted funds — 2) Restricted funds required

Activities dependant on resource availability — 3) Reserves of free funds required

Source: NCVO

Assessment of reserve needs

The charity's reserves policy should be based on:

- Its forecast for levels of income in future years, taking into account the reliability of each source of income and the prospects for opening up new sources;
- Its forecast for expenditure in future years on the basis of planned activity;
- Its analysis of any future needs, opportunities, contingencies or risks, the effects of which are not likely to be able to be met out of income if and when they arise;

- Its assessment, on the best evidence available, of the likelihood of each of those needs etc arising and the potential consequences for the charity of not being able to meet them.

FURTHER READING AND RESOURCES

Merger: an option for charities? CAF Consultants 1997.

Redefining core capabilities: a business guide to outsourcing. KPMG Management Consulting.

Charities and contracts (CC37). The Charity Commission 1998.

Charities' reserves (CC19). The Charity Commission 1997.

Not just for a rainy day: guidelines on developing a reserves policy and putting it into practice. NCVO 1997.

A range of brokered deals are available through NCVO. Please call the HelpDesk for information.

Struggling to Survive, Centre for Voluntary Organisation, LSE, 1988.

Appendix A: Case studies

1. The Womens' Centre

This case study looks at the challenges faced by a voluntary organisation that has just lost its funding. It examines how the organisation can exploit its resources to ensure survival; the issues discussed are not exclusively financial ones.

The case study examines the following areas:

- Initial reaction.
- Longer term response.
- The impact on the organisation.
- Determining factors.
- Lessons.
- Conclusions.

The Women's Centre was set up in an outer London borough by a group formed in 1993. Working as a collective, the centre provided a women-only space; ran activities such health groups, support groups and adult education; provided drop-in and advice sessions; and campaigned on women's issues locally. In a borough that rejected the idea of a women's centre, they turned to a Londonwide funding body for capital and revenue funding. This enabled them to open the centre three weeks before the funding body was abolished, funding was lost and the staff made redundant.

Applications for replacement funding to the local borough and the London Boroughs Grant Scheme were unsuccessful. By this time the centre was running on an entirely voluntary basis – the running costs were covered by the residue of the grant funding – but was exploring other sources of funding.

Initial reactions to loss of funding

Inevitably, the reactions of paid staff and the management committee/unpaid collective members differed: the livelihood of paid staff was under threat, whereas unpaid members often had other things to move on to.

For many voluntary organisations – and the Women's Centre is no exception – funding is a form of recognition; and so, when that funding was taken away, so was the recognition.

However, the fact that the centre had opened its building just before the loss of funding seems to have lightened some of the gloom.

Longer term responses

Although the loss of funding was in some sense an ending for the Women's Centre, the opening of its new building marked an important beginning. This gave the women considerable energy to face the future.

Although uncertainty about future funding made it difficult to plan, the clear priority was to get the new building used. It was therefore decided to staff the centre with a rota of volunteers, holding self-financing Workers' Education Association classes and renting out space to other organisations (such as the local Legal Resource Centre) for specific sessions.

Before the funding cut, the centre had invested in some useful equipment, including a camera, video equipment and a minibus; the minibus brought in some income from hire fees. It was also agreed to encourage the women using the centre to make a contribution by standing order and paying subscriptions for newsletters.

The collective also changed its method of operation. In the absence of a central decision-making body, and because of the difficulty of finding new women to join the group, the responsibility for specific tasks (such as newsletter production, dealing with correspondence, minibus bookings or garden maintenance) was taken on by volunteers identified from the mailing list.

The impact on the organisation

This can have wide-ranging effects, at a personal level on individuals and at an operational level on the work programme. It was a particularly difficult time for paid staff, who went through long periods of uncertainty and then, in some cases, had to face redundancy and unemployment.

Staff and others felt that the withdrawal of funding showed that their work was not valued. As a result, the centre lost some of its most active members, and the increase in workload and responsibilities this brought for the remaining members led to exhaustion. This temporary crisis was overcome by changes in the organisation's structure and the allocation of work.

It was not long before conflict broke out between management and staff about who held the power in the organisation. This power struggle was not new. In the past it had been papered over or ignored, but now, as the threat to the organisation and fears about its future raised the stress level, it came to seem more important.

At the operational level, the loss of funding caused the Centre to restrict the work it did; as is usual in these situations, outreach and development were the main casualties.

In addition to the effects of losing its paid staff, the Centre's ability to carry out its work was seriously hindered by the amount of time that had to be spent in fundraising, filling in grant applications and lobbying potential funders.

One positive result was that members felt that the loss of paid staff had strengthened the collective. The disagreements between paid workers and members were now behind them; members had to have a genuine commitment to working for the centre if they wanted it to survive. They had learned to cut out unnecessary areas of work and concentrate on the essential. The women felt more motivated because they felt that they had something to contribute.

Determining factors

The Centre was seen as the example of an ideology that was represented nowhere else in the area; this further increased its determination to survive.

Some lessons

Having one main funder. This made them feel insecure and severely limited their options. However, having more than one funder was considered to be too time consuming; also, the interest of funders might have conflicted, causing problems for the organisation.

Ways of working. There had been a lack of urgency in what was done before funding was lost: applications should have been made sooner and there should have been more planning.

Dependence on paid workers. This had caused problems when funding ran out. The paid staff who left had a lot of valuable information in their heads, but they had not been properly debriefed; as a result, unpaid members lost the benefit of that information.

Some conclusions

The Women's Centre managed to survive, but not without difficulty. It achieved this by exploiting a number of assets:

- A clear and adaptable organisational structure.
- A supportive governing body.
- Clear aims and priorities.
- A long existence.
- Strength of members' commitment.
- Contacts and support within the community.
- Economic resources (such as skills, premises, equipment).
- Political resources (the support of powerful people and organisations).
- An understanding of the situation in which it found itself.
- An awareness of the options open to it.

Many of these assets are a source of competitive advantage, arising either from the voluntary organisation's internal strengths or its position within the sector (see Chapter 2).

One of Women's Centre's strengths has been its ability to adapt to its new situation and develop a more appropriate structure. It has managed to persuade a large number of women to work at the centre on a voluntary basis, perhaps because it is focused on its aims. It had strong links with the community and important material resources (including the building and the minibus); these tangible assets have been used to generate income. On the other hand, as a radical women's organisation it lacked political resources, and its limited knowledge of the situation it found itself in meant that its choices were restricted.

With acknowledgement to Centre for Voluntary Organisation, LSE

2. BCD

This case study examines the familiar situation where a voluntary organisation has obtained funding for a project from a variety of sources, but the total funds are still insufficient. The organisation turned to commercial lenders for the remainder, but without success. Finally, the organisation approached the Local Investment Fund (LIF), a charity in its own right. LIF provides:

- Loans to community enterprises that are unable to obtain all the funds they need from a bank.
- Help to community groups that are meeting local need by providing goods, services and jobs, and are aiming to be self sufficient.
- Funding exclusively to non-profit organisations.
- Loans from £25,000 to £250,000 at near commercial rates.
- Loans that are only part of the total amount needed.

The case study provides a valuable insight into how a project is assessed and some of the concerns of a lender when evaluating the project for funding.

Background

BCD was set up in 1979 to alleviate poverty and advance education by supporting workers' co-operatives and small starter businesses, and by providing training courses for co-operatives and ethnic minority and other disadvantaged groups. It is a company limited by guarantee and controlled by a voluntary management committee elected annually by the membership, which is composed of representatives of the co-operative movement, the local community and tenants. Any surplus goes to the improvement of BCD services and resources.

BCD's flagship project was the short-life rehabilitation of over 10,000 square feet of retail and office space in Acer Street, leased from the London Borough of Conifer.

BCD has a record of success in enabling women, ethnic minorities and refugees to gain a foothold in the market, and in providing suitable facilities for small voluntary sector and community groups. Its training courses are targeted on existing co-operative businesses, refugees and local people in need of business skills.

Working closely with other local agencies, BCD is now taking advantage of the myriad opportunities brought about through City Challenge, the European Regional Development Fund (ERDF), the Single Regeneration Budget and the local authority.

BCD's current plans for rehabilitating Acer Street will involve the retention of existing businesses in the area and the opening of many new units for community business start-ups and youth enterprise activity. These units will be let to community organisations on flexible terms that take account of the fact that many such groups do not have a track record.

These measures are enabling BCD to bring about an integrated range of new openings and a coherent infrastructure in which Conifer's community-based business and voluntary sector is set to flourish.

The funding proposition
The overall costs of the Acer Street refurbishment and lease purchase are estimated at £837,500.

The project is being supported by ERDF (£212,500) and City Challenge Gap Funding (£350,000). Commercial finance of £175,000 is required in the development phase, with a further £100,000 needed to purchase a 99-year lease from the London Borough of Conifer at the end of the refurbishment period. A total of £275,000 therefore remains to be financed.

In 1995 BCD approached the Local Investment Fund (LIF) for a £275,000 loan as part of the package of finance required for the refurbishment of Acer Street.

The project met the criteria set by LIF for such projects; what remained to be decided was the amount of finance LIF would provide. Among the documents submitted to LIF was a rent budget, reproduced as Figure 4.11.

Project viability
LIF was particularly concerned about the assumption underlying the level of voids and areas (that is, the periods between lettings and the common areas which are not lettable), which was that they would reduce from 70 per cent to 35 per cent in the year 1997 and then to 20 per cent for the remainder of the projection. These targets would have to be met if the loan repayments were to not become a drain on the organisation.

Strengths
- BCD Limited appears to be a well managed and efficiently run organisation.
- The loan will be fully secured in the event of the failure of BCD.
- The proposal meets LIF criteria in supporting regeneration of impoverished communities through providing economic opportunity.
- The project has the support of local agencies including the Government Office (ERDF/ SRB) and City Challenge.
- The project professionals are experienced, with goods track records.

Weaknesses
- The project must build occupancy levels quickly to 80 per cent and maintain them in order to meet projected loan payments.
- This project taken together with other development projects in the pipeline may exceed staff capacity.

Conclusion
The LIF Council of Management agreed finance of £175,000 for BCD. Although this means that £100,000 remains to be financed, the organisation was able to reasonably secure this from the proceeds of an option to sale on another property within their portfolio.

With acknowledgement to LIF.

Figure 4.11: BCD Acer Street post-development rent budget

Year	1996	1997	1998	1999	2000	2001	2002	2003	2004	2005	2006	2007	2008	2009	2010
% voids	70	35	20	20	20	20	20	20	20	20	20	20	20	20	20
Sub rent rise 20% every five years						20%					20%				
Head rent review & costs rise 20% every five years						20%					20%				
Rent receivable	79,738	79,738	79,738	79,738	79,738	91,698	91,698	91,698	91,698	91,698	105,453	105,453	105,453	105,453	105,453
Less: voids and areas	55,817	27,908	15,948	15,948	15,948	18,340	18,340	18,340	18,340	18,340	21,091	21,091	21,091	21,091	21,091
Total rental income	23,921	51,830	63,790	63,790	63,790	73,358	73,358	73,358	73,358	73,358	84,362	84,362	84,362	84,362	84,362
Head lease rent	6,000	0	0	0	0	0	0	0	0	0	0	0	0	0	0
Repair/ maintenance	0	1,000	4,000	4,000	4,000	4,800	4,800	4,800	4,800	4,800	5,760	5,760	5,760	5,760	5,760
Advertising	1,000	1,000	1,000	1,000	1,000	1,200	1,200	1,200	1,200	1,200	1,440	1,440	1,440	1,440	1,440
Legal/ technical	2,000	1,000	1,000	1,000	1,000	1,200	1,200	1,200	1,200	1,200	1,440	1,440	1,440	1,440	1,440
Staff costs	12,000	12,000	12,000	12,000	12,000	14,400	14,400	14,400	14,400	14,400	17,280	17,280	17,280	17,280	17,280
Establishment, admin & overheads	2,000	4,500	4,500	4,500	4,500	5,400	5,400	5,400	5,400	5,400	6,480	6,480	6,480	6,480	6,480

Figure 4.11—continued

Year	1996	1997	1998	1999	2000	2001	2002	2003	2004	2005	2006	2007	2008	2009	2010
% voids	70	35	20	20	20	20	20	20	20	20	20	20	20	20	20
Sub rent rise 20% every five years						20%					20%				
Head rent review & costs rise 20% every five years						20%					20%				
Rates liability	0	2,000	3,190	3,190	3,190	3,827	3,827	3,827	3,827	3,827	4,593	4,593	4,593	4,593	4,593
Total expenditure	23,000	21,500	25,690	25,690	25,690	30,827	30,827	30,827	30,827	30,827	36,993	36,993	36,993	36,993	36,993
Net Income	921	30,330	38,100	38,100	38,100	42,531	42,531	42,531	42,531	42,531	47,369	47,369	47,369	47,369	47,369
£275,000 repayment	450	33,000	33,000	33,000	33,000	33,000	33,000	33,000	33,000	33,000	33,000	33,000	33,000	33,000	33,000
Balance carried forward	0	471	-2,199	2,902	8,002	13,102	22,634	32,165	41,697	51,228	60,759	75,129	89,498	103,868	118,237
Balance	471	-2,199	2,902	8,002	13,102	22,634	32,165	41,697	51,228	60,759	75,129	89,498	103,868	118,237	132,606

RESOURCE MANAGEMENT 143

3. ChildCare

This case study illustrates how a voluntary organisation can calculate the level of reserves it needs by examining the risks involved. This means asking the question 'How likely is . . .?' Reserves are for future use, so it is necessary to look to the future, applying the information obtained from Chapter 2.

Background
ChildCare is a fundraising and grant-receiving charity whose concerns are underprivileged children and young people in this country and abroad. It has a database of regular donors and supporters which it seeks to expand and develop through appeals and fundraising activities. Whenever possible, it rents or leases its premises and equipment.

Some of its projects are entirely under its own discretion, and others are undertaken solely according to grant funding received from various agencies. Projects may be short term in response to emergencies or longer term and include development work.

The trustees are considering a fresh approach to evaluating the funds they believe need to be retained and tying their perceived requirements directly to their future planning. In addition to setting up a designated Fixed Assets Equivalent Fund, they are thinking about revising their Operating Reserve – representing nine months' anticipated net voluntary income – so that it is related to the perceived risks attaching to various strands of income and expenditure.

Net voluntary income for next year is budgeted at £8,000, so under the old basis the Operating Reserve would have been £6,000.

Significant factors
In evaluating the risks, the following are considered relevant:

- Personal donations and covenants from known supporters for ongoing activities are more predictable than those from the general public.
- Special Appeals are launched for particular emergencies. This money is obviously earmarked, but sometimes it has to be supplemented from general funds, and there is frequently the need to pump-prime ahead of responses. Appeals vary in response according to several factors, and thus can range from low to high risk.
- Fundraising activities fall into two categories: low risk and high risk. The budget endeavours to strike a balance between the two.
- Trust income for general activities can be irregular, depending upon factors outside the control of the charity, and is considered to be moderate to high risk.
- The charity's budgeting for legacy income is considered to be conservative (following under-performances in the past owing to slow property sales). The risk attached to budgeted legacy income is therefore considered to be low.
- Certain projects are undertaken solely from the specific grants. If the funding is not renewed, the project will be discontinued. The ending of one of these grants

would result in unfunded winding-up costs equivalent to two month's costs for the programme.
- The allowance for administration attached to grants varies from one funder to another.
- Employment costs in the UK are mainly for established positions, which would require between one and three months' compensation should there be a need to reduce staff levels. A reduction of 20 per cent is considered to be the maximum without longer notice.
- Other UK commitments are minimal.
- Emergencies Expenditure can vary considerably owing to the nature and locations of the work.
- Tangible fixed assets acquired in connection with an emergency are considered to be a sunk cost. Therefore no adjustment is to be included in the evaluation.
- Most projects do not incur significant local legal commitments (though there is a strong moral intention to complete the work). From a risk assessment point of view, therefore, it is not considered that a provision is necessary.

Figure 4.12: Risk evaluation

	Budget £000	Risk percentage Min	Max	Evaluation Min £000	Max £000
INCOME STRANDS:					
1a Database support	2,000	7.5	12.5	150	250
b New supporters	600	17.5	30.0	105	180
2 Appeals income	2,500	15.0	60.0	375	1,500
3a Fundraising: low risk	1,000	5.0	15.0	50	1,500
b Fundraising: high risk	600	20.0	50.0	120	300
4 Trusts	500	20.0	40.0	100	200
5 Legacies	800	5.0	12.5	40	100
	8,000				
EXPENDITURE:					
6 Programme closure	700	10.0	20.0	70	140
7 Grant administration	300	5.0	20.0	15	60
8 Employment costs	300	10.0	20.0	30	60
9 Other UK costs	400	5.0	15.0	20	60
10 Emergencies Expenditure	2,500	25.0	80.0	625	2,000
TOTAL RISK				1,700	5,000

Source: NCVO

The revised requirement would therefore range from £1,700 to £5,000, represented by a designated Rapid Response Fund and unrestricted Reserves. The Appeals Income and Emergencies Expenditure would comprise the Rapid Response Fund, which would be available as the name implies, subject to planned replenishment.

As the charity's Operating Reserve of nine months equated to £6,000, the trustees could therefore consider a reduction ranging from the significant to the draconian! They should, however, take into account any planned growth indicated in the Three Year Plan (since this would itself require increases in Reserves) as part of any phased reduction.

The new basis and the effects of its introduction, including how and over what time scale any surplus might be applied, would appear in the Treasurer's Report, with appropriate references in the Notes.

Appendix B: Outsourcing

Objectives
There should be:

- Clear objectives, the implications of which have been thought through.
- A recognition that cost is only one aspect.
- A commitment on the part of the organisation to manage the relationship.
- Reliance on the contract as a manual rather than as a set of legal rights and obligations.
- A focus on people, those who are to be outsourced and their importance to the organisation.
- Clarity about what services are required and how they are currently being provided.

The supplier
The prospective supplier should offer:

- Specialist assistance: the supplier should have an excellent track record for the services being outsourced, so the organisation can obtain greater specialist input than it is able to develop in-house.
- Economies of scale, since the supplier is performing a similar function for other organisations.
- Access to technology: the supplier has a better opportunity to be at the forefront of developments.
- Costs savings.
- Shared risks: suppliers are better equipped to handle many types of risks, such as those related to volume.
- The chance to free up management to concentrate on the organisation's core services.

The contract
This should offer:

- Terms for checking the supplier's performance.
- Flexibility to implement contract variations.
- Terms dealing with charges and compensation.
- Flexibility for new services and projects.
- Terms for developing existing services.
- The means of resolving day-to-day operational problems.

APPENDIX C: TRUSTEE INVESTMENT ACT 1961

Narrower range investments
These include the following:

- Government bonds and securities.
- Treasury Bills.
- National Savings Certificates.
- Deposits in the National Savings Bank and most government and local government borrowing, including nationalised industries; debentures issued by a company incorporated in the UK with a share capital of not less than £1 million which has paid a dividend on all its share capital in the last five years.
- Authorised gilts unit trusts.
- Building society deposits.
- Mortgages on freehold property or leasehold property where there is at least a further 60 years left on the lease.

Wider range investments
These can be summarised as follows:

- Any quoted shares of an EU company with a share capital of not less than £1 million which has paid a dividend on all its share capital in each of the five preceding years.
- Shares in a building society

Special range investments
There are also certain investment vehicles which are considered to be particularly low risk, mainly Common Investment Funds. Trustees may invest from either fund into these securities.

Appendix D: Investment policy – the issues to consider

Does the Trustee Investment Act apply?
Or are there other express powers contained in the governing documents?

For what length of time can the funds be invested?
The organisation's liquidity needs to be projected into the future for a number of years. In choosing a suitable investment, the organisation must know when or if the funds might be needed to pay future operating expenses: for example, to build a new community centre or to meet some other financial obligation.

Can the voluntary organisation afford to lose any of the money?
The answer to this question indicates the level of risk the organisation can take. The rate of return from interest, dividends and/or increase in underlying value of assets is related to the possibility that the original investment (also called 'principal sum') can be lost. The higher the risk of loss, the higher the expected return, as explained below.

How secure are the organisation's funding sources?
The organisation must evaluate the stability of its funding sources to project the level of contingency or emergency reserves it may require. Such funds would be placed in investments with a low risk of loss of principal value.

Are the organisation's staff capable of overseeing the investment?
Special skills and training are required to manage successfully a fully diversified investment portfolio. As shown by the stock market crashes in recent years, no one knows whether stock values will go up or down. A voluntary organisation's financial managers must assess their own knowledge and experience and consider whether there is a need to engage outside professional investment managers.

Are there any ethical considerations the charity can legitimately pay heed to?
See section on ethical investments.

How will the rate of inflation or deflation affect the investment?
Fixed money investments, such as Government Gilts, do not fluctuate in value according to the overall economy. Equity stocks, real estate and tangibles may increase in value as a result of deflation. The voluntary organisation must project expected future inflation or deflation to properly diversify its investments.

Appendix E: Types of investment

Deposit account with bank or building society
These give immediate access, or they may be on seven-day or longer notice periods.

- Rate of interest will usually increase as the amount invested and the period of notice increases.
- Be wary of depositing large sums with less well known financial institutions.

Common Deposit Fund
This is a special deposit fund available only to charities in England and Wales. It uses a system of pooling cash deposits so that the amount available for investment is increased and the return improved. The fund manager will invest these funds with several different banks or deposit takers so that the risk is spread.

- Immediate access.
- Interest is paid gross.

Equities
These are shares in quoted companies.

- Dividends usually paid twice yearly, with no guarantee of how much.
- Market value can go up as well as down.
- Risk can be diversified by investing in companies operating in different market sectors.

Gilts
These are fixed interest securities, such as government stocks, bonds, debentures and preference shares issued by central and local government.

- Risk of losing the principal capital is negligible, hence the rate of return is low.
- Investment portfolios may well include gilts because they are a way of balancing the overall risk profile.

Unit Trust
A pooled investment fund that invests in quoted shares.

- Allows the charity to enjoy the benefits of more diversification than it would otherwise be capable of, as the portfolio will comprise fixed interest and equities.
- An entry and exit charge, as well as annual management charges, is usually levied.

Common Investment Funds (CIFs)
Pooled funds similar in many ways to unit trusts but with additional benefits to charities. CIFs have the same advantage of diversifying investments across different stocks and shares.

They are approved by the Charity Commission and are themselves registered as charities.

- Tax free so they are able to pay income gross.
- Administration charges are lower than with ordinary unit trusts.

Property
Investment suitable only for voluntary organisations with large investment portfolios and governing documents that give them the power to do so. They are long-term investments and cannot readily be sold should the organisation require quick access to resources.

- There are costs associated with managing and maintaining the property.
- Trustees are likely to need professional advice on the long term growth and income prospects of property.

5.
Special financial procedures

---

1. Performance monitoring by financial Indicators
2. Cost accounting
3. Using costs for decision making
4. Breakeven analysis
5. Marginal analysis

This chapter expands on the procedures that will prove useful to the financial planner. Specialised financial analysis can provide answers not evident from the financial reports described earlier. Using ratio analysis to assess performance sheds a different light on resource flows and allows the evaluation of revenue sources. Cost accounting allows the voluntary organisation to control and calculate the costs of services and programmes. Money spent is reclassified according to functional category – for example, counselling, vaccinations and food services – in addition to generic type, such as supplies, salary and rentals.

1. Performance monitoring by financial indicators

Ratio analysis permits financial planners to identify trends, recognise strengths and pinpoint weaknesses that may not be readily apparent. As an addition to the financial statements and budgets, ratios provide an alternative view of a voluntary organisation's financial health.

The overall financial condition of an organisation can be measured with capital structure ratios. The current, or 'acid test', ratios are widely used by banks and financial advisers to assess financial health. The ratio of available cash to the liabilities or debts to be paid reveals the outlook for continued operation. The higher the cash flow is in relation to total debt or expense, the better. The ratio of debt to net assets also indicates the voluntary organisation's ability to take on additional debt or to self-finance a new project. The ratio of existing debt to current assets also indicates the degree of leverage, or ability to afford more debt: the lower the ratio the better.

A wide range of operational indicators can be useful. Comparing the various types of income received over a five-year period can reveal trends that could be meaningful. Knowing how much it costs to serve a user is necessary to evaluate whether the price of services is appropriate.

Figure 5.1 uses ratio analysis to test a voluntary organisation's financial situation; the calculations used are based partly on the financial statements. The implications of the results are discussed.

Figure 5.1: Current ratio

	Holy Spirit Church ratio		Ass'n of NPO Managers ratio	
expendable current assets*	£20,000	1	220,000	1.9
current liabilities**	£80,000	4	116,000	1

*expendable cash and assets convertible to cash
**debts payable within the next 12 months

The current ratio compares the organisation's resources available to pay the bills during the coming year. The classic view is that the current ratio of assets to liabilities should be at least 2:1; a ratio lower than that means short term liquidity problems. With its 1:4 ratio, the church obviously has a serious problem. With its 1.9:1 ratio, the Association of Non Profit Managers can comfortably pay the bills and have some cash left over. What if the ratio was above 2:1? Too high a ratio sacrifices income for safety. The difference between current assets and current liabilities is also called working capital. When working capital is adequate, a voluntary organisation may be in a position to make long term investments, or begin a new project. This formula can also be calculated and compared for restricted and unrestricted fund current ratios.

The acid tests, or quick ratio tests, shown in figure 5.2, to see if the organisation

Figure 5.2: Acid test ratio

	Holy Spirit Church ratio		Ass'n of NPO Managers ratio	
Cash or assets due in one month	£20,000	1	£110,000	1.5
Total expenses in same period	£40,000	2	£74,000	1

Figure 5.3: Overall liquidity ratio

	Holy Spirit Church ratio	Ass'n of NPO Managers ratio
Expendable fund balances	£20,000	£220,000
Total monthly expenses	£10,833	£67,000
Number of months	1.8	3.3

Figure 5.4: Income source comparison (version 1)

	Year 1	Year 2	Year 3
Membership dues & donations	£105,000	£100,000	£95,000
Total Income and support	£300,000	£320,000	£340,000
Ratio	35%	31.2%	27.9%

can pay its bills for this current month or quarter if calculated on a quarterly basis. Ask the question, 'Is the acid test or quick ratio at least 1:1?' If the ratio is below 1:1, the planners ask, 'Can the organisation survive the month if receipt of funding is delayed?' The church finance committee may wish it had asked these questions sooner as it faces what is now a serious financial situation: debts equalling two times its assets available to pay the debt.

The overall liquidity ratio, shown in figure 5.3, measures how long the organisation could survive if it received no new money. The Association of Non Profit Managers has enough money to pay its normal bills for a little more than three months, but the Church has only 1.8 months of money. For an organisation with an endowment or other permanent funds, a similar calculation would be made to compare the permanently restricted, or unexpendable funds, with total annual expenses.

Figure 5.4 analyses the percentage of the organisation's support received from members' subscriptions and general donations over a three-year period to see if this funding has changed significantly. The example shows a 7 per cent decline over three years and could indicate a serious problem unless the organisation has deliberately focused on developing other sources.

How does the current year's income portion for a particular income source compare with last year's? (see figure 5.5) Is the change planned or expected? Should the reasons for the change be analysed? Should any action be taken in response to the change?

Figure 5.5: Income source comparison (version 2)

	Association of Non Profit Managers	
	Prior Year	Current Year
	£	£
Corporate members fees	258,000	270,000
Individual members fees	87,800	90,000
Information services	147,000	150,000
Publication sales	215,000	230,000
Professional training	108,000	110,000
Annual meeting	42,000	20,000
Interest income	3,000	1,000
TOTAL INCOME	860,800	913,000

Figure 5.6: Cost Ratios (version 1)

	Year 1	Year 2	Year 3	Year 4
POUNDS SPENT ON:				
Direct charitable objectives	280,000	300,000	320,000	304,000
Fundraising & publicity	100,000	110,000	120,000	140,000
Management & admin	10,000	20,000	40,000	50,000
	390,000	430,000	480,000	494,000
PERCENTAGE RATIO:				
Direct charitable objectives	71.8	69.8	66.7	61.5
Fundraising & publicity	25.6	25.6	25.0	28.3
Management & admin	2.6	4.7	8.3	10.1

The Charity Accounting Statement of Recommended Practice (SORP) requires total expenditure to be classified under the above three headings in the annual accounts. It is therefore important to monitor how these figures change. They may serve as some measure of worth for a grant provider, which will be interested to see how much of its money is used directly in charitable service provision. Many grant making bodies shy away from funding groups with apparently high administration expenses. The example in figure 5.6 shows that expenditure on charitable objectives has fallen by 10 per cent over four years while administration costs have increased from 2.6 to 10 per cent.

Figure 5.7 shows how reliant the voluntary organisation is on particular sources

Figure 5.7: Cost ratios (version 2: individual income sources)

	Association of Non Profit Managers			
	Prior Year		Current Year	
	£	Ratio	£	Ratio
Donations and gifts	890,677	53%	1,647,832	70%
Legacies	668,278	40%	815,872	34%
Grants received	42,500	3%	134,432	6%
NLCB grants	–	–	159,634	7%
Investment income	48,378	3%	77,605	3%
Other income	116,187	7%	130,486	6%
Profit on disposal of investments	3,929	–	15,532	–
TOTAL INCOME	1,769,949		2,981,393	
Total expenditure	1,676,419		2,366,483	

of income to fund its total expenditure. In this example, the organisation is heavily dependent on donation and gifts (which may include income from fundraising events and appeals). This source of income has funded just over half the total expenditure in the first year, rising to almost three-quarters in the second year.

Other ratios are also useful:

- *Staff cost as a percentage of total expenditure.* This indicates the proportion of the total expenditure that is (at least in the short term) fixed. Further analysis can distinguish between the staff costs of those who deliver the organisation's mission and those in management and administration.
- *Fundraising costs as a percentage of total expenditure.* This shows the relative efficiency of fundraising appeals and events, at least in financial terms. The recent decline in giving has had the effect of increasing this percentage, as fundraising generally has become more competitive.

SERVICE DELIVERY INDICATORS

Non-financial indicators can also be used when planning services, preparing funding applications or bidding for contracts. Here are some examples:

- Number of beneficiaries overall and for each service.
- Number of staff per beneficiary by service and overall.
- Cost per beneficiary overall and for each of the main areas of service.
- Number of information requests on a rolling average.
- Number of press mentions on a rolling average.
- Capital cost of buildings per beneficiary and per unit.

2. Cost accounting

This section will demonstrate why costs are important in voluntary organisations and look at some techniques for cost management.

The terms 'cost' and 'cost accounting' have many definitions; here are some useful ones:

- Cost is 'a measure of the resources used up in obtaining goods and services'; 'the amount of expenditure (actual or notional) incurred on, or attributable to, a specified thing or activity'; 'to ascertain the cost of a specified thing or activity'.
- Cost accounting is 'the establishment of budgets, standard costs and actual costs of operations, processes, activities or products; and the analysis of variances, profitability or social use of funds'.

Here are some of the issues that cost accounting seeks to address:

Figure 5.8: Cost accounting

ISSUE TO ADDRESS:	Why this is an issue?
What to charge for services/products	Establishes a pricing structure that covers total costs and thus helps to ensure future viability of service
Determining the total cost of a project for which funding/contract is sought.	Helps to ensure that funding/contract fee is based on a 'competitive price' and covers its costs
Negotiating charge for internal services/ general overheads	Ensures that core costs of organisation are allocated to projects on a reasonable basis
Whether the organisation should accept the contract price given by a local authority	Organisation must be certain about project's total costs if it is to accept a contract
Cost control for budget reporting purposes	Ensures that budget parameters (e.g. balanced budget) set at planning stage are met
Cost management for cost reduction purposes	Ensures long-term financial viability
Identifying internal strengths and weaknesses	Exploits cost advantages and/or commits to corrective action
Maximising resources employed by organisation	Enables a strategic review of activities to consider possibility of outsourcing, alliances etc
Performance evaluation	Maximises outputs/impact on society for minimum costs
Following fund accounting principles	Trust law requires the separation of funds provided for specific purposes, and the Charity Accounting SORP requires classification of expenditure according to functional categories

Figure 5.8 includes some of the most fundamental issues that voluntary organisations have to cope with. It is therefore crucially important, in the interests of both

internal cost measurement and management and external reporting, that proper techniques exist to address these issues.

In this section, cost accounting techniques will be described under the following headings:

- Cost ascertainment: how much does a service, product or activity cost?
- Planning: what level of activity and resource allocation can the voluntary organisation undertake?
- Resource maximisation: are we making the best use of available resources?

COST ASCERTAINMENT

The question of what a product, service or activity costs is becoming more important for voluntary organisations. Furthermore, as conditions of funding become more stringent and core funding becomes increasingly difficult to obtain, organisations need to be very clear about costs not only at the organisational level, but also at project level.

The total cost of a service or product can be broadly divided into:

- *Direct costs.* These are costs incurred as a direct result of carrying out a particular activity. Running educational courses, for example, would involve the cost of trainers, room hire, course materials and probably most of the education officer's time; but if the organisation did not run courses, it could probably avoid these costs.
- *Indirect costs.* These are shared organisational costs which are difficult to apportion to a specific project or activity; examples include the project manager's time, some administration costs and some premises costs. Organisations are finding it increasingly difficult to obtain funding for indirect costs if these have not been apportioned across other project costs.

In most cases, it is possible to identify accurately the direct costs of a project or service. What is less clear is how to identify indirect costs and the share of these costs that should be allocated to the end product or service.

The process of sharing out the indirect costs among a number of products or services is called 'overhead absorption' or 'overhead recovery'. It can be a very arbitrary process: for example, how much of the account clerk's salary cost should be allocated to each service or product? It may be easiest simply to divide the total salary cost by the number of projects served. However, this may not reflect the true cost of serving a project or product; later in this chapter we will see how the absorption of overheads can be a more sophisticated operation.

WHY ABSORB OVERHEADS?

Overhead absorption is often criticised for its arbitrary nature. So why should the finance officer undertake the task at all? Why not simply concentrate on the direct costs that *can* be accurately allocated to services and products?

There are two main reasons why it is important to calculate the fully absorbed costs of a product or service:

- To understand the long-run costs of products and services. This can be useful in many decisions, including pricing. Some voluntary organisations take the total cost and add a percentage to determine the selling price. This is known as 'cost-plus' pricing, but it is not always appropriate in a competitive market: suppliers may have to set prices according to what the customers are prepared to pay, rather than what the supplier would like to charge!
- Under the fund accounting principles specified in the Charity Accounting SORP, most organisations are required to identify separate expenditure on restricted funding projects. This means that they will need to allocate indirect or support costs to services or projects.

At this stage an example may prove helpful. This has been adapted from *The Complete Guide to Business and Strategic Planning For Voluntary Organisations* by Alan Lawrie. The Community Health Project is a voluntary health education project with five main activities:

- Education and training: courses for teachers and health workers.
- Youth project: specific health work with 12-22 year olds.
- Public enquiries: enquiry point for a wide range of public calls.
- Resource centre: producing and disseminating teaching and resource materials.
- Rural project: community health work with isolated communities.

The current budget is:

INCOME	£	EXPENDITURE	£
Health Authority contract	115,000	Salaries	100,000
Income from courses	19,000	Administration	20,000
Income from sale/hire of resources	5,000	Minibus	5,000
Trust grant for rural work	15,000	Telephones	6,000
		Building costs	20,000
TOTAL	154,000	TOTAL	154,000

The staff costs are analysed as:

	£
Manager	28,000
Education Officer	23,000
Information Officer	22,000
Resources Officer	19,000
Clerk (part time)	8,000
TOTAL	100,000

The change to a project-based accounting system came about for the following reasons:

- The budget did not show the cost of individual projects.
- Funders and purchasers wanted to become more 'project' based.
- There was an urgent need to cost and price contracts properly.
- The difficulty of raising money for core costs.

The treasurer and manager have reviewed the projects and identified the following cost centres; all future income and expenditure will be allocated to one of them:

- Education.
- Resource centre (including public enquiries).
- Youth work.
- Rural work.

The first task will be to identify and allocate direct costs to each of the above cost centres. The treasurer and manager have together identified the following basis of apportionment. Firstly, for non staff costs:

- Building costs: fixed percentage (based on floor space occupied by each activity).
- Resource materials: actual usage (based on review of last twelve months' invoices).
- Minibus: approximate costs of past usage.
- Telephone and admin: a quarter of all telephone costs (£1,500) and one-tenth of admin costs (£2,000) were estimated to be the direct costs of the resource centre's public information work.

The results of this review are shown in figure 5.9.

Figure 5.9: Direct non staff costs per cost centre

	Admin	Materials	Minibus	Telephones	Building Costs	Total allocation
BUDGET	20,000	3,000	5,000	6,000	20,000	
Cost Centre						
Education		1,500			6,000	7,500
Res. centre	2,000	800		1,500	8,000	12,300
Youth work		500	1,000		4,000	5,500
Rural work		200	3,500		2,000	5,700
Not allocated	18,000	0	500	4,500	0	31,000

The treasurer and manager have now looked at staff costs and have broadly agreed the allocation of time spent by each staff member to the four cost centres. The results of the exercise are shown in figure 5.10.

Figure 5.10: Allocation of staff costs to cost centres

COST CENTRE	Manager	Education Officer	Info Officer	Resources Officer	Clerk	Total allocation
Education	30% i.e. 8,400	70% i.e. 16,100	20% i.e. 4,400		10% i.e. 800	29,700
*Resource centre	20% i.e. 5,600	15% i.e. 3,450	60% i.e. 13,200	75% i.e. 14,250	20% i.e. 1,600	38,100
Youth work	5% i.e. 1,400		20% i.e. 4,400	25% i.e. 4,750		10,550
Rural work	5% i.e 1,400	15% i.e. 3,450				4,850
Not allocated indirect cost	40% i.e 11,200				70% i.e. 5,600	16,800
TOTAL	28,000	23,000	22,000	19,000	8,000	

It was also agreed that 40 per cent of the manager's time and 70 per cent of the admin clerk's time could not be allocated to a particular project and would therefore form part of indirect costs.

At this stage, only the direct costs have been allocated to cost centres, and the position so far can be summarised as follows:

Figure 5.11: Total staff and non staff costs per cost centre

COST CENTRE	Direct non staff costs £	Direct staff costs £	TOTAL DIRECT COSTS £
Education	7,500	29,700	37,200
Resource centre	12,300	38,100	50,400
Youth work	5,500	10,550	16,050
Rural work	5,700	4,850	10,550
Total	31,000	83,200	114,200

The amounts still to be allocated (indirect costs):

Non staff costs (see figure 5.9)	23,000	Staff Costs 16,800 (see figure 5.10)	Total 39,800

The remaining £39,800 (£23,000 non staff costs and £16,800 staff costs) represents the indirect costs of the community health project, and is now allocated to the four cost centres according to the floor space occupied shown in figure 5.12.

Figure 5.12: Allocation of indirect costs

COST CENTRE	Share	Indirect £	Direct costs £	TOTAL COST CENTRE £
Education	30%	11,940	37,200	49,140
Resource centre	35%	13,930	50,400	64,330
Youth work	20%	7,960	16,050	24,010
Rural work	15%	5,970	10,550	16,520
TOTAL		39,800	114,200	154,000

Having reassigned the information from the income and expenditure budget into a cost centre framework, the treasurer and manager now have a much better idea of the true cost of running the current services. For example, although the trust grant for rural work is £15,000, the total cost of carrying out this work is in fact £16,520, which suggests that it is losing the Community Health Project £1,520 in the current year. The project is now in a much better position to decide whether to continue this work (and subsidise the loss from other income) or to approach the trust for extra funding.

Developing a cost-centred approach can raise a number of other issues:

- Many voluntary organisations are very poor at costing their work: the cost involved in operating and providing good management is often underestimated, not properly identified or even ignored. This attempt to do 'quality' work on the cheap can easily lead to a long-term crisis.
- Many organisations that have adopted a cost-centred approach have found that the true cost of providing a service or activity is greater than the funding being offered. This information enables the organisation's managers to be more assertive when negotiating with funders or taking the strategic decision to subsidise and/or fundraise to cover the loss.
- Problems may arise when people in one cost centre believe they are more 'profitable' than another centre. Cost accounting and absorption costing are management tools that allow decisions to be made about priorities; they are not concerned with assigning value to an activity. Normally, value will be measured in non-financial terms.

The absorption costing model discussed above is not without its weaknesses, however. Amongst the chief of these is the arbitrary way in which indirect overheads are allocated to services or products. With the Community Health Project this was done on a simple percentage basis, and as a result the rural work was seen to be losing the organisation money. However, the results may well have been different had the percentages used to allocated overheads been different – and hence a different decision about continuing with the rural work might possibly have been made.

A further weakness of absorption costing is that it fails to explain to management *why* costs are incurred. This is because, under most accounting systems, costs are accumulated in the general ledger using a natural classification system of salaries, printing, rents, insurances etc and then reported by the department or project manager responsible. As a result, the project manager lacks any real understanding of the activities or processes that are ultimately responsible for these costs. This means that, whenever cost cutting is needed, management will tend to reduce headcount first, since this is by far the largest cost item. But the work remains untouched, to be shared out between fewer people!

To address these weaknesses, a system of Activity Based Costing (ABC) has been developed and has gained some acceptance within the voluntary sector. At its simplest, ABC attributes the costs incurred by an organisation to processes or activities. It therefore cuts across the departmental boundaries that often appear in organisational charts. An example of such a process in a commercial company is order fulfilment: from persuading the customer to receiving their order, from fulfilling the order to receiving the cash, each process is performed in different parts of the company.

However, most business activities are organised not on the basis of processes but on a functional basis: for example, sales, accounts and legal. The same is true for voluntary organisation, which are divided into fundraising, accounts, personnel and so on. In accordance with this functional split, costs tend to be collected by department and when appropriate may be allocated out to other departments as a general overhead. The reporting of costs to the department head is also usually by cost type: for example, salaries, travel, overheads and computer costs. Although this is important to the department head for internal budgetary control purposes, it gives no insight into the business processes which caused the costs to be incurred in the first place. It tells the management the What but not the Why.

Take, for example, the finance department, which performs the functions of invoicing, payroll, general accounting, cash receipts and payments – all of them activities that exist as a result of other business processes. They are not an end in themselves, but a consequence of other activities. In most commercial organisations these costs are treated as overheads and may be reallocated to other departments.

However, as we have seen, the allocation is very arbitrary. Take the cost of running the payroll: a detailed analysis of how costs were incurred would probably show that it costs very little more to run a payroll for 200 staff than it does for 150. But a common basis for allocating payroll costs is the number of employees. As a result, a department employing 150 staff would receive a disproportionately higher charge than one employing only 50. In addition, allocating costs to a department rather than to business processes reinforces the organisational/functional structure at the expense of giving a genuine insight into costs.

The critical difference under ABC accounting is that costs should, if possible, be charged directly to the service or project in such a way that the amount charged reflects as closely as possible the actual cost of the service.

ABC AND CHARITIES

Despite the benefits it can bring, ABC does have a number of problems associated with it. Some of these are peculiar to the voluntary sector:

- When setting up the system it is easy to make it too complicated. Only the most important business processes need to be identified, and the components of those processes should be kept to a minimum. If for some reason more detail is required, this can be obtained by a one-off exercises rather than by building it into the system.
- A balance needs to be struck between reasonable approximations and excessive detail. This is particularly important when costs have to be allocated.
- Full implementation of ABC requires a sophisticated accounting system to collect and hold data.
- Maintaining time sheets to record how staff spend their time is commonly used as a basis for attributing staff costs and some services to the identified business processes or products. Maintaining such a system, with its associated complications, is an additional overhead that would need to be justified.
- Unlike their commercial counterparts, voluntary organisations often receive donations of time, goods and services that enable them to provide a much better service. How should these donations be valued and how should they appear in management reports?
- To be effective, ABC needs the involvement and commitment of all staff, not just senior management. It may, however, be seen as a threat by staff, as business processes cut across departmental boundaries and challenge work practices or unproductive activities.

Although direct implementation of ABC across the voluntary sector may not be appropriate, there are some organisations – in particular, the larger charities and those actively engaged in commercial operations – that should seriously consider introducing it. ABC is probably unsuitable for smaller voluntary organisations, however, because it needs sophisticated computer systems to provide information on a regular basis. But such organisations should at least think about conducting a one-off study to identify the business processes and determine what the real costs of each one are. There may be misconceptions about the true cost of a particular process, product or service that could have serious consequences for the future of the entire organisation.

3. Using costs for decision making

This section of the guide will examine: using costs to help managers in their decision making activities; cost behaviour patterns; and different classifications of costs for decision making.

Cost behaviour patterns

The term 'cost behaviour patterns' is used to describe how costs behave in relation to the level of activity; essentially, it involves asking the question, 'Does this cost increase in line with activity or does it remain constant?' A variety of factors can cause costs to change – for example, inflation, scarcity in supply – but cost accounting focuses on how they change in response to the level of activity. Activity can be measured in a variety of ways, depending on the organisation, the type of costs being analysed and the reasons for analysing the costs. Common measures of activity might include the level of service provided (local, regional or national), the number of training courses run, the number of beneficiaries using the service, the number of employees, the number of telephone calls to a helpline etc.

Fixed costs

Fixed costs are those that do not vary with the level of activity of a project and remain constant for a limited period of time. Figure 5.13 shows fixed costs of £10,000.

Figure 5.13: Fixed costs

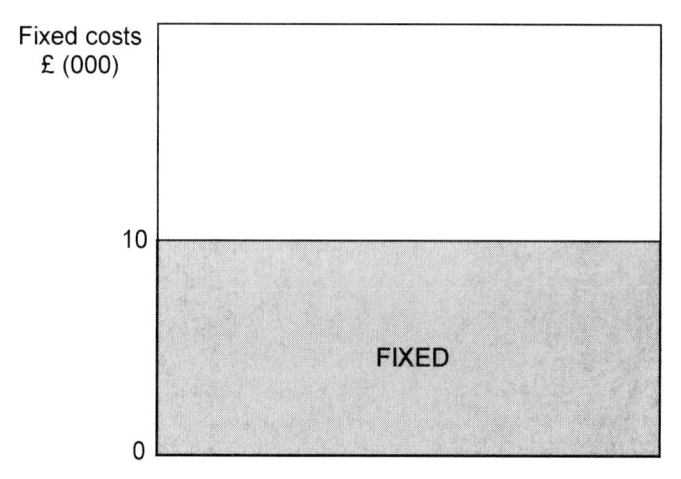

The total cost incurred in the period is £10,000 for all activity levels, even at zero activity. In the short term, therefore, an organisation will have to pay all its fixed commitments even if activity drops to zero. Another term used to describe fixed costs is 'period costs'; this highlights the fact that a fixed cost is incurred according to the time elapsed rather than the level of activity.

Examples of fixed costs for a community centre operating a kitchen preparing food for homeless people on a contract basis would be:

- Rent and rates.
- Salaries of kitchen staff.
- Insurance.
- Depreciation of equipment.

These costs will probably be unaffected by the number of homeless people served over a period. But there may come a point when demand for the service expands and more staff or bigger premises are needed. There will then be corresponding increases in salaries, rent and rates etc.

A fixed cost is therefore unaffected by changes *within a relevant range of activity*. If activity extends beyond this range, then the fixed cost behaviour pattern previously identified may no longer be applicable. Figure 5.14 demonstrates this.

Figure 5.14: Stepped fixed costs

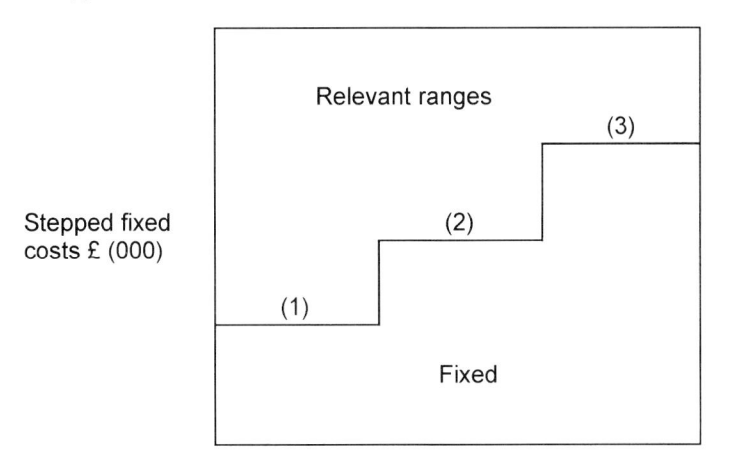

Activity level: number of units

The above diagram could be taken as depicting the cost of kitchen staff's salaries. The costs remain fixed for a certain range of activity. Within this range it is possible to serve more homeless people without needing extra staff, and therefore the salary cost remains constant. However, if activity is expanded to the critical point where another staff member is needed, then the salary cost moves up to a higher level. The cost then remains constant for a further range of increases in activity until another staff member is needed and another step occurs. The critical points illustrated in the diagram are often referred to as 'break points'.

Out of a desire to serve as many beneficiaries as possible, voluntary organisations often increase their levels of activity beyond the relevant break point. This situation cannot be sustained in the long term without affecting the quality of the services provided. Furthermore, it is seldom possible to obtain extra funding to allow for this expansion; a commercial provider, by contrast, is more likely to secure further investment. Identifying the relevant range and break point is therefore crucially important for voluntary organisations.

Variable costs

Variable costs are those that vary according to the amount of activity undertaken or goods produced. The higher the level of activity, the higher will be the cost incurred. Figure 5.15 below shows a linear variable cost line.

Figure 5.15: Linear variable costs

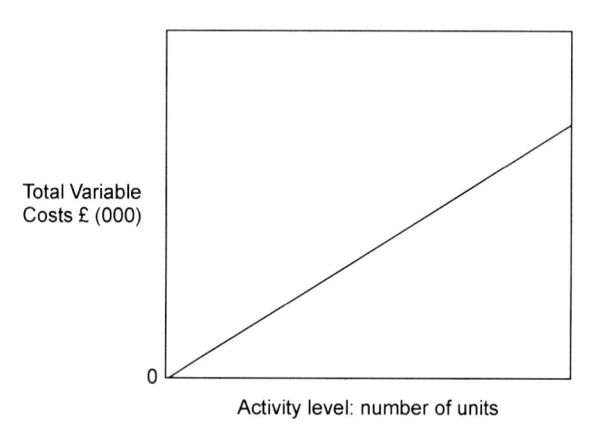

Total Variable Costs £ (000)

Activity level: number of units

The graph is a straight line, which means that the cost at zero activity level is nil. When activity increases, the total variable cost increases in direct proportion: i.e. if activity goes up by 10 per cent, the total variable cost also increases by 10 per cent, as long as the activity level is still within the relevant range.

Using the community kitchen as an example, the two costs likely to be variable are food and fuel.

Planning and decision making often assumes that variable costs are linear. This is not always a safe assumption: as depicted in Figures 5.16 and 5.17 below, a variable cost may be non-linear.

The graph of cost A becomes less steep as the level of activity increases. Each successive unit of activity adds less to the total variable cost than the previous unit. An example of a variable cost that follows this pattern is the cost of obtaining food ingredients where quantity discounts are available.

The graph of cost B becomes steeper as the level of activity rises. This indicates that each successive unit of activity is adding more to the variable cost than the previous unit. An example of a variable cost that follows this pattern could be where specialist food ingredients are in short supply and it is necessary to pay higher prices to acquire the larger quantities needed when more homeless people are served.

Figure 5.16: Non-linear variable costs (Cost A)

Cost A

Total Variable
Costs £ (000)

0

Activity level: number of units

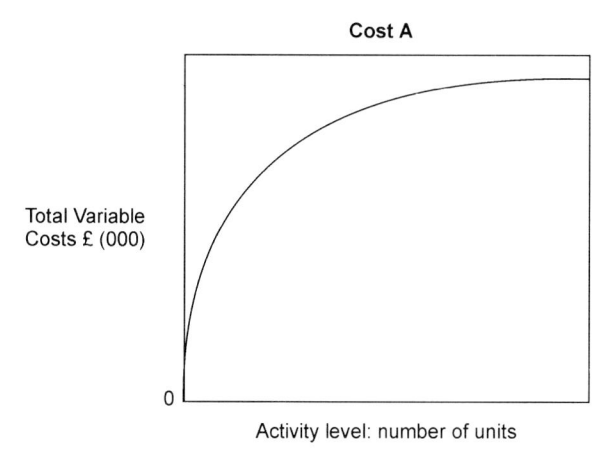

Figure 5.17: Non-linear variable costs (Cost B)

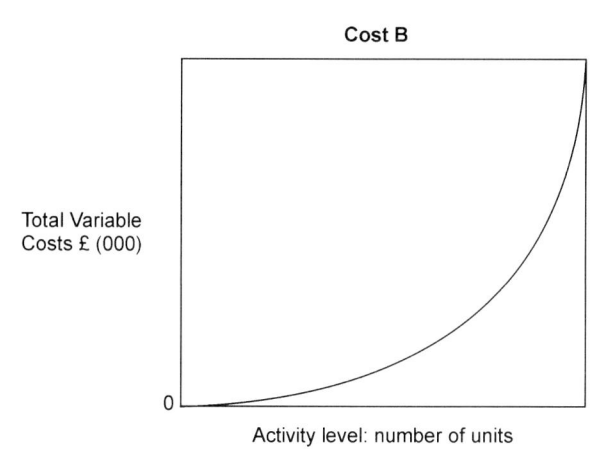

Cost B

Total Variable
Costs £ (000)

0

Activity level: number of units

Semi-variable costs

Also referred to as a 'semi fixed' or 'mixed' cost, this is a cost which contains both fixed and variable components and is therefore partly affected by fluctuations in the level of activity. Figure 5.18 shows the graph of a semi-variable cost.

This particular semi-variable cost has a basic fixed component of £60,000 which is incurred even at zero activity. As levels of activity increase, a variable component is incurred in addition to the basic fixed cost. Examples of semi-variable costs for the community kitchen could be telephone, gas, and electricity. Each of these has a basic fixed component and then a variable element increasing with usage.

Figure 5.18: Semi-variable cost

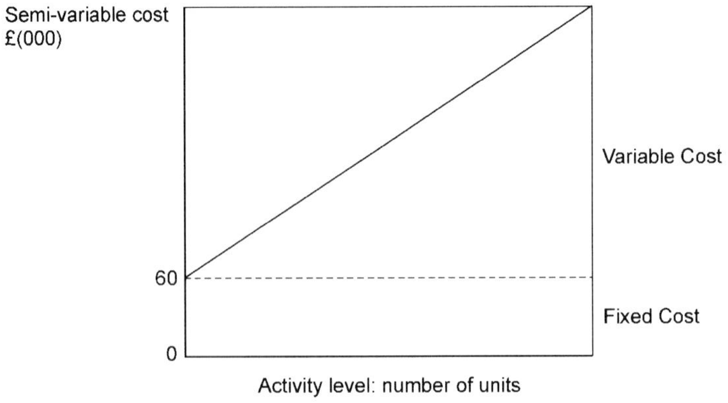

4. BREAK-EVEN ANALYSIS

The next section looks at a type of analysis that depends on an understanding of cost behaviour. Suppose the community centre was faced with the original decision of whether it should accept the fixed-price contract with the local authority to operate a community kitchen. One key factor in the decision will be: 'How many homeless people does the community centre need to attract in order to break even each month?'

CALCULATING THE BREAK-EVEN POINT

Suppose that you have produced the following estimates of the monthly costs:

Fixed Costs	£ per month
Rent and rates	800
Salaries	1,500
Insurance	100
Other	100
	2,500

Variable Costs	£ per person (average)
Food and drink	3
Laundry	1
Other	1
	5

The contract with the local authority will provide a fixed fee of £10 for every homeless person fed. It is now possible to calculate the break-even point. The first step is to calculate the contribution from each person.

Every time the community centre serves a homeless person it receives £10 and has to pay £5 for food etc. The management accounting term for this difference of

£5 is the 'contribution'. Therefore the community centre gets a contribution of £5 per person:

contract income less variable costs = contribution (£10–£5=£5)

The contribution is so called because it literally contributes towards the fixed costs, which are incurred no matter how many persons are served. Therefore, if the community centre has one homeless person walk in, there is a £5 contribution towards the fixed costs of £2,500. If there are two customers, there is a £10 contribution towards the fixed costs of £2,500; and so on.

To break even, the community centre needs sufficient contributions to pay all the fixed costs. The centre will then have nothing left: no surplus and no deficit – the break-even point will have been reached.

$$\text{Breakeven point} = \frac{\text{Fixed costs}}{\text{Contribution per person}} = \frac{£2,500}{£5}$$

$$= 500 \text{ persons per month}$$

LIMITATIONS OF BREAK-EVEN ANALYSIS

The example of the community centre shows that break-even analysis can be useful for investigating the relationship between an organisation's costs and income. However, it does have its limitations, most of which stem from its underlying assumptions:

- Costs are assumed to behave in a linear fashion. Unit variable costs are assumed to remain constant and fixed costs are assumed to be unaffected by changes in activity levels. Break-even charts can be adjusted to cope with non-linear variable costs or steps in fixed costs, but too many changes in behaviour patterns can make the charts very cluttered and difficult to use.
- Sales revenues are assumed to be constant for each unit sold. This may be true where, as in the community centre, there is a contract for services. But it may be unrealistic in situations where 'products' are sold, because of the necessity at times to reduce price in order to increase volume.
- It is assumed that activity is the only factor affecting costs and revenues. Other factors such as inflation and technology changes are ignored.
- The analysis can only be applied to a single product or service. Most voluntary organisations have more than one product or service, and the sale or take-up of each may be affected by the other.

5. Marginal analysis

The guide will now look at a number of common decision-making situations to see how choices are made between alternative courses of action.

If alternative courses of action are being compared, there is little point in including data that is common to all of them. Management's attention should be focused on the costs and revenues which will differ as a result of the decision. In other words, the *incremental* costs and revenues should be highlighted. In many cases, the fixed costs will not be altered by a decision; since they are not incremental costs, they should therefore be excluded from the analysis. However, in some situations there may be a step in the fixed costs, and this extra, or incremental, fixed cost should be taken into the analysis. The following examples illustrate this.

Hamilton Care provides residential care for young people in need under contract from the surrounding local authorities. The contract price paid is on the basis of the number of young people cared for (i.e. spot purchase). Hamilton Care has the capacity to provide 100 beds in total. These facilities are available for 200 days of the year; at present, 80 beds are occupied for the full term (200 days p/a). Extracts from their management accounts reveals the following:

Figure 5.19: Residential care facilities

	£	£
Contract income for services		480,000
Variable costs	320,000	
Fixed costs	100,000	
		420,000
Surplus		60,000

A private sector competitor has recently gone out of business and Hamilton Care has been approached to take the competitor's place. The regional authority will refer 20 young people a year, but is only prepared to pay 75 per cent of the normal contract price per person.

Variable unit costs will not be altered by the proposal, but fixed costs would increase by £5,000, as extra staff would be needed to help with supervision.

Is it a worthwhile proposal from a financial point of view? Hamilton Care needs to determine the incremental costs and income that will arise from this proposal.

The current spot purchase price per person: £30
(contract income divided by total "bed nights") £480,000
                                                 ───────
                                                  16,000

("bed nights" is equal to total days multiplied by 200 x 80
current capacity)

Therefore the proposed contract price is: £22.50
(75% x £30)
Variable cost per "bed night"   £320,000   £20
                                                 ───────
                                                  16,000

A financial outline for the proposal has been prepared as shown in figure 5.20.

Figure 5.20: Financial evaluation of proposal

	£	£
Incremental income: 200 × 20 × £22.50		90,000
Variable costs: 200 × 20 × £20	80,000	
Incremental fixed costs	5,000	
		85,000
Incremental surplus		5,000

The proposal would generate an extra £5,000 and is therefore worthwhile from a financial point of view.

CLOSING A PROJECT

A national voluntary organisation, which provides support services and information for elderly people and campaigns on their behalf, has a chain of retail shops through which it sells donated goods. A financial review of the shops is currently under way, and three shops have been identified with a view to perhaps closing at least one of them. The results for the latest period are shown in figure 5.21.

The directors are considering closing down shop C because it makes a loss. But the fixed costs would be incurred even if this were done. The organisation's profit on its retail shops as a whole would fall to £16,000 per year if shop C is closed.

The £5,000 contribution from Shop C would be lost, and so this shop should *not* be closed unless a more profitable use can be found for the space it occupies.

The financial affect of closing shop C is shown in figure 5.22. These examples have been evaluated on purely financial terms; it is important to consider the non-financial consequences of such decisions as well.

Figure 5.21: Summary of financial results for shops

	Shop A £000	Shop B £000	Shop C £000	Total £000
Sales revenue	78	120	21	219
Variable cost of sales	48	68	16	132
Contribution	30	52	5	87
Fixed cost	23	34	9	66
Profit/ (loss)	7	18	(4)	21

Figure 5.22: Effects of closure of shop C

	Shop A £000	Shop B £000	Total £000
Sales revenue	78	120	198
Variable cost of sales	48	68	116
Contribution	30	52	82
Fixed cost			66
Profit			16

RELEVANT COSTS

Relevant costs are those that will be affected by the decision being taken. In management decision making, all relevant costs should be considered. If a cost will remain unaltered regardless of the decision being taken, it is called a 'non-relevant cost'.

NON-RELEVANT COSTS

Costs that are not usually relevant in management decisions include:

- *Sunk or past cost.* Money already spent that cannot now be recovered: for example, expenditure incurred in developing a new fundraising campaign. Even if a decision is taken to abandon further work, the money cannot be recovered. The cost is therefore irrelevant to future decisions concerning the product.
- *Absorbed fixed overheads.* These will not increase or decrease as a result of the decision being taken; see the example above on the closure of retail shops.
- *Expenditure that will be incurred in the future, but because of decisions taken in the past cannot now be changed.* Although this is a future cost, it will be incurred regardless of the decision being taken and is therefore not relevant. An example is expenditure on training material that has been delivered but not paid

for; the organisation is obliged to pay for the material even if it subsequently decides not to proceed with the training courses.
- *Historical cost depreciation.* Depreciation calculations do not result in any future cash flows. They are merely bookkeeping entries designed to spread the original cost of an asset over its useful life.

FURTHER READING AND RESOURCES

Management accounting: official terminology. CIMA 1996

Marginal costing. CIMA 1995

Finance for the non-specialist. CIMA 1997

The Complete Guide to Business and Strategic Planning for Voluntary Organisations by Alan Lawrie, Directory of Social Change, 1994.

Appendix A: Case Study

Womens' Building Project

This case study looks at the use of marginal costing to help a voluntary organisation determine which projects should be accepted in order to ensure maximum contribution to core costs.

The Women's Building Project (WBP) is a recently-established charity that seeks to provide women who are disadvantaged (either because of low income or otherwise) with opportunities to gain new skills that can then be usefully employed within the construction industry. This is a unique project that offers training to reskill women, and initial information-gathering has identified a number of government and voluntary agencies that have indicated willingness to refer on to WBP.

WBP operates from premises in west London. The site was previously used as a warehouse storage facility and covers about 15,000 square feet. This has been modified by allocating 5,000 sq ft to office and administration functions and the remaining 10,000 sq ft to be space for training workshops.

WBP has applied to a well-known charitable trust set up by the construction industry for funding for both the running costs of the premises and the provision of free training to women. The trust agreed to provide £50,000 towards the core costs of running the premises, but no funding for the provision of training, which it argued should be self-financing through course fees. Further negotiations resulted in the trust agreeing to provide materials and trainers at heavily subsidised rates; however, WBP would still have to levy a charge to ensure that its costs were covered.

The training courses that WBP plans to offer are:

- Utility installation: this will provide the skills and knowledge needed to install electricity, water and gas supplies to new residential premises;
- Woodwork and joinery: this will provide women with the hands-on experience and skills they need to use different types of timber in the construction and decoration of residential premises;
- Metal work: this will provide women with the basic skills they need to use metal structures in the construction of industrial premises;
- Brickwork: this will provide women with the basic skills necessary to use brick materials in the construction of residential properties.

The training programmes are planned to provide as much hand-on experience as possible within a workshop environment. They will last for three months each, and will be repeated three times a year. The site will be closed for the remaining three months. To ensure maximum learning, the number of women allowed on to the training programmes at any one time will be restricted to 12.

Because of the workshop approach of this training, it has become apparent that only three of the planned programmes can be accommodated in the 10,000 sq ft space. Any unused space may be offered to another community organisation wanting office space at £5 per sq ft. Each training programme will require its own set of materials, to be used and facilitated by a skilled supervisor.

Detailed costings for each of the four training programmes and the premises as a whole are provided in figure 5.23. A unit of output has been defined as a 'training day' for the maximum of 12 women. For the nine months available in each year, the number of 'training days' will be 180 days per annum or 60 days per term. The costs for each training day will differ according to the type of training programme being run. For example, brickwork training requires more materials (cement, sand, bricks etc) than utility training.

Figure 5.23: Training programme costs

	Utilities	Woodwork	Brickwork	Metalwork
Per training day	£	£	£	£
Materials	30	35	40	60
Supervisors' staff costs	75	22	30	60
Consumables	15	10.50	10	20
Floor space required (sq ft)	2,000	2,000	3,000	5,000
Training course fees (per term)	£750	£700	£600	£650
Expected take-up rate (%)	90	80	75	95

The other fixed premises costs are estimated at £50,000 p.a. and indirect overhead costs are estimated at £30,000 p.a.

At the next trustees meeting, the management team needs to be able to recommend which training programmes to offer. An initial examination of the information has led the project manager to conclude that first priority should be given to Utilities, then Metalwork, and finally Woodwork, as these have the highest course fees and take-up rate.

The treasurer, who is also studying to be an accountant, has decided to take a more rigorous approach. He is particularly concerned that, in view of the restriction imposed by the available floor space, only those training programmes that maximise the contribution per square foot to the annual fixed overheads should be accepted. His calculations are shown in figure 5.24.

As can be seen, the conclusions of the project manager and the treasurer are very different. The treasurer is recommending that the Metalwork programme be dropped, whereas this was the project manager's second favourite.

The financial effect on WBP as a whole of the two proposals is shown in figure 5.25.

Figure 5.24: Contribution per training programme

	Utilities	Woodwork	Brickwork	Metalwork
Total variable costs per training day (a) (material +staff+consumables)	£120	£67.50	£80	£140
Total variable costs per term (b) (a) multiply by 60 days	£7,200	£4,050	£4,800	£8,400
Expected variable costs per term (c) (b) multiply by take-up %	£6,480	£3,240	£3,600	£7,980
Expected course fees per term (d) (total course fees (for 12) multiply by take-up %)	£8,100	£6,720	£5,400	£7,410
Expected contribution per term (e) (d) minus (c)	£1,620	£3,480	£1,800	£(570)
Floor space required in sq ft (f)	2,000	2,000	3,000	5,000
Contribution per sq ft (g) (e) divided by (f)	£0.81	£1.74	£0.60	£(0.114)
Treasurer's ranking	2	1	3	not run
Project manager's ranking	1	3	not run	2

Figure 5.25: Financial results of the recommendations

	Treasurer's proposal	Project manager's proposal
Contribution for year: (e) multiplied by 3 terms		
1: Woodwork	£10,440	
Utilities		£4,860
2: Utilities	£4,860	
Metalwork		£(1,710)
3: Metalwork	£5,400	
Woodwork		£10,440
	£20,700	£13,590
Remaining floor space available to rent	3,000 sq ft	1,000 sq ft
Rental income @ £5 per sq ft	£15,000	£5,000
Total contribution to overheads	**£35,700**	**£18,590**

The information on fixed premises costs and indirect overhead costs will be the same for whatever course of action.

6.
Charity accounts and financial management

1. **Who uses financial statements?**
2. **Converting management accounts to SORP accounts**

This chapter looks at the different users of charity accounts and the type of information that is particularly relevant to them.

It is important for the trustees of a voluntary organisation to be able to understand the annual report and accounts, because it is the chair of the trustee board who signs the report and, together with the honorary treasurer, the financial statements.

Trustees are often unclear about how the information and figures in the management accounts – which they will be familiar with – become the annual accounts. There are three key reasons for this:

1. The purpose of management accounts is monitoring and control, whereas the annual accounts are for an external audience.
2. The format of annual accounts is prescribed by the Charity Accounting SORP and other regulations, while management accounts should be in a format that informs the management of the organisation.
3. A number of adjustments may be needed to the management accounts – e.g. for accrual and prepayments – in order to arrive at a set of figures that complies with accounting principles.

Later on, this chapter uses the example of the Environ Alliance Trust to illustrate how the information from management accounts is translated into a format that complies with SORP.

1. Who uses financial statements?

The list of people who might need the information provided by financial statements seems to grow longer every day. Some of them are directly connected with the organisation: for example, its employees and managers. Others are not directly connected, but may be affected by its management of finance or its financial stability: for example, the general public.

Here is a list of user groups which is by no means exhaustive but which covers the main categories:

- The trustees of voluntary organisations.
- Managers, employees and prospective employees.
- Donors and sponsors.
- Grant-making bodies.
- The beneficiary stakeholders using the services of the charity.
- Suppliers.
- Lenders and potential lenders.
- The government, including the Charity Commission, Companies House, Inland Revenue and Customs.
- The public.

TRUSTEES OF VOLUNTARY ORGANISATIONS

The trustees are legally responsible for the financial resources entrusted to the organisation, and therefore need to assure not only that the accounts comply with the Charity Accounting SORP, but also that they properly describe the voluntary organisation's activities and financial position.

MANAGERS, EMPLOYEES AND PROSPECTIVE EMPLOYEES

The managers of a voluntary organisation need financial information to help them manage the business. They need past information to help them monitor the progress of the business (or their part of it), current information to carry out day-to-day operational management and control, and forecast information to plan activities in the future.

Employees and trade unions may consult the financial statements when they are negotiating pay and terms of employment. Current and prospective employees might be wise to examine the accounts to assess whether the organisation is likely to grow and prosper, or whether it (and the job!) will have disappeared by this time next year.

DONORS AND SPONSORS

People and organisations who donate money to voluntary organisations, or who otherwise sponsor their activities, might use the financial statements to check that they are happy with the way the organisation is handling its funds.

GRANT MAKING BODIES

Many grant making bodies will use the financial statements to obtain a better appreciation of what the organisation does and how it is managed. In particular, they often use the financial statements – wrongly, in my view – to determine the level of reserves available to the organisation, and on this basis decide whether funding will be granted.

For many voluntary organisations, restricted project funding may form a large part of their reserves as disclosed in the financial statements. However, since these project funds are restricted, they are not available for another purpose.

Grant making bodies will also use financial statements to determine how well the voluntary organisation is managed. Although useful insights can be obtained by using key ratios, sometimes grant makers pay too much attention to the figures for management and administration costs in isolation.

The beneficiary stakeholders using the services of the charity

This group of users may be paying for services or receiving them free of charge, but in either case they will want to use financial statements to assess how effectively and efficiently those services are being delivered. Their particular concern will be whether the voluntary organisation has sufficient resources, present and future, to support their continuing needs.

Suppliers

Potential suppliers want to know whether their customer will be able to pay for the goods and services supplied. Furthermore, many customer-supplier relationships are long term and require a considerable investment of time and money. A supplier will want to be sure of the long-term viability of the other party before making the effort.

Lenders and potential lenders

Banks and others who lend money to voluntary organisations will need information about the organisation's ability to make interest payments in the short term and ultimately to repay the loan on its due date. They will also be concerned about the security for their loan: does the organisation have valuable items, or assets, that could be sold to raise the money to repay the loan if necessary?

The government, including the Charity Commission, Companies House, Inland Revenue and Customs

The Inland Revenue, for example, will need to consult the voluntary organisation's financial statements to determine whether there is a tax liability arising from any trading activities. The Charity Commission in general will require financial statements and annual returns from registered charities as part of its monitoring activities. Other government departments and agencies may require financial and non-financial statistics to monitor the state of the economy.

The public

Voluntary organisations rely to a large extent upon the goodwill of the public in donating money to their causes, and are also able to take advantage of a range of tax concessions. As taxpayers and ratepayers, the public often use financial statements to decide whether to give to a particular charity or not, on the basis of how efficiently it is managed.

2. Converting management accounts to SORP accounts

Converting internal management accounts, prepared on an income and expenditure basis, to a set of final year and accounts is essentially a process of apportionment. The management accounts contain the income and expenditure results for the different departments of the organisation, reflecting the structure of the organisation. These may be departments involved in the provision of charitable services or departments that support the organisation as a whole: for example, the finance or human resource departments.

The expenditure within each of these departments must be identified and apportioned between the main expenditure headings identified in the SORP: direct charitable expenditure, fundraising and publicity, management and administration.

The income within each department must be reviewed to identify, firstly, that which represents restricted funds and that which is unrestricted funds; and secondly, the different sources of income, such as donations, grants etc.

Figure 6.1 uses the Environ Alliance Trust budget results (see figure 3.10) to show how this process of apportionment is carried out. A number of assumptions and simplifications have been necessary:

1. The basis of apportionment is the number of staff in each department:
- *Services development:* three project staff and one director.
- *Research and policy:* three project staff and one director.

Figure 6.1: Staff and running costs

DESCRIPTION	This forecast £	DESCRIPTION	This forecast £
STAFF COSTS		**RUNNING COSTS**	
Chief executive	45,000	Chief executive	7,930
Research and policy	77,011	Research and policy	62,731
Services development	121,940	Services development	88,060
Membership	10,638	Membership	37,162
Non-team	16,675	Non-team	30,375
TOTAL STAFF COSTS	271,264	TOTAL RUNNING COSTS	226,258

Figure 6.2: The allocation table

The headings in this table correspond to the information required in the notes to the accounts; the split between headings for the purpose of this example is arbitrary.

	Salaries	Other staff costs	Premises	Dep'n	Other running costs	Total Expenditure	
Non-team running costs			14,825	3,400	12,150	30,375	
Internal recharge			−14,825	−3,400	−12,150	−30,375	
NON TEAM	0	0	0	0	0	0	
Chief executive's office	42,500	2,500			7,930	52,930	
Internal recharge	−42,500	−2,500			−7,930	−52,930	
	0	0	0	0	0	0	
Services development:							
Director	36,000	585			6,280	42,865	
S1	30,000	2,010			30,365	62,375	
S2	27,500	1,840			36,790	66,130	
S3	22,500	1,505			14,625	38,630	
Internal recharge from							
1) CEO	**14,167**	**833**			**2,643**	**17,643**	
2) Non-team			4,941	1,133	4,050	10,124	
Internal recharge to							
1) Management & admin @ 5%	**−1,800**	**−29**			**−314**	**−2,143**	2,143
	128,367	6,744	4,941	1,133	94,439	235,624	

- *Membership services:* one staff member and one director.
- *Fundraising, finance and administration:* one staff member spending half her time on fundraising activities and the other half on finance, and one part-time director.
- The total headcount for the organisation equals 12 which is used when apportioning non direct costs.

Figure 6.2—continued

Research & policy:

Director	23,000	103			7,758	30,861	
P1	18,650	1,458			25,870	45,978	
P2	18,256	1,427			15,950	35,633	
P3	13,094	1,023			13,153	27,270	
Internal recharge from							
1) CEO	**14,167**	**833**			**2,643**	**17,643**	
2) Non-team			**4,942**	**1,133**	**4,050**	**10,125**	
Internal recharge to							
1) Management & admin @ 5%	−1,150	−5			−388	−1,543	1,543
	86,017	4,839	4,942	1,133	69,036	165,967	

Membership services:

Director	5,375				3,704	9,079	
M1	4,500	763			33,458	38,721	
Internal recharge from							
1) CEO	**7,083**	**417**			**1,322**	**8,822**	
2) Non-team			**2,471**	**567**	**2,025**	**5,063**	
Internal recharge to							
1) Management & admin @ 5%	−269	0			−185	−454	454
	16,689	1,180	2,471	567	40,324	61,231	

Non-Team staff :

Director	5,000					5,000	
Finance, fundraising and admin	11,000	675				11,675	
Internal recharge from							
1) CEO	**7,083**	**417**			**1,322**	**8,822**	
2) Non-team			**2,471**	**567**	**2,025**	**5,063**	
	23,083	1,092	2,471	567	3,347	30,560	
Internal recharge to							
1) Management & admin (2/3)	15,389	728	1,647	378	2,231	20,373	+ 4,140 = 24,513
2) Fundraising (1/3)	7,694	364	824	189	1,116	10,187	
	23,083	1,092	2,471	567	3,347	30,560	

Figure 6.3: Restricted funds from budget

Description	This forecast £
INCOME	
Chief executive	100
Research and policy	93,912
Services development	99,785
Membership	121,000
Non-team	196,980
TOTAL INCOME	511,777

	Total Expenditure	Restricted Income	Project Restricted Expenditure	Unrestricted Expenditure
Services Development:	235,624	85,000	85,000	150,624
Research & Policy	165,967	55,650	55,650	110,317
Membership	61,231			61,231
	462,822	140,650	140,650	322,172
Fundraising	10,187			10,187
Management & Admin	24,513			24,513
	34,700			34,700
	497,522	140,650	140,650	356,872

2. Because Environ Alliance is a membership-driven organisation providing services that are mainly financed by unrestricted funds, there are no restricted fund balances carried forward.
3. Non-team running costs comprise premises costs, depreciation and other running costs; the directors of each department spend 5 per cent of their time and running costs on administration.
4. The last forecast results, as shown in the September budget (figure 3.10), are those used to produce the year end results.

The same process is followed for the other departments as shown in figure 6.2-continued.

Figure 6.4: Extract from statement of financial activities

ENVIRON ALLIANCE TRUST
Year ended 31 March 19X9

	Unrestricted fund £	Restricted funds £	Total funds 19X9 £
INCOME AND EXPENDITURE ACCOUNT			
Incoming resources			
Grants received	108,697	85,000	193,697
Donations and other voluntary income	141,330	55,650	196,980
Membership subscriptions	121,000	–	121,000
Total incoming resources	371,027	140,650	511,677
Resources expended			
Direct charitable expenditure			
Policy and research	110,317	55,650	165,967
Services development	150,624	85,000	235,624
Membership services	61,231	–	61,231
	322,172	140,650	462,822
Other expenditure			
Fundraising	10,187	–	10,187
Management and administration	24,513	–	24,513
Total resources expended	356,872	140,650	497,522
Net incoming resources for the year	14,155	–	14,155

The next stage is to identify restricted funding for the different departments. This has been done in figure 6.3.

The figure shows the total expenditure for each department, including the apportionments made for CEO and non-team costs. This is then set off against the restricted funding received (in this example arbitrary), leaving the remainder financed from unrestricted funds.

The final stage is to fit these figures into an extract of a Statement of Financial Activities as shown in figure 6.4.

7.
Tax and voluntary organisations

1. VAT and voluntary organisations
2. Questions and answers about VAT and the voluntary sector
3. VAT planning for voluntary organisations
4. The currrent system of Tax relief on giving
5. Review of charity taxation

This section highlights key aspects of taxation and how they affect voluntary organisations. The purpose of including a description of taxation in a financial management guide is to help voluntary organisations maximise their resources by maximising the use of the many tax advantages that exist.

Voluntary organisations enjoy a range of tax benefits by virtue of their charitable activities and their role in society. These concessions are given under direct tax (income tax) when donations are received by deed or gift aid; and indirect tax (VAT) when certain expenditures qualify for zero-rating, for example.

This section aims to ensure that organisations are aware of how these concessions operate and how to organise their activities so as to maximise the value of the concessions.

Commercial organisations that trade act on 'behalf' of Customs when accounting for VAT. Such organisations generally charge VAT on the products and services they supply, and will incur VAT on supplies brought in. The company will account to Customs, periodically paying over or reclaiming the net amount (the difference between VAT charged and incurred) There is a cash flow effect, when the company must either pay the net amount to Customs or claim a refund.

As a general rule, it will only be possible to set off VAT incurred on trading expenses if VAT was charged on the initial sale of goods. In the company's accounting statements both income and expenditure will be shown net of VAT; therefore VAT does not affect the profitability, or otherwise, of commercial organisations.

The VAT treatment of voluntary organisations and charities is different, however. VAT is a tax on sales, and is therefore applicable when a trade or business is being carried on. Voluntary organisations do not generally carry on trading activities, and yet, as an end purchaser of products and services, will incur VAT on supplies they buy in. Unlike commercial organisations that charge VAT on products and are therefore eligible to reclaim by set-off VAT on supplies brought in, most voluntary organisations and charities have a mixture of income sources, some liable to VAT (for example, sponsorship) and some outside the scope of VAT (for example, voluntary donations). Because voluntary organisations and charities have this mixture of income sources, their ability to reclaim by set-off VAT on supplies brought in is restricted to those activities which are VAT liable.

It should by now be apparent that, for voluntary organisations and charities, VAT is a genuine expense. It is commonly referred to as 'irrecoverable VAT' and has to be written off as an expense. One objective of financial management is to minimise the amount of irrecoverable VAT; this can usually be done by taking maximum advantage of the VAT reliefs available when supplies are made to charities and by planning, for example, fundraising and the provision of services in a way that minimises the risk of such activities being liable to VAT.

It is estimated that the voluntary sector as a whole loses up to £400 million a year in irrecoverable VAT. There has been much campaigning, by NCVO and others, to have this situation rectified. At the time of writing, the government had launched a review of charity taxation and was inviting submissions from all interested parties. The sector is awaiting publication of a consultation paper setting out the government's proposed intentions. However, any reforms, particularly concerning VAT, might well be limited because of EU restrictions.

1. VAT AND VOLUNTARY ORGANISATIONS

Voluntary organisations are under increasing pressure to generate income through fundraising, trading and contracts. Some of these activities can lead to VAT liabilities, and incorrect treatment of VAT may result in penalties being imposed. Every organisation must acquire a basic understanding of VAT and be able to identify potential problems which may have to be referred to a specialist adviser.

This section gives the essential background to VAT. It addresses the main issues for voluntary organisations through a question and answer section; and it gives valuable planning points and information about how to find out more.

INPUT TAX AND OUTPUT TAX

Value Added Tax (VAT) is a tax on the supply of goods and services. It is administered by HM Customs and Excise (referred to hereafter as Customs), and is distinct from Income Tax and Corporation Tax, which are administered by the Inland Revenue. VAT was introduced in the UK by the Finance Act 1972 and came into force from 1 April 1973. It operates in all the countries of the European Union, although the rates and applications vary to some extent. VAT law in the European Union is governed by various directives, notably the Sixth VAT Directive

(1977). The main UK legislation is the Value Added Tax Act 1994 as updated by amending legislation and through changes made in the Finance Acts following the Chancellor's budget. The Customs booklet entitled *The VAT Guide* (ref 700) covers all the main rules and procedures, and is essential reading.

Broadly, an organisation that is registered for VAT is required to pay to Customs in a given accounting period the VAT charged to customers (output tax) after deducting the VAT paid to suppliers (input tax).

When an organisation sells goods and services to others, and adds VAT to the amount charged, this is known as output tax. Output tax is VAT levied on sales. When an organisation purchases goods and services from others and is charged VAT, this is known as input tax. Input tax is VAT incurred on purchases. The Customs pamphlet *The ins and outs of VAT* (ref 700/15) is a brief guide to output tax and input tax.

From a consumer's point of view, VAT is a tax on the final transaction in the chain of supplying taxable goods or services. As there is no way of knowing whether a transaction is going to be the final one, VAT is charged at every stage, with provision for credit to be given to the supplier for the VAT that has been charged at the stage before. From the tax gatherer's point of view (i.e. Customs), the tax is the sum total of the amounts collected on the value added at successive stages from manufacture to retail sale.

If organisation A sells goods to organisation B and charges VAT on the sale, this VAT is output tax from the point of view of organisation A, the supplier. However, it is input tax from the point of view of organisation B, the purchaser. Figure 7.1 illustrates this.

Figure 7.1: VAT claim purchase of a computer by a voluntary organisation

	Goods	VAT Charge (e.g.)		Net VAT
Component company	Components	100		100
Manufacturer	Finished computer	250	(100)	150
Wholesaler	Computers	300	(250)	50
Retailer	Computer	400	(300)	100
Charity	No business supply			

Source: NCVO

WHAT FALLS WITHIN THE SCOPE OF VAT?

The EU sixth Directive defines activity within the scope of VAT as 'the supply of goods and services . . . by a taxable person'. A 'taxable person' is defined as 'any person who independently carries out any [of the above] activities, whatever the purpose or results of that activity'. Furthermore, it specifically includes producers, traders and persons supplying services – including mining and agricultural activities – and the activities of professionals. The exploitation of tangible or intangible property to obtain income on a continuing basis is also included. UK legislation provides additionally that the activities of clubs and societies shall be deemed to be within the scope of VAT if they would not otherwise fall under the criteria set out above.

Thus it can be seen that the scope of VAT is wide. But beware of equating this concept with taxable activities: bizarre as it may seem, an activity can be exempt from VAT but still within its scope. It is a good rule of thumb to think of business activities as falling within the scope of VAT and non-business activities as falling outside its scope.

As a consequence, activities within the scope of VAT can be treated as (a) positive rated, (b) zero rated and (c) exempt. There are considerable practical differences between these three categories, to which we shall return later. At this stage, however, it seems appropriate to look at the other side of the coin, and to ascertain what falls outside the scope of VAT.

WHAT IS OUTSIDE THE SCOPE OF VAT?

An organisation that does nothing but provide free services funded by donations and grants will not be treated as a business and so will be entirely outside the scope of VAT. This means that it does not charge VAT on its outputs, but neither can it reclaim VAT on its inputs. As a result, it will have to bear the cost of VAT on its purchases, like any private individual buying goods.

But an organisation usually has a mixture of supplies, both within and outside the scope. Money flows that are not 'in consideration' (see glossary) of goods and services are not counted as being in the course or furtherance of a business, and are thus outside the scope of VAT. They can never give rise to a VAT charge. Examples are gifts of money (for example, donations, legacies) and dividends from stocks and shares.

Income that is outside the scope of VAT includes:

- Donations, legacies and bequests.
- Membership subscriptions, provided they are not in exchange for any benefits.
- Funds raised for no return (e.g. flag days, sponsored walks), but not sales or admission fees.
- Grants from public funds, provided they are not in return for services.
- Dividends from equities (but not bank deposit interest and other loan interest, which is technically exempt).
- Trading of equities (only where a charity is concerned; otherwise it would be exempt).

For a donation to be outside the scope of VAT, it must be freely given, with no prospect of a benefit being gained in return; and for a grant to be outside the scope, it must not relate to specific services performed in return. This is often difficult to judge. In very general terms, however, a payment is a grant if the charity sets the agenda and seeks a grant to match expected spending, whilst if the grant maker sets the agenda, the payment is probably consideration for services rendered.

Figure 7.2 illustrates how the activities of an organisation may fall inside or outside the scope of VAT:

Figure 7.2: Activities within and outside the scope of VAT

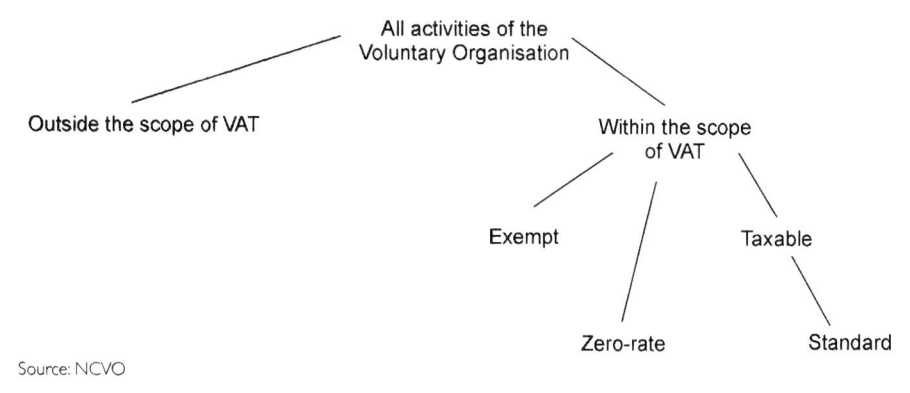

```
              All activities of the
              Voluntary Organisation
           /                         \
Outside the scope of VAT          Within the scope
                                      of VAT
                                  /           \
                               Exempt        Taxable
                                 /              \
                            Zero-rate        Standard
```

Source: NCVO

VAT REGISTRATION

An organisation is required to register for VAT if its' taxable supplies, taken together, exceed a certain figure per annum (£50,000 as at April 1998). This is known as the 'registration threshold'. In addition to standard rated supplies, zero-rated and lower rate supplies count towards the registration threshold.

The difference between zero rated and exempt

This is one of the most difficult concepts to grasp in VAT. Essentially, the zero rate provides that:

- No VAT is chargeable, but a registered person may recover the input tax on related expenses.
- Examples of zero-rated supplies that may be made by voluntary organisations (as at October 1997) are books, periodicals and other publications, certain aids designed for use by handicapped persons, the sale of donated goods, distribution of goods overseas.

Exempt supplies are:

- Excluded from registration threshold calculations.
- No VAT is chargeable.

- VAT is not recoverable on related expenses, subject to certain special exceptions; see questions B2 and C6 and de minimis rules (see VAT Notice 706).
- Examples of exempt supplies (as at October 1997) include youth club services, welfare services, education, research, vocational training, provision of health care by a relevant body.

An organisation is not required to charge VAT on goods and services which it supplies (output tax) unless it is registered or registrable for VAT.

Once registered for VAT, it is important for the organisation to distinguish between zero-rated supplies, exempt supplies and supplies that are outside the scope of VAT altogether. Although all result in a nil VAT charge, they are treated differently in respect of reclaiming VAT.

PAYING AND RECLAIMING VAT

There is no general relief giving charities or voluntary organisations exemption from VAT; this is a mistaken idea held by a large number of enquirers to NCVO. Under normal circumstances, when a voluntary organisation buys goods and services, it has to pay any VAT charged by the supplier.

Broadly speaking, all organisations have to pay VAT on their purchases and expenses. If an organisation is registered for VAT, it also has to charge VAT (output tax) on goods and services that it supplies to others and pay it over to Customs, unless the goods and services are outside the scope of VAT, exempt or zero-rated.

However, if an organisation is registered for VAT, it is able to reclaim some or all of the VAT paid on its purchases and expenses (input tax). It does this by reducing the amount of output tax payable to Customs, by deducting any input tax charged on related supplies.

For example, a charity might sell calendars to raise funds, on which it charged VAT at the standard rate to its customers. The same charity might also provide vocational training (usually exempt from VAT). Any input VAT paid when buying equipment to be used in providing training services could not be reclaimed, as the related outputs are exempt (subject to the partial exemption de minimis limits). The charity could claim back VAT on inputs related to its standard rated supplies, such as paper for the calendars, but could not claim back VAT related to its exempt supplies, such as VAT paid when purchasing equipment to be used in providing its training services.

Figure 7.3 illustrates when VAT on inputs can be reclaimed.

Input VAT may relate partly to a business supply and partly to a non-business supply, or partly to a taxable supply and partly to an exempt supply. For example, general office expenditure such as telephone and photocopier costs may not be directly attributable to any particular supply. It should be apportioned between the different supplies, to calculate the proportion of the VAT which can be reclaimed. See question C6 below for an explanation of partial exemption and apportionment.

Figure 7.3: Reclaimable VAT

Input VAT related to output of:	Can input VAT be recovered?
(a) Non-business supply (outside the scope of VAT)	No VAT recovery
(b) Business supply:	
Taxable supply (standard or zero-rated)	Full VAT recovery
Exempt supply	No VAT recovery (unless below de minimis limits; see question B2)

Source: NCVO

CAN OUR ORGANISATION BE CLASSED AS A CHARITY FOR VAT PURPOSES?

The VAT law provides for certain specific supplies made to or by charities to be zero-rated or exempted from VAT where they would otherwise be positive rated. These are not available to voluntary organisations which are not classed as 'charities'. So it is important to know whether your organisation is treated as a charity for VAT purposes. Such organisations include:

- *Registered charities:* charities in England and Wales registered with the Charity Commission under the Charities Act 1993.
- *Exempted charities:* certain charities, such as universities, places of worship and industrial and provident and friendly societies, are exempted from Charities Act registration, as are charities in Scotland and Northern Ireland.
- *Non profit making bodies with charitable objects:* certain bodies are publicly recognised as charitable although not registered as such. For VAT treatment as charities, they must be able to demonstrate that they are non profit making bodies with written charitable objects. These objects include the relief of poverty, the advancement of education, the advancement of religion, and certain other activities beneficial to the community.

There is no cut and dried definition of 'charity' and you may need to check the circumstances of your organisation against existing case law. The Charity Commission and the Inland Revenue can give guidance.

2. QUESTIONS AND ANSWERS ABOUT VAT AND THE VOLUNTARY SECTOR

This section further explains how VAT affects voluntary organisations and charities by using frequently-asked questions. These questions have been categorised as follows:

A: About VAT and voluntary organisations
B: Exemptions and reliefs
C: Specific cases
D: Administration of VAT

A1. Why do we have to bother about VAT?
Charities and other voluntary organisations are not exempt from VAT and are treated by Customs in the same way as any business. There are severe penalties for failing to register for VAT at the correct time for any organisation whose 'taxable' income exceeds the compulsory registration threshold. Indeed, it may even be beneficial to register voluntarily to enable the recovery of all or part of the VAT you pay to your suppliers. You can register voluntarily as long as you make some taxable supplies, however low the value.

A2. Does charitable status mean we do not have to pay VAT?
No. Charitable status only relieves charities from paying VAT on an extremely limited number of purchases (see question B1 below).

A3. When must we register for VAT purposes?
There are two main criteria for determining when you must register for VAT:

- If at the end of any month the value of your taxable supplies (i.e. sales of goods and services excluding capital assets) made in the course of business activities in the previous 12 months or less has exceeded the registration threshold.
- If at any time, there are reasonable grounds for believing that the value of your taxable supplies in the next 30 days alone will exceed the registration threshold.

You should notify Customs within 30 days of either of these criteria being met. In the case of the first criterion, you will be registered with effect from the beginning of the month following notification. For the second criterion, the registration will be effective from the beginning of the month in which the qualifying supplies will be made.

Additionally, under EU law, if you are not VAT registered under the above criteria, you may be liable to register if you purchase goods from suppliers in other EU member states, or sell goods to customers in other EU member states or purchase services from abroad

A4. My suppliers say we can recover the VAT they charge – true or false?
VAT incurred which is wholly attributed to a non-business income – such as donations, grants, collections etc – cannot be recovered. VAT which cannot be attributed to any particular supply, such as general office expenditure (e.g. telephones, photocopier), must be apportioned. Only that element which relates to your business supplies can be recovered. You can normally only recover the VAT you are

charged when it can be wholly attributed to a 'taxable' business supply (i.e. a supply liable to positive-rate or zero-rate VAT). VAT incurred which can be wholly attributed to an exempt business supply can only be recovered if it is under the de minimis limit (see question B2 below).

A5. Even if our organisation does not have to register, what do we need to know about VAT?

If your organisation makes taxable supplies you should ensure, at the end of each month, that the registration threshold has not been exceeded. If you are a charity, certain purchases you make are relieved from VAT (see question B1).

A6. Does VAT apply differently to a voluntary organisation as compared to a charity?

Generally speaking the answer is no. However, there are certain reliefs over and above the general zero-rate and exempt supplies available to all, which enable charities to purchase and supply certain goods and services without the need to incur or charge VAT (see question B1).

A7. What is the difference between a voluntary organisation and a commercial organisation as far as VAT is concerned?

There is little difference, for VAT purposes, between a voluntary organisation and a commercial organisation. Both must administer VAT under the same regulations. In practice, a voluntary organisation will have greater difficulty in recovering the VAT it is charged by its suppliers because of the restriction on the recovery of VAT incurred on both its exempt and 'non-business' activities.

A8. We have heard that other charities register for VAT in order to claim their VAT back. How can we arrange to do this?

You are allowed to register for VAT if you have some taxable supplies, even if these are less than the registration threshold. But you cannot register if you do not intend to make taxable supplies. Even if you register, this does not automatically give you the right to reclaim VAT (see the sections on exempt and non-business activity). Otherwise, if you register voluntarily, you may find that the VAT cost on your supplies outweighs the VAT you could claim and you would then be worse off.

A9. How do we calculate the value of our taxable turnover to decide if we must register?

Taxable turnover is the value of all business supplies made in the UK within the last 12 months or less, that are liable to VAT at either the standard, reduced or zero rate. Supplies of goods or services that are 'capital assets' of the organisation can be disregarded, with the exception of any interest in, right over or licence to occupy any land which is not zero-rated. For example, if you sold your office computer, the sale proceeds would be disregarded when calculating taxable turnover to decide whether you must register.

B1. What special exemptions and reliefs are there for charities?
The VAT reliefs available to charities may be placed in one of two categories:

1. Those which enable certain purchases to be made without incurring a VAT charge.
2. Those which enable certain supplies of goods and services to be made without the need to make a VAT charge.

The main reliefs include purchases that can be zero-rated:

- Construction costs of a building to be used for certain residential and certain charity 'non-business' uses.
- Some advertising and printing costs.
- Certain medical and scientific equipment and medicinal products.
- Certain equipment designed for use by handicapped people.
- Talking books and wireless sets for blind people.

Supplies on which VAT need not be charged: (a) zero-rated:

- Sales of goods donated to the charity, so long as the goods are offered to the general public and not sold by way of private deal. The relief does, however, include sales of substandard items to recycling agents. The relief also applies to taxable persons who have covenanted to give all the profits of that supply to a charity, but only if they are selling donated goods in the manner described above.
- Goods which are exported free of charge by a charity are deemed to be zero rated supplies made in the course of business. Where exports are paid for, these are zero rated for all types of organisation.

Supplies on which VAT need not be charged: (b) exempt:

- Income from one-off fundraising events. In order to be classified as 'one-off', the events must not be part of a series and must take place sufficiently infrequently to be regarded as having no impact on local commercial providers. It is possible to hold the events more frequently if they take place at considerable distances from each other. Customs does not usually accept dinners and participative sports as such events unless there is an unequivocal fundraising aim or objective. This is an area where law and practice changes frequently, and it is therefore wise to take professional advice.
- Certain welfare services and related goods. Welfare provided otherwise than for profit is included in the exemption. Where medically trained personnel provide the services, or supervise it closely, this is also included.
- Certain educational supplies. This will usually involve training carers, be they voluntary or professional, or training sufferers of various conditions to deal with their circumstances.

- The supply of spiritual welfare in a religious community.
- The supply of transport services for sick or injured persons in vehicles specially designed for that purpose.

B2. What is the difference between exempt status and zero-rating?

Although you do not need to charge VAT on any supply which is exempt or zero-rated, it is essential to establish into which category a supply falls. This is to determine how much VAT you can recover as input tax. VAT incurred which can be attributed to a zero-rate supply can be recovered in full, subject to the normal requirements. VAT incurred which can be attributed to an exempt supply can only be recovered if it falls below the partial exemption de minimis limit (currently £625 per month on average, and the exempt input tax should be no more than 50 per cent of total input tax) in any given VAT year. The means of calculating the amount of VAT attributed to exempt supplies can be complex and will often require special negotiation with Customs.

B3. What is the significance of certain incomes we receive being classed as 'non-business' income?

Examples of non-business incomes include: donations, street collections, grants, bequests and legacies. VAT should not be accounted for on these incomes because they are not consideration for a supply of either goods or services (see VAT glossary for definition of 'Consideration'). However, VAT which is incurred on attributable costs cannot be recovered as input tax. As with B2 above, the means of calculating the tax related to non-business activities can be complex. It is sometimes possible to ignore non-business income (e.g. grants) if it supports taxable activities.

C1. What is the difference between grants and contracts for VAT purposes?

A grant, for VAT purposes, is money freely given at the discretion of the donor without prospect of anything in return. On the other hand, for example, payment from a local authority in return for services under a contract is subject to VAT, unless the supply is contained within the general exemption reliefs: for example, certain educational, health care and welfare services. In practice, the difference between these two can be difficult to determine, and there are many borderline cases.

C2. We have been told to charge VAT on our membership services – is this a new ruling?

No. In order to determine the VAT liability of a membership subscription, it is necessary to establish all the benefits received by the member. Each benefit must be valued on either a cost basis or an open market value basis. The appropriate VAT liability is then applied to each benefit. A membership subscription may include supplies which are standard-rated, zero-rated (e.g. publications), exempt (e.g. insurance) and outside the scope of VAT altogether, such as a donation. Such calculations must be done on a regular basis and details recorded, and should usually be agreed with your local VAT office.

A subscription to a charity is treated as a donation when it entitles the member to nothing more than the right to receive copies of financial accounts and reports on the charity's activities, and to vote at general meetings.

C3. What exemptions are there for welfare services?

For VAT purposes, welfare services include 'the provision of care, treatment or instruction designed to promote the physical or mental well being of elderly, sick, distressed or disabled people'. It also includes the protection of children and young persons, and certain religious activities. To be exempt, the welfare services must be provided 'otherwise than for profit'. This means that if a profit is made, it is applied solely to the furtherance of the welfare activity that generated it. If any profit is used for a different charitable activity, albeit within the same charity, then the supply of welfare is standard-rated.

Welfare supplies made by charities at 'below cost' are classed as non-business supplies. For this purpose Customs has indicated that it will accept that an activity is carried on below cost if the cost of providing the welfare supply is subsidised by at least 15 per cent from the charity's other funds. This calculation of cost and subsidy should include organisational overheads (e.g. accommodation and team services). However, the legislation does not include this formula and there may be room to negotiate a better deal with Customs.

C4. Our landlord has charged VAT on rent – is there a way round paying the VAT element?

Rents payable under a lease agreement are exempt from VAT. In order for a landlord to charge VAT, he or she is required formally to waive their exemption over his/her interest in the property. This is commonly termed 'opting to tax' the property. The landlord who elects to do so can charge VAT unless the lease contract specifies otherwise. If you are being charged VAT, you should ensure that your landlord has opted to tax by requesting to see his or her notification to Customs.

If you are a charity, your landlord is not, however, able to charge VAT on any rent which relates to an area of the property which is used solely for non-business activities. A landlord is entitled to opt to tax the rent of office premises, even if they are to be used to support the non-business charity purposes. Offices used to carry out the non-business purposes, as opposed to supporting them, are usually treated other than as an office.

When negotiating a lease, your charity might wish to have a clause in the agreement that would prevent your landlord from increasing your rent charge by opting to tax. Further information is contained in the Customs leaflet *Land and property* (ref 742).

C5. We receive income for sponsorship from commercial organisations – should we charge VAT on this income?

Such income tends to arise in two circumstances. First, a payment may be made by a company for allowing them to sponsor an aspect of the charity's work. Typically, this will involve the sponsor's logo and advertisement appearing in connection with the charity activity. Second, the sponsor will ask the charity to associate itself and its own logo with the sponsor's product. For example, in the case of affinity cards, the logo of the charity is used to promote financial services.

In both cases the payment received is consideration for promotional services. These are usually standard rated. This may not be the case if the sponsor is based entirely overseas. It may not be the case if the sponsorship is associated with a one-off fund raising event, as it will then probably be exempt. Typically, only one-fifth of the payment associated with affinity cards need be taxable, as long as contracts are carefully structured. Affinity card arrangements can also sometimes be exempt from VAT. This is a complex area on which you will probably need to take professional advice

C6. What is partial exemption/apportionment?

As discussed in question A4, you can normally only recover VAT you incur when it can be wholly attributed to a taxable business supply and not when it relates to an exempt supply, subject to the partial exemption de minimis limit of £625 per month on average. An annual adjustment is carried out at the end of each VAT year to ensure that monthly fluctuations are averaged over the year.

VAT which cannot be apportioned to any particular supply, such as that incurred on general overhead costs (e.g. telephones, photocopier etc), must be apportioned between an exempt and taxable element so that only that element deemed to relate to your taxable supplies can be recovered. The standard method of apportionment, which can be used without Customs' prior permission, is based on the ratio taxable turnover bears to total business turnover. Any other method (for example, staff ratios or values of purchases for each sector) requires Customs prior approval. See Customs Notice (ref 706) on partial exemption.

D1. What are the penalties regarding VAT and what are the liabilities for trustees?

Customs may apply the following civil penalties:

For belated notification of requirement to register
Up to 9 months late: 5 per cent of net VAT due
More than 9 months: 10 per cent of net VAT due
More than 18 months: 15 per cent of net VAT due

For late payment of tax due on a VAT return (default surcharge
First late payment: no surcharge, warning liability notice issued
Second late payment within 12 months of first: default surcharge of 2 per cent of net VAT due

Third and subsequent late payment: 5 per cent, rising in 5 per cent increments to 15 per cent

Default interest
Interest is payable on certain underdeclarations and overclaims of VAT either notified to Customs or identified by them on inspection. The interest is seen by Customs as representing commercial restitution. Accordingly, it will not levy the interest where it can be shown that the person who would have paid the VAT charge would have been able to recover it.

Misdeclaration penalty
15 per cent penalty if undisclosed error on VAT return is discovered by Customs and the error exceeds 30 per cent of gross amount of tax (output tax plus input tax on return), or £1 million or more.

There are numerous other civil penalties which Customs can apply, including persistent misdeclaration penalty of 15 per cent, incorrect certificates claiming zero-rating and breaches of regulatory provisions (e.g. failure to keep the required books and records). Trustees are liable for the VAT debts of charities just as they are for other classes of debt.

D2. If I raise a query with the Customs Office, will this lead to an inspection?
It is unlikely that a general enquiry made at your local VAT office will generate an inspection of your VAT affairs. However, should your enquiry imply that you have been incorrectly accounting for VAT, a Customs Officer may wish to pay you a visit.

3. VAT PLANNING FOR VOLUNTARY ORGANISATIONS

VOLUNTARY REGISTRATION
If your organisation is not required compulsorily to register for VAT, it may be advantageous to consider applying for what is termed a 'voluntary' registration. This may enable a partial recovery of the VAT you incur. If you make 'taxable supplies' in the course of a business activity, no matter how small, you are entitled by law to apply to be registered for VAT purposes.

Before an application is made, you should establish that the VAT you will be able to recover will exceed that which you will have to declare to Customs on your standard-rate activities. This may, however, be less of a problem if your taxable supplies are made to commercial organisations who can recover the VAT you charge to them: for example, sponsorship or advertising services. This is because you would add the VAT on top of your usual charge. You should also bear in mind that, once registered, you will need to maintain the necessary books and records and complete a VAT return either monthly or quarterly.

Maximising VAT recovery

A problem encountered by all voluntary organisations and similar bodies is how they can recover as much of the VAT they are charged as possible. The restriction is caused by the fact that the activities undertaken by such organisations are predominantly outside the scope of VAT (i.e. non-business) or exempt.

VAT incurred which is wholly attributable to non-business and exempt supplies is irrecoverable (subject to the partial exemption de minimis limits). This being so, the scope for increasing recoverable VAT is limited to VAT incurred on non-attributable costs: for example, HQ expenses, general overheads, telephones, rents.

Can you increase your VAT recovery by apportioning this non-attributable VAT using a different method? Consider using:

- Output values (taxable turnover ÷ total turnover).
- Input tax values.
- Staff employed on different activities (taxable staff ÷ total staff).
- Floor area used on different activities (taxable floor area ÷ total floor area).
- Any other method which produces a 'fair and reasonable' result.

You must agree the method with Customs before applying it, but first work out which is best for your recovery rate. Note that where the word 'total' is used, there is room for flexibility; for example, it might exclude areas that have general use only.

Subscription income

The VAT liability of a subscription is determined by the liability of the individual benefits afforded to members. The benefits will often include several publications which are currently zero-rated: common examples are magazines, newsletters, leaflets, handbooks, accounts and reports.

It is possible to minimise the VAT due on subscription income by ensuring that all such publications are correctly valued. Customs will accept valuations based on the cost to the organisation of providing the benefit or valuations based on open market values (OMV). Where it is beneficial to use the OMV basis, those items which are not available to non-subscribers can be given an OMV by applying the average mark-up achieved on other benefits to the item's costs.

Customs are normally willing to repay VAT previously overdeclared on subscription income which has not been correctly apportioned, subject to a three-year cap.

Where a subscription entitles the member to nothing more than the right to receive copies of financial accounts and reports, and the right to vote at general meetings, it is outside the scope of VAT and should be treated as non-business income.

Cash accounting

Your charity may be eligible to account for VAT purely on a cash basis: for example, if its taxable turnover does not exceed £350,000. It is also possible to join the annual accounting scheme (only one VAT return per year) if the taxable turnover is less than £300,000 per year.

Conclusion

VAT and how it affects voluntary organisations and charities is a complex subject that often defies both logic and common sense. It is continually being updated with new provisions contained in Finance Acts, after each Budget, and the results of tribunal cases. Of necessity, it is not possible to provide a detailed explanation of VAT within this book. Further references are given at the end of this chapter for those needing more information.

Appendix A provides a registration checklist and Appendix B is a useful glossary of common VAT terms.

4. The current system of tax relief on giving

There are currently four different ways in which taxpayers can give to charity in a tax-efficient manner: covenanted giving, Gift Aid, payroll giving and legacies. (Individuals can also get inheritance tax relief on bequests to charities; however, this subject is beyond the scope of this guide).

Covenants

Under the longest-running scheme for tax relief on contributions, individuals and companies can set up a covenant committing them to donate a fixed amount to a particular charity each year. As long as the covenant runs for a minimum of four years, covenanters can get relief from income or corporation tax on their donations. There is no upper limit on the size of covenanted gifts. The charity claims back basic-rate tax on the gift; higher-rate taxpayers can claim the difference between the basic rate and the higher rate from the Inland Revenue tax office. Covenants are the single biggest form of tax-free giving. In the last year for which information is available (1997-98), a total of £1,125 million was donated by companies and individuals, with an associated tax expenditure of some £310 million.

To satisfy the requirements of the Inland Revenue, a number of criteria must be met. The way in which the covenant is worded is of paramount importance.

- A covenant form must state that it is a deed.
- It must be signed and delivered by the covenanter in the presence of a witness.

- The covenant must provide for annual payments to be made year by year and must cover the minimum period of four years.
- A covenant cannot be back-dated. Previous Revenue practice was to allow a payment earlier in the tax year to be validated retrospectively by a deed of covenant. This practice no longer applies after 31 July 1990.

The Inland Revenue publishes a model deed for a form of covenant by an individual to a charity (see Appendix C).

A covenanted payment to a charity must represent pure income profit for the charity. Therefore the charity cannot give any benefit to the donor in return for the covenanted payment. In practice, the Revenue are prepared to accept small benefits (up to 2.5 per cent of a subscription payment) without invalidating the covenant.

The Finance Act 1989 introduced legislation to enable certain charities to grant free admission to their sites in return for a covenanted membership subscription. This allows charities such as the National Trust to grant free admission to members, even though this benefit is perhaps not small relative to the cost of the membership subscription. However, the legislation only applies to a charity if its sole or main purpose is:

- The preservation of property for the public benefit; *or*
- The conservation of wildlife for the public benefit.

Gift Aid

Established in 1990, the Gift Aid scheme provides a way for individuals and companies to get tax relief on one-off donations of money, so long as the donation exceeds a minimum threshold. Originally, the threshold was set at £600 (after deduction of basic rate tax), but this was reduced to £400 from May 1992 and to £250 from March 1993. An original upper limit of £5 million was abolished in March 1991. Donors cannot meet the threshold through a series of smaller gifts or pass on money raised through fundraising by others.

An extension, the Millennium Gift Aid scheme, was introduced in July 1998 to run until 31 December 2000. The scheme reduces the lower limit to £100 on donations to charities supporting education, health and anti-poverty projects in 80 nominated 'poor countries'. The scheme also allows smaller donations to be bundled up and still qualify for tax relief.

Gift Aid as a method of giving money to charity has two major advantages over a deed of covenant. The first is that it is significantly simpler to administer. The donor simply completes a form stating that tax has been deducted from the payment and passes this to the charity with the donation. Indeed, it is not strictly necessary to complete the form at the time the donation is made. It can be completed, often at the charity's request, after the donation has been received. Secondly, Gift Aid applies to one-off payments and thus there is no necessity to commit the donor to regular giving over four years.

The operation of Gift Aid is very similar to that of a covenant. Donations are made net of basic-rate tax; the charity recovers the basic-rate tax, and higher-rate taxpayers may claim additional tax relief on the grossed-up amount from their Inland Revenue tax office. A total of £583 million was donated in 1997-98, of which £260 million was donated by individuals. Tax repayments to charities on these gifts amounted to £177 million.

GIVE AS YOU EARN

Payroll giving schemes, or Give As You Earn (GAYE), were established in 1987. Under such schemes, employees can authorise their employer to deduct amounts from their pay and nominate the charities to which their gifts should go. This requires the employer to contract with a collection agency approved by the Inland Revenue. The donation is deducted from pay *before* calculating tax due under Pay As You Earn (PAYE). The key difference between tax deductions and conventional tax credits is the possibility (as with pension deductions, for example) that giving to charity can move taxpayers to a lower marginal tax rate. Since an individual's taxable income is calculated net of all donations, the deduction itself could move the individual from higher to the basic rate. This is also true of covenanted payments.

On GAYE's introduction, gifts made under payroll-giving schemes could not exceed £120 a year. Since then, the upper limit has been raised from time to time and it currently stands at £1,200. By 1996-97, 370,000 employees were participating (reflecting 5,200 contracted employers), although the total amount donated through payroll-giving schemes is considerably less than that given by covenant or Gift Aid: £27 million in 1997-98. The cost of the income tax relief was £6 million.

5. REVIEW OF CHARITY TAXATION

The review of charity taxation was announced by the Chancellor in the July 1997 Budget. It is intended to create a system which:

- Is more coherent and consistent.
- Is simple to administer.
- Reduces charities' compliance costs.
- Reduces the scope for charity tax reliefs to be exploited for tax avoidance purposes.
- Is more receptive to the needs of today's charities.

The review will consider incentives to encourage giving to charities and voluntary organisations, and is taking place over an eighteen-month period. The deadline for initial responses was 1 December 1997.

A summary of the NCVO submission to the government is presented below as an indication of how the future taxation of charities may develop:

Encouraging individual giving

The government should commission and fund research examining whether the US model of tax relief on giving, if adopted in this country, would generate additional income for charities. Such a change could potentially make giving much more attractive to the general public, but this hypothesis needs to be tested.

All donations to charitable organisations should be eligible for tax relief. Rather than a reclaim scheme, the government should consider making 'relief' payments in the form of a partnership grant. This grant could be set at a level higher than the basic rate of income tax.

At the very least the government should:

- Remove the current ceiling on payroll giving or replace it with a cap expressed as a percentage of earnings.
- Reduce the Gift Aid threshold to £100.
- Review the complex rules and procedures involved in covenanting.

In the US and Canada, schemes have been developed which encourage the rich to make large gifts of capital to charitable trusts and foundations. NCVO recommends that the government should consider whether similar initiatives could usefully be developed in this country.

The government should develop and promote a campaign aimed at encouraging individuals to give to charity as part of its commitment to creating a 'giving age'.

Encouraging corporate giving

The government should allow companies to offset all donations in either cash or goods against their corporation tax bill.

Companies with a significant programme of employee volunteering should pay either a reduced rate or no employer's national insurance contributions.

Government could also consider setting a lower rate of corporation tax for companies that show a genuine commitment to sustainable community development by providing:

- Significant funding for community projects.
- Significant volunteer input to community projects.
- Match funding for their payroll giving schemes.

Social investment

NCVO supports CAF's view that the government should consider how socially directed investment could best be encouraged:

- Donors could be provided with an income/corporation tax break equivalent to the interest lost because they invested in a social rather than a commercial project.
- Funds loaned for social purposes for a qualifying period before death could be excluded from the estate when inheritance tax is being calculated.

Encouraging volunteering

A standard minimum allowance should be introduced for volunteer expenses.

Reducing charities' tax burden

NCVO supports the Charity Tax Reform Group's (CTRG) argument that the government should compensate charities for all the irrecoverable VAT incurred on their charitable activities.

It also accepts CTRG's contention that government should ensure that changes made on the way towards European economic convergence should maintain the current status quo as regards charitable income. It asks the government to consider CTRG's proposal that a super-reduced rate of VAT on outputs or sales for charities should work alongside a grant-back scheme for the VAT incurred in providing services.

It would greatly assist the voluntary sector if an interpretation of the rules as they affect particular types of organisation could be negotiated by voluntary sector umbrella organisations and the agreements reached communicated to local VAT offices.

Unincorporated groups – for example, community centres or village halls running small trading enterprises – should be allowed to group register their trading and other activities for VAT purposes.

Trading income

Charities should be allowed to trade without incurring any tax liability, provided that profits are used in pursuit of the objects of the charity. NCVO acknowledges that such a change would require an amendment to charity law.

A less radical proposal, and one easier to implement, would be to allow charities £50,000 per annum of trading income tax free.

At the very least, however, the government should simplify the procedures that have to be followed when a wholly owned subsidiary covenants back profits to its parent charity.

Rate relief

Voluntary organisations should receive full mandatory rate relief. Business rate relief for charity shops should be maintained, and consideration given to the issue of zero rates and their importance in the context of the income from charity shops.

FURTHER READING

VAT for Voluntary Organisations, NCVO, 1998.

Appendix A: VAT registration checklist

1. Are any of your activities 'taxable' for VAT purposes?

- If no, you are not able to register for VAT.
- If yes, you are able to register for VAT.

2. Does the income generated by your taxable activities exceed the compulsory registration threshold?

- If yes, you should notify your local VAT office to apply to register for VAT within 30 days of exceeding the limit. Your effective date of VAT registration will be the first of the month following this 30-day period, unless you intend to exceed the threshold in the next 30 days, in which case you will be registrable immediately.
- If no, you are still able to register voluntarily for VAT.

3. Do you import any services from abroad in respect of your business activities, or make acquisitions of goods from the EU in a business context?

- If so, there are further registration requirements, and you should take professional advice.

4. If you are required to or voluntarily register for VAT, you will need to submit a monthly or quarterly VAT return and maintain books and records to include the following:

- Simple sales day book.
- Simple purchase day book.
- VAT summary.
- Copies of purchase invoices.
- Copies of sales invoices.
- Bank statements.
- Accounts

You are required to retain these records for a period of six years.

5. Have you been charged VAT before you are registered?
You can recover on your first VAT return submitted (subject to the normal rules) VAT you have been charged on services in the six months prior to the effective date, to the extent that they relate to your business activities. VAT you have been charged on assets held on the effective date of registration can also be recovered, again subject to the normal rules. But you cannot reclaim VAT on costs the benefits of which have been 'consumed' prior to registration.

6. Once you are registered for VAT you should issue a tax invoice for any 'taxable' supplies you make to other registered persons. A tax invoice should include the following information:

- An identifying number.
- The date of the supply (tax point).
- The date of issue.
- Your name, address and VAT registration number.
- Your customer's name and address.
- Type of supply (sale, loan etc).
- Description of the goods or services supplied.
- Quantity of goods or extent of services.
- VAT rate applicable.
- Net charge in sterling.
- VAT charge in sterling.
- The rate of any cash discount offered.
- Gross invoiced amount.

7. Subject to the conditions explained in this guide, you will be able to recover all or some of the VAT you are charged. You should ensure that trustees/employees obtain and forward suppliers' invoices for all purchases made.

8. Any changes in trustees should be notified to Customs within 30 days.

9. If the value of your taxable supplies falls below the deregistration threshold, you are able to cancel your VAT registration. If this is considered beneficial, you should notify your local VAT office.

10. If you cancel your VAT registration, you must declare VAT to Customs on your business assets on which VAT has previously been recovered, if this VAT exceeds £250 in total.

11. When completing your VAT return, refer to Customs leaflet (ref 700/12/93).

Appendix B: VAT glossary

apportionment
The term used for dividing a sum of VAT incurred on a general overhead expense e.g. between different relevant activities conducted by the organisation. This will assist in determining how much of the VAT can be recovered as input tax.

business supplies
Activities which are liable to VAT at either the standard or zero-rate, or which are exempt from VAT.

consideration
The term used to describe everything received in return for the supply of goods or the provision of services. Consideration is normally made in the form of money.

de minimis
Describes a level of activity or value which is not considered significant: for example, the partial exemption de minimis limit.

European Union (EU)
Formerly the European Community, this is the collective designation of the member states of the European Coal and Steel Community (ECSC), the European Economic Community (EEC) and the European Atomic Energy Community (EAEC).

exempt supplies
These are activities which are specifically exempted from a VAT charge but are considered to be business supplies for VAT purposes. However, VAT on related purchases and expenses (input tax) cannot normally be recovered.

HM Customs & Excise
The government department which is responsible for the administration, collection and enforcement of Value Added Tax in the United Kingdom.

input tax
The VAT which your organisation incurs on purchases of goods and services. Input tax can also consist of VAT due on the acquisition of goods from another EU member state and any VAT due on the importation of goods from a country outside the EU.

irrecoverable VAT
VAT incurred which cannot be recovered as input tax, either because the organisation is not registered for VAT or if it is, because the expense relates to a non-business activity or an activity exempt from VAT.

LVO
A local VAT office staffed by HM Customs and Excise.

non-business supplies
Activities which are outside the scope of VAT. VAT incurred which can be attributed to these activities cannot be recovered as input tax.

open market value
The price a person would have to pay for goods in their present condition and age.

output value
The value of a sale excluding any VAT which has been charged (termed net value).

output tax
VAT due on business supplies which are liable to VAT at either the standard rate (currently 17.5 per cent) or a reduced rate or zero rate.

partial recovery
When it is possible for an organisation only to recover part of the VAT charged on the purchase of goods or services.

registration
The collection of VAT is administered by the registration with Customs of those persons who either exceed the registration threshold or who wish to register voluntarily.

standard rate
The term used to describe the rate of VAT applied to the supply of those goods and services for which there is no relief from VAT. The standard rate of VAT is currently 17.5 per cent. VAT can be recovered on associated inputs.

taxable supplies
Activities which are liable to VAT at either the standard, reduced or zero-rate.

UK
For VAT purposes the UK includes the Isle of Man and Northern Ireland but excludes the Channel Islands.

VAT return
The form upon which a VAT registered organisation declares to Customs the VAT due on its activities in the period covered by the return. The form is also used to recover VAT which may be treated as input tax, thus resulting in a net payment to, or repayment from, Customs.

VAT period
The period of time covered by a VAT return. A period is normally three months long, but those receiving regular repayments may submit monthly returns.

VAT year
Usually the 12 months ending either 31 March, 30 April or 31 May, depending upon VAT periods.

wholly attributable
The term used to describe an expense which solely relates to a specific activity of the organisation.

zero rate
The term used to describe the rate of VAT applied to certain specifically relieved supplies of goods and services. VAT can be recovered on associated inputs.

Appendix C: Deeds of covenant

Model version approved by the Inland Revenue:

Form of covenant by an *individual* to a *charity* for use in *England and Wales* from 31 July 1990.

Deed of Covenant
Notes
To..
[name of charity]
I promise to pay you for ....years, or until I die if earlier,   1
such a sum as after deduction of income tax at the basic rate amounts to
£.................   2
each [week] [month] quarter] [year]   3
from [the date shown below] [   ]   4
Signed and delivered   5
Date..
Full Name..
Address ....
Witnessed by:
Signed ....
Full Name..
Address ....

Notes

1. Enter the period of the covenant, which must be longer than *three years*.
2. Enter the amount you will be paying to the charity
3. Delete as appropriate to show how often you will make the payment
4. Delete as appropriate. If you choose to enter an actual date, *it must not be earlier than the date you sign the deed.*
5. You must sign the form and enter the date you actually sign it in the presence of a witness, who should also sign where shown.

Glossary

accounting systems
The series of tasks and records of a organisation by which the transactions are processed as a means of maintaining financial records.

advanced corporation tax
An amount payable in respect of the final corporation tax liability arising whenever a dividend is made by a company

annual report and accounts
A set of statements which may comprise the trustees report and the financial statements of the charity

break-even point
The level of activity at which there is neither a surplus or deficit: total income equates to total cost.

budget
A quantitative statement, for a defined period of time, which may include planned income, expenses, assets, liabilities and cash flows. A budget provides a focus for the organisation, helps the co-ordination of activities and facilitates control.

budget forecast
A prediction of future income and expenditure or receipts and payments for the purpose of preparing budgets.

budget profiling
The assignment of annual income and expenditure figures to relevant months in the year when the income or expenditure is likely to be receivable or incurred.

budget variances
The difference, for each expense or income element in a budget, between the budgeted amount and the actual expense or income.

budget worksheets
Standard templates used for the preparation, update and consolidation of budgets; often produced using a spreadsheet package.

budgetary control
The establishment of budgets relating the responsibility of individuals or departments to the requirements of a financial policy, and the continuous comparison of actual with budgeted results.

conflict of interest policy
A statement which seeks to identify instances when the judgement of trustees of a charity may be unduly influenced by their connections with other persons or bodies.

controllable costs
A cost that can be influenced by the budget holder.

cost accounting
The establishment of budgets, standard costs and actual costs of operations, processes, activities or products; and the analysis of variances, social use of funds.

cost centre
A service location, function or activity for which costs are accumulated.

current liabilities
Liabilities that fall due for payment within one year.

direct cost
Expenditure that can be identified and specifically measured in respect of a relevant activity.

endowment funding
An endowment is a special type of restricted fund that must be retained intact and not spent.

equities
Shares in a company. Equity shares normally entitle the holder to a dividend and are traded on an exchange.

external environment
Key factors that have their origins outside the voluntary organisation, but may affect its activities and the fulfilment of charitable objectives.

financial procedures manual
A document outlining the key responsibilities of trustees, management and staff, and the controls in place to regulate financial activity.

general charities
Private, non profit making bodies serving persons.

governance
A function of trustee boards who are concerned with the fulfilment of strategic objectives.

governing document
The instrument that defines the reasons why the charity exists and how it is to conduct its internal affairs; may be in the form of a written constitution, memorandum and articles of association or deed.

income
Money that the organisation is legally entitled to receive. The accounting records will recognise this by recording an entry as soon as legal entitlement exists. To be distinguished from receipts, which are recorded when the money is actually received.

incremental budgeting
A method of budgeting that uses the previous period's results and inflates these by a fixed amount to account for increase in retail prices, for example.

indirect costs
Expenditure on labour, materials or services that cannot be identified with a specific activity.

internal audit
An independent appraisal function established with an organisation to examine and evaluate its activities as a service to the organisation. The object of internal auditing is to help members of the organisation to discharge their responsibilities effectively.

investment assets
Assets held by a charity for the purpose of deriving income and/or capital growth; for example, property, equity shares and antiques.

investment policy
A statement that defines the objectives for holding investments; will therefore include details of what type of investments are to be held and in what proportions.

investment portfolio
A basket of investment assets held collectively with the intention of reducing the risk that would arise if these assets were held separately.

irrecoverable VAT
The proportion of VAT that is incurred and relates to non-business activities.

joint venture
A project undertaken by two or more persons or entities joining together with a view to profit, often in connection with a single operation.

liquid assets
Cash and other assets readily convertible into cash: for example short-term investments.

liquidity
Condition in which assets are held in a cash or near-cash form.

mission
The fundamental principles by which an organisation exists and operates.

non-profit organisations
Any organisation whose primary objective is not exclusively orientated towards the maximisation of wealth for its owners and/or profit. This need not be a registered charity.

outcomes
Used in performance measurement. Outcomes or impacts are difficult to identify and measure, but might be considered as the desired end results from the outputs of the organisation. However, it can be difficult to prove that a cause and effect relationship exists.

outputs
Not always measured in money terms, but represent some delivery, service or result of special interest.

outsourcing
The buying in from a third party of services or goods that had previously been produced internally. The day-to-day management of the process is also delegated to the third party.

project charges
Expenditure incurred by the organisation which cannot be easily traced to a project or department and is therefore charged using a variety of bases.

relevant costs
Costs appropriate to a specific management decision.

reserves
Income available to be spent at the trustee's discretion in furtherance of the charity's objects but which is not yet spent, committed or designated; in other words, 'free' reserves.

restricted fund
A fund subject to specific trusts within the objects of the charity (for example, by a letter from the donor at the time of the gift or by the terms of a public appeal). It may

be a capital fund which cannot be spent but must be retained for the benefit of the charity; or it may be an income fund which must be spent on the specified purpose within a reasonable time.

shareholder value
The maximisation of economic value for shareholders, as measured by share price performance and flow of dividends.

stakeholders
Any group of people (either internal to the charity or not) or organisations externally that may be affected by the decisions and policies of the charity.

static budget
The original budget that has been approved by the trustees and is not changed to reflect either changes in the underlying assumptions used to prepare the budget or inaccurate forecasts.

strategic planning
The formulation, evaluation and selection of strategies for the purpose of preparing a long-term plan of action to attain objectives.

treasury management
The handling of all financial matters, the generation of external and internal funds for an organisation, the management of currencies and cash flows.

trustee board
A collective body of trustees responsible in law for the activities of the charity, whether officially designated as trustees or not.

vendorism
The practice of charging fees for the provision of services or activities which the organisation exists to supply.

venturing
Non-related commercial activities whose sole rationale is to raise money for the agency.

virement
The authority to apply savings under one subhead of a budget to meet excesses on others.

working capital
The capital available for conducting the day-to-day operations of an organisation; normally, the excess of current assets over current liabilities.

zero-based budgeting
A method of budgeting which requires each cost element to be specifically justified as though the activities to which the budget relates were being undertaken for the first time. Without approval, the budget allowance is zero.